MINISTERIAL CAREERS AND ACCOUNTABILITY IN THE AUSTRALIAN COMMONWEALTH GOVERNMENT

MINISTERIAL CAREERS AND ACCOUNTABILITY IN THE AUSTRALIAN COMMONWEALTH GOVERNMENT

Edited by Keith Dowding and Chris Lewis

Australian
National
University

E PRESS

ANU
E PRESS

Published by ANU E Press
The Australian National University
Canberra ACT 0200, Australia
Email: anuepress@anu.edu.au
This title is also available online at http://epress.anu.edu.au

National Library of Australia Cataloguing-in-Publication entry

Title: Ministerial careers and accountability in the Australian Commonwealth
              government / edited by Keith Dowding and Chris Lewis.

ISBN: 9781922144003 (pbk.) 9781922144010 (ebook)

Series: ANZSOG series

Notes: Includes bibliographical references.

Subjects: Politicians--Australia.
              Politicians--Australia--Ethical behavior.
              Political ethics--Australia.
              Politicians--Australia--Public opinion.
              Australia--Politics and government.
              Australia--Politics and government--Public opinion.

Other Authors/Contributors:
              Dowding, Keith M.
              Lewis, Chris.

Dewey Number: 324.220994

Cover design and layout by ANU E Press

Contents

1. Hiring, Firing, Roles and Responsibilities

Keith Dowding and Chris Lewis

Accountability for government action and inaction has always been central to the study of government in political science and public administration. In Westminster systems such as Australia's, the heart of academic and media discussion lies in the issue of ministerial accountability. Traditionally the idea behind the Westminster system is that whilst civil servants advise and administer policy, their public face is their minister, who promotes policy and defends department action in parliament and in public. Naturally this directs public attention to ministers and to the processes by which ministers and, through them, public servants are held to account. The manner in which ministers are chosen, how they see their jobs and how they do their jobs are thus key aspects of the governmental and accountability processes.

This book examines the roles, responsibilities and accountabilities of Australian Commonwealth cabinet ministers. We will examine what sorts of jobs ministers do, what is expected of them and what they expect of the job. We will examine how they (are supposed to) work together as a team. We will consider aspects of how they are chosen to become ministers, how they are scrutinised by parliament and to some extent by the media, and how ministers view the accountability mechanisms themselves. Subsequent chapters will then explore what the public often considers to be the heart of ministerial accountability: the issues that lead to calls for them to resign. We examine in some detail scandals around ministers. Our final chapter assesses ministerial accountability.

This first chapter will examine the roles that ministers are asked to perform and establishes some background theory. We consider the traditional constitutional account of responsibility as well as positive theories about how we can expect accountability mechanisms to work in practice. We explore issues that prime ministers might take into account when choosing ministers and when releasing them from their duties. The chapter performs most of these tasks by reflecting upon and introducing the more detailed accounts to be found in the chapters that follow.

The Role and Responsibilities of Ministers

The Governor-General officially appoints Australian ministers under Section 64 of the *Constitution*. In practice, within the Labor Party, until Kevin Rudd, the party caucus chose ministers though not necessarily their portfolios. Within the Coalition, Liberal prime ministers need to take account of the Country or National Party partners. Powerful ministers with strong party backing, notably those who lose leadership contests, become deputy prime minister and choose their own portfolio, often finance. These complications aside, we can think of ministers as agents of the prime minister. A cabinet forms a single government and it is in each member's interest to work together as a team—as John Wanna describes in Chapter 2—despite conflicts of interest and rivalries.

Until 1987 when legal advice changed, all ministers had to be appointed to their own department; now they can be appointed 'to administer' a department. Ministers often take on more than one portfolio or area of responsibility. They have 'individual ministerial responsibility' not only for their own personal conduct but also for their portfolios. Traditionally this involves administering their department and taking ultimate responsibility for what goes on in their area of responsibility. This includes reporting on the activities of their department to parliament and the public, either directly, through public statements or the prime minister answering on their behalf; explaining why problems emerge in implementation or execution and taking action to make improvements through new administrative procedures, oversight of or direct action by public officials; or through introducing new legislation.

Parliamentary democracy thus operates through a 'chain of delegation' (Strøm 2003) that links the electorate to the executive. The link runs from voters as principals to Members of Parliament (MPs) as agents. MPs are organised as collections of parties and from these the government is formed. The backbenchers and party then form the principals with the executive as the agent. The parliament delegates to the government the role of initiating policies. The prime minister is thus an agent of her party in parliament, and she in turn acts as a principal to the minsters who form her cabinet. Finally cabinet ministers act as principals and their public servants act as their agents. Each link in the chain is an important part of accountability within parliamentary democracies.

These are the important aspects of individual ministerial responsibility. The public face of such individual responsibility is generally witnessed when the minister is 'sacrificed' (read resigns) over some scandal or issue within his remit. In some sense 'sacrificial responsibility' is a minor part of individual ministerial responsibility, but it is a key element in accountability; if ministers never felt threatened then they would feel less pressure to demonstrate competence in administering, reporting, explaining and improving within their remit. Chapter 6 examines the operation of sacrificial responsibility in recent years in Australia, but we should acknowledge that what there is described as 'forced exit' is only one stark aspect of a minister's career prospects that makes him accountable. Ministers might not resign at the time they are criticised but, in the United Kingdom at least, it has been shown that ministerial durability is affected by the number of times they are criticised and the number of times their colleagues are criticised (Berlinski et al. 2010, 2012). The prime minister and her party want ministers who perform well; those who perform badly will leave the cabinet and often parliament at the same time or shortly thereafter. Any minister who is seen as an electoral liability will be less durable than those who perform well. Of course, if a government does badly as a whole then all the ministers will pay the price.

Individual ministerial responsibility is thus inextricably linked to collective responsibility. Any minister who is deemed to be in trouble can expect the support of his colleagues. First, any organised collective that sees one of its members under fire is likely to want to defend that member since damage to one will damage them all. There is a collective interest in defending ministers. Second, ministers will have an individual interest in seeing their colleagues defended by their prime minister and party since they might be under fire themselves in the future; however, such defence will only continue whilst the damage can be limited. If a minister is severely damaging the government's re-election prospects then support will be withdrawn. Having said that, governments can weather much criticism of individual ministers; what matters is the relative popularity of the government. The key minister with regard to the government's re-election prospects is the prime minister herself.

Collective ministerial responsibility requires that ministers support each other and the government. In its traditional garb it requires that whilst ministers might debate furiously behind the scenes or in cabinet over some political issue, once the government line has been laid down they will all publicly support it. Again important for re-election prospects, this ensures that the government team at least looks unified. It supports individual responsibility to the extent that each minister is responsible for their own area of responsibility, so ministers should support each other's policies as developed within their own remit. In practice most policies encroach upon several areas of responsibility and much of the work of public servants, these days, in the early stages of policy formation involves liaising across ministers and departments to ensure agreement. Such liaison, whether through official cabinet committees or informally, has always been the real heart of cabinet government. Nevertheless, in Australia, more so than in the United Kingdom, the formal cabinet meeting remains an important decision-making forum.

Ministers do come into conflict over policy and vie with each other for pre-eminence or dominance. Parliamentary sitting times are short and there is limited time to introduce legislation; ambitious ministers will want their bills as high on the agenda as possible. Some ministers will be seen as more important and awarded portfolios where the prime minister wants action. In Australia ministers have scope for putting themselves forward, through major speeches, appearances on television, in newspaper articles or new media. Whilst prime ministers take collective responsibility seriously, sometimes they have had to ignore or selectively interpret statements by ministers, effectively skirting the boundaries of collective responsibility (Weller 1985). Ministers can also allow the public to glimpse conflict through leaks and through friendly journalists reporting and speculating. Prime ministers despair of such selective leaking—and are the most assiduous practitioners of it. John Wanna in Chapter 2 carefully examines what collective responsibility has been interpreted to mean in Australia.

Many commentators argue that prime ministers have become more powerful, not only in Australia but also in all the Westminster countries and indeed other parliamentary democracies (Pogunkte and Webb 2005). In part this is presentational. With increasing media attention focusing on people, there has been, worldwide, a personalisation of politics (McAllister 2007). How far this media presentation reflects the actual running of government, however, is another issue. Robert Menzies, partly due to his long tenure, which lent him authority and caused his ministers to owe him their position, was certainly a dominant figure—more so than his immediate predecessors. Malcolm Fraser and Rudd both required detailed information about all areas of government, whereas Bob Hawke was seen as the supreme chairman of cabinet, allowing ministers their own initiative but intervening where necessary (Weller 2007). Gough Whitlam wanted to run everything—an approach that can become disastrous if the prime minister cannot control his cabinet (as was the case with William McMahon). John Howard and Rudd were decisive, setting the agenda and making decisions—in Rudd's case, often without even consulting the relevant minister. Rudd's domination of his cabinet in this manner was not unimportant in his rapid demise (see Chapter 2), which tells us as much about cabinet government as the fact that he had the resources to dominate in such a manner. If we want to study the growing centralisation of policy making and the ability of prime ministers to control their cabinets—sometimes dubbed 'prime ministerialisation' (Dowding 2012)—we need to look at the growth of their resources.[1] The Prime Minister's Office (PMO) and the Department of the Prime Minister and Cabinet (PM&C), which provide the central coordinating machinery and planning for the prime minister, have grown in personnel and

---

1 The 'prime ministerialisation' designation was chosen to counter the institutionally and behaviourally naive 'presidentialisation of prime minister' thesis.

resources; however, governments have always struggled and will continue to struggle to keep abreast of the complexities and interrelationship of policies across the spectrum of government.

The role and responsibilities of ministers have changed over time, as Anne Tiernan and Patrick Weller discuss in their book (Tiernan and Weller 2010). Nevertheless, there are a number of general functions performed by ministers that have altered relatively little. Ministers are responsible within the remit of their job in several senses, to announce, explain and to defend the policies and actions of their department but also to initiate some of the policies and actions. An important aspect of their role is to represent their departments in interdepartmental forums and when negotiating policy, and to fight for time to get their legislative agenda through parliament. To be sure, public servants and policy advisers do the bulk of such work, but at times, as advised by these staff, ministers do get involved. Departments compete with each other over scarce resources and ministers help their public servants in negotiations with finance, meeting with clients and pressure groups. Again, public servants conduct the bulk of such work, but ministers need to be prepared to take on the responsibility of making as well as signing off on decisions and agreements when required. Ministers will engage in cabinet and cabinet committees, and defend their department and represent its views, in discussion of the policies and plans of other ministers. Of course as elected Members of Parliament they retain their parliamentary roles of representing constituents and their factions within the party.

One of the problems of the ministerial role is that the choice mechanism does not necessarily reflect the job that a minister has to do. To become a minister a person has to convince first the party and then the broader electorate of their qualities. He then has to convince the party hierarchy. This can be achieved partly through the organisational qualities displayed in his party work or previous occupations; but crucially he must be able to demonstrate that he can handle the rough and tumble of politics. Ministers' public exposure has increased with the onset of the 24-hour media cycle and social media; ministerial offices are now expected to respond almost instantly to emails or Twitter gossip.

Cabinet Composition and Teamwork

Most of the items on the list of ministerial functions relate to their roles as individual ministers, and in that sense they concern individual ministerial responsibility. Within that framework the public image and the public manner of the minister are important, as is their role as part of the government. John Wanna in Chapter 2 considers the role of ministers as part of a cabinet team. As we have suggested, cabinets are composed of ambitious sets of politicians who are rivals as well as colleagues. The strong party nature of Australian politics ensures that ministers share some sets of policy preferences and ideological concerns, but within broad lines their views can differ sharply. Cabinets are composed of powerful figures who represent factions where conflicts can run deep and have long histories. Cabinet members are likely to have known each other for many years and to be strong personalities who have previously clashed over policy or even stood against each other for party positions or for seats at local, State or even national levels.[2] Despite all that, they must pull together and be part of a government team. The convergent and divergent sets of interests create a collective-action problem, with incentives, at times, pulling in different directions. Ministers are agents of their party and of the prime minister, and if any one of them is seen as too divisive, and so damaging the government and ultimately the party's chances of re-election, he will be punished by their backbenchers. Ministers must therefore provide a semblance of coherence and consistency. More than that, however, they must work together as a team.

The prime minister is the key player in forging the cabinet as a team, but other powerful ministers also play key roles; and we have seen over the years rivalries that have damaged the team: Hawke and Paul Keating, Howard and Peter Costello—both to some extent because of supposed deals over the leadership formerly agreed. The main thrust of Wanna's chapter, however, is a consideration of what collective responsibility really means in practice. His discussion helps mitigate the imbalance of so much concentration upon individual ministerial responsibility. His major conclusion is that collective responsibility is as much about the appearance of a unified government and the interpretations of working together that a prime minister is prepared, or sometimes forced, to accept, given the personalities and conflicts amongst his team. Importantly, the idea (the 'myth' perhaps) of collective responsibility is something that has to be accepted by all, under a broad interpretation, in order for government to work. Furthermore, what some prime ministers (Rudd might be an example) sometimes seem to forget is that collective responsibility holds for them too. As Wanna suggests, cabinet is a bridge between the prime minister and the party; but it also acts as the party's leash upon the prime minister—a leash that is slackened depending on how successful the government appears to be.

---

2   A story told of Winston Churchill is as relevant to Australia as it is to the United Kingdom. A newly elected MP leaned forward and whispered to Churchill how good it was to face the enemy across the House of Commons. 'The enemy is beside and behind us', replied Churchill, 'facing us is merely the Opposition.'

Choosing Ministers

John Wanna describes elements of that team and how a government must have some overarching principles that govern the whole. Furthermore, teamwork in a complex organisation like government is not simply pulling together like a tug-of-war side but rather entails different members doing different jobs. A good governing team will have within it elder statesmen, Rottweilers to maul the opposition, those with dynamic ideas and those considered safe pairs of hands. The prime minister will also want a set of loyal lieutenants. Biographies show that prime ministers usually have a strong idea of who they want in most positions, and probably agonise more over the final few places than over the bulk of them. In Australia it is important that the cabinet is representative of the different States roughly in proportion to the size of their population, and leaders these days want some degree of gender balance. Nevertheless, there might be specific qualities leading some parliamentarians to ministerial posts that even prime ministers themselves do not fully recognise. These are the qualities that Michael Dalvean attempts to uncover in Chapter 3.

Dalvean uses words as data to try to examine the psychological characteristics that lead some to become ministers. He tries to predict who will be chosen as a minister, and who will be successful once there, based upon the maiden speeches of parliamentarians. Given those data, he adds other factors, such as the member's State, gender, educational background, and so on, to predict who will be ministers. In fact, he argues that representativeness does not add anything to his predictive model. His argument here is subtle and open to misunderstanding. He does not claim that prime ministers do not explicitly take into account representativeness when considering candidates for ministerial position; indeed we know from biographical accounts that such discussions about representativeness do take place during the composition of the cabinet. He argues, however, that representativeness does not really explain the actual composition. How can that be?

One way of thinking about the issue is to imagine the choice of, say, 20 stones from six urns. There are 150 stones overall distributed among the urns in the proportions 10, 10, 20, 20, 45, 45. Now say we want to choose the 20 smoothest stones, and the stones have been randomly assigned to each urn. If we were to randomly pick a stone from the 150 we would have a one in 7.5 chance of picking one of the 20 smoothest. The chance of one of the smoothest being in any given urn is thus $(1/7.5)^*n$ where n is the number of stones in the urn. Now consider a non-random choice. Imagine we get to feel each of the stones in turn and choose the 20 smoothest. How many are likely to be picked from each urn?

The answer of course is $(1/7.5)^*n$. So we would expect to pick one–two stones from the first two urns (prob. = 1.3), two–three from the second two (prob. = 2.6) and five–six (prob. = 5.3) from the two largest urns.

Now consider that each urn has stones of a different colour in it and we want to choose stones representative of the urns. So now we want to choose 20 stones out of the 150 in proportion to how many of the stones are in each urn. Our calculation is $(20/150)^*n$ from each urn. Of course, this is the same calculation, so we would expect one–two stones from the smallest urn, two–three from the middle and five–six from each of the largest. Either way of choosing cannot distinguish the stones by the numbers chosen. We can of course understand which way of choosing occurs by inspecting the colours or the smoothness. If only colour matters then we might assume that representativeness has been the key element. If smoothness is what matters then we can assume stones have been chosen by shape. Michael Dalvean argues that the most predictive way of seeing who becomes a cabinet minister is from their personal characteristics as identified by their maiden speech in parliament and not from their State. It is smoothness = psychological characteristics, not urn = State, that gives the predictions of the actual stones = members chosen. Dalvean does not need to deny that representativeness seems to matter but it seems to matter only because the personal characteristics that cause someone to be seen as a viable minister are normally distributed across the States. It might be true that a prime minister plumps for candidate B over candidate A simply because he is from one of the States that otherwise might be under-represented, but that is only because the number of qualified candidates (given some stochastic variance) does not equal the precise number of ministers required. In other words, even if Australia were not a federal system with State boundaries and some constitutional niceties of representativeness, much the same cabinets would be chosen anyway. If we could operate the counterfactual—what if the qualities that make ministers were not normally distributed across representatives of the States?—then we might see whether State representation matters more than candidate quality.

So Dalvean looks to personal psychological factors. Examining the maiden speeches of Members of Parliament through computer-assisted word search, he statistically collates sets of words and phrases that are strongly correlated with future office, distinguishing those MPs who become ministers from those who do not. He predicts who can become a minister through analysis of MPs' maiden speeches. He then psychologically analyses those words and phrases to see if he can demonstrate what characteristics are associated with becoming a minister (as opposed to not becoming one) and what is associated with longer ministerial careers (as a proxy for being a successful minister). He finds that ministers have qualities that distinguish them from MPs. He also finds that there are differences between Labor and Coalition governments.

We have seen that prime ministers might not always get the cabinet team they fully desire. Even when the prime minister does control the process, he or she will be forced to find jobs for the big beasts, and those beasts might demand specific roles. They have to keep different factions happy and sometimes find a role for someone whose time has passed perhaps, but who is still important politically. Dewan and Hortala-Vallve (2011) discuss the three As of government formation: appointment, allocation and assignment. Often we concentrate upon the appointment aspect, but prime ministers can hide ministers in unimportant portfolios, assign them to unpopular ones and to some extent reassign the nature of the responsibilities within a portfolio. Peter Costello (2008, 55) describes the last (albeit in opposition):

> When we got back to Canberra after John Hewson appointed me shadow attorney-general, Hewson called me down to his office. He explained that he had previously appointed [Andrew] Peacock to the job because he needed to give him a portfolio as senior as that held by John Howard. He told me: 'It was a clever strategy. No one caught on that in fact I had gutted the portfolio and given the substantive responsibilities to you.'

Prime ministers have some discretion as to what specific responsibilities are assigned to each portfolio; they can move the chairs around within departments as well as assigning the chairs to departments. They control more than the actual appointments.

Ministerial Accountability

Where Dalvean uses quantitative techniques, James Walter in Chapter 4 uses the qualitative technique of in-depth interviews to examine the attitudes of ministers to their job and to the issue of executive accountability. He draws upon two sets of interviews: one conducted when the interviewees first entered parliament about 30 years ago, and the second more contemporary. He compares the attitudes of his interviewees towards executive accountability when they first entered parliament and again after they had held office; and compares the attitudes of those who held office with those who did not. In doing so he explores whether the experience of ministerial office leads to a change in attitudes to executive accountability, especially in relation to party and parliamentary oversight. Interestingly, he finds that even prior to high office some different attitudes emerge. The more ambitious backbenchers tend to rate the processes by which the executive makes decisions, and the decisions themselves, more highly than the less ambitious. The latter recognise the realities that the legislature is not very influential in executive decisions but believe it ought to have a bigger role. Backbenchers also rate their role of representing their constituency more highly. Walter categorises the parliamentarians according to the sorts of answers they give. Some are policy activists who see their careers in terms of how they influence policy—they tend to be more ambitious for an executive role. Parliamentarians see their role in parliament and the caucus of their party as important; delegates put their constituency representation at the forefront. Those who later made it to the executive recognise the accountability function of parliament but also see its limitations. They also tended to see the party caucus as less important to the executive than they did as backbenchers. This might reflect the fact that whilst caucus might seem to direct, often since the cabinet is chosen by caucus (or chosen by the prime minister who is chosen by caucus), the views of the executive and caucus are not so far apart. On those few occasions when views diverge, the executive prevails most often.

Walter chronicles change. He chronicles the greater ambition of later generations, how the age profile is getting younger and the growing professionalisation of politics—the last marked by the greater numbers who have always worked in politics as opposed to those who had more life experience prior to their political careers. Importantly, as his title suggests, he finds a democratic ambivalence towards attitudes to accountability. The greater ambiguity lies in those who are more ambitious.

Phil Larkin looks carefully at the formal processes of parliamentary scrutiny, carried out both through the chamber and the committee system. He examines the contested decline of parliament as a mechanism of accountability. First, we ought to acknowledge the counterfactual. We might lament that ministers do not fear parliament as much as they might, or believe that parliament ought to have more powers, or perhaps just use the powers they have more often and more effectively. But we should begin by considering what the executive might do if there were no parliament. That is, we must first recognise the vast difference between the behaviour of the executive in parliamentary democracies and dictatorships and their puppet legislatures.

Parliament can ensure that ministers explain their decisions and account for their policies and the public service. That in itself is an important function. Larkin also brings out the fact that parliament is not a single actor, and there is a series of relations—between ministers and their own backbenchers, and between ministers and the opposition parties. He argues that Question Time is not a very effective process; rather we need to look to the committee structure for more effective means of accountability. His careful study brings out the strength and the weakness of the committees in both houses, but also acknowledges that trying to understand or quantify their effectiveness is exceedingly problematic. He highlights the importance in this respect of the bicameral system. The Senate by repute is a more deliberative assembly that stands a little aside from the day-to-day affray of government versus opposition. Given that it is elected by a different system, ensuring that neither Labor nor the Coalition will normally have majorities there, can the Senate perform a more reflective role? Or do we find that the rough and tumble of adversarial politics override any institutional differences? Larkin also considers the important change we have seen in the past two or three decades: the rise of the ministerial adviser and the fact that parliamentary rules and accountability conventions have not fully adjusted to this innovation.

Keith Dowding, Chris Lewis and Adam Packer take a longer look at accountability, especially that aspect of accountability that has been dubbed 'sacrificial accountability' (Woodhouse 1994). To be sure, such accountability is only part of the nature of ministerial responsibility. In the popular mind, however, ministerial accountability involves resigning for personal mistakes. Academics have long argued that government accountability is much broader than this (Dowding 1995, Ch. 7; Dowding and Kang 1998; Mulgan 2000; Robinson et al. 1987; Weller 1999; Woodhouse 1994, 2002, 2003), while also recognising that resignation needs to underpin accountability for grave errors (Page 1990; Thompson and Tillotsen 1999). Both John Howard and Kevin Rudd made it clear that they saw it as an important aspect of responsibility, at least at the beginning of their office, by bringing in codes of conduct (Howard 1996; Rudd 2007). Dowding et al. use a unique data set that examines all forced exits from the cabinet since 1947 to make judgments about whether ministers are more or less accountable now than in the past. These questions have taken on a more vibrant tone in the past 20 years, largely because it was thought that John Howard's ministers seemed teflon coated—continuing in office despite many scandals. Dowding et al. demonstrate that in fact the rate at which Howard lost ministers relative to calls for resignation was not so different from the past; what differed was that he lost so many in his first two years and then seemed determined to keep them.

Dowding et al. argue that the rate at which ministers forcibly exit relative to calls has gone down, but that this is due to the greater number of calls that are made. They argue that issues that once were not considered worthy of public examination now are. In that sense public scrutiny and ministerial accountability have increased not decreased, but consequently public confidence and trust in government have gone down. Scott Brenton continues this theme, examining in more detail scandals involving ministers in the past 50 years to judge whether ministerial behaviour has deteriorated over time. Chris Lewis takes a detailed look at a recent executive problem—the debacle of the Home Insulation Program—and argues that it is one of the worst failures of the executive in recent years. Caused by haste and ignoring the proper internal checks, it demonstrates a lack of accountability.

We can, though, place too much weight on sacrificial accountability. Even if ministers do not resign at the time there are calls for them to do so, their careers may still be affected. Just because a minister does not forcibly exit— is 'sacrificed'—it does not mean he or she has not been held accountable for their actions. Ministerial careers might still end: the minister might move to the backbenches after the next election or not stand at all. Howard might have defended his ministers during times when they were criticised, but he was not averse to moving them out or demoting them after the Christmas break. Australian governments—possibly because of the short terms (a three-year maximum as opposed to the United Kingdom's five years)—do not have the UK tradition of the 'mid-term reshuffle', but prime ministers do choose to shift ministers around and move some on occasionally. And not standing for another term is more common in Australia, partly again because of the short terms but largely because of the relatively small size of parliament and the preselection process where most constituency parties would sooner have members who are going somewhere than those who have been somewhere. In other words, ministerial durability is more important than the rate of forced exits in making judgments about the nature of ministerial responsibility.

The final chapter in the book, by Richard Mulgan, takes a careful look at ministerial accountability. He suggests that over-reliance on the concept of ministerial as opposed to governmental responsibility is the major problem with Westminster systems such as Australia's. Public servants no longer enjoy anonymity, making televised appearances before parliamentary scrutiny committees; the old distinctions between administration and policy no longer (if they ever did) hold; and the increasing complexity of government makes individual ministerial responsibility something of a misnomer. Furthermore, Mulgan suggests that accountability agencies like the audit office and ombudsman are important and more attention should be devoted to their role when considering governmental responsibility. He argues that the focus we often direct to individual ministers, which his extended analysis of the Home Insulation Program illustrates, deflects attention away from others who share responsibility. We should pay less attention, Mulgan advises, to individual ministerial responsibility and more to the collective aspects of ministerial responsibility; and we should pay more attention to the government machine as a whole and less to individual ministers.

Conclusions

In parliamentary systems of government, and in Westminster-style democracies especially, the role of ministers is a key element in the democratic and accountability processes. They form the public face of the political and administrative processes. Their role both as individuals and as a collective is a vital aspect of how we can hold executive processes together. In this book, we examine how ministers come to gain office in Australia, how well they represent different parts of the community, how they operate as a team, their behaviour in office and how they are held to account through parliamentary and public processes. Aspects of ministerial accountability are not the be-all and end-all of accountability structures in democratic systems: audit systems, ombudsmen and the judiciary all form part of the constitutional fabric of accountability. The media and the public themselves are also vital aspects of accountability.

In the end, how far ministers and governments sustain themselves relies upon their standing in the public eye, and it is this knowledge that, together with their own normative and moral principles, leads politicians to act as responsibly as they do. Richard Mulgan's concluding chapter brings us to realise that perhaps at times we place too much emphasis on individual ministerial responsibility—failures in government often result from collective failures in organisation—and perhaps we might move too quickly to blame a public face both for our own convenience and for that of the executive. Nevertheless, ministers will always remain a vital part of the accountability process in parliamentary democracies.

Bibliography

Berlinski, S., T. Dewan and K. Dowding. 2010. 'The Impact of Individual and Collective Performance on Ministerial Tenure'. *Journal of Politics* 72: 1–13.

Berlinski, S., T. Dewan and K. Dowding. 2012. *Accounting for Ministers: Scandal and Survival in British Government 1945–2007*. Cambridge: Cambridge University Press.

Costello, P. 2008. *The Costello Memoirs*. Melbourne: Melbourne University Press.

Dewan, T. and R. Hortala-Vallve. 2011. 'The Three A's of Government Formation: Appointment, Allocation, and Assignment'. *American Journal of Political Science* 55: 610–27.

Dowding, K. 1995. *The Civil Service*. London: Routledge.

Dowding, K. and W.-T. Kang. 1998. 'Ministerial Resignations 1945–97'. *Public Administration* 76: 411–29.

Dowding, Keith 2012 'The Prime Ministerialization of the British Prime Minister' *Parliamentary Affairs,* Advance Access 6 April 2012 — DOI: 10.1093/pa/gss007

Howard, J. 1996. *Guidelines on Ministerial Conduct*. Canberra: Australian Government Publishing Service.

McAllister, I. 2007. 'The Personalization of Politics'. In *The Oxford Handbook of Political Behavior*, eds R. Dalton and H.-D. Klingemann, pp. 571–88. Oxford: Oxford University Press.

Mulgan, R. 2000. 'Accountability: An Ever Expanding Concept'. *Public Administration* 58: 555–74.

Page, B. 1990. 'Ministerial Resignation and Individual Ministerial Responsibility in Australia 1976–1989'. *Journal of Commonwealth and Comparative Politics* 28: 141–61.

Poguntke, T. and P. Webb. 2005. *The Presidentialization of Politics: A Comparative Study of Modern Democracies*. Oxford: Oxford University Press.

Robinson, A., F. F. Ridley and G. W. Jones. 1987. 'Symposium on Ministerial Responsibility'. *Public Administration* 65: 61–91.

Rudd, K. 2007. *Standards of Ministerial Ethics*. Canberra: Australian Government.

Strøm, K. 2000. 'Delegation and Accountability in Parliamentary Democracies'. *European Journal of Political Research* 37: 261–89.

Strøm, K. 2003. 'Parliamentary Democracy and Delegation'. In *Delegation and Accountability in Parliamentary Democracies*, eds K. Strøm, W. C. Muller and T. Bergman. Oxford: Oxford University Press.

Thompson, E. and G. Tillotsen. 1999. 'Caught in the Act: The Smoking Gun View of Ministerial Responsibility'. *Australian Journal of Public Administration* 58: 48–57.

Tiernan, A. and P. Weller. 2010. *Learning to Be A Minister: Heroic Expectations, Practical Realities*. Melbourne: Melbourne University Press.

Weller, P. 1985. 'The Hawke Cabinet: Collective or Responsible?'. *Australian Quarterly* 57: 319–32.

Weller, P. 1999. 'Disentangling Concepts of Ministerial Responsibility'. *Australian Journal of Public Administration* 58: 62–4.

Weller, P. 2007. *Cabinet Government in Australia, 1901–2006*. Sydney: UNSW Press.

Woodhouse, D. 1994. *Ministers and Parliament: Accountability in Theory and Practice*. Oxford: Oxford University Press.

Woodhouse, D. 2002. 'The Reconstruction of Constitutional Accountability'. *Public Law*: 73–90.

Woodhouse, D. 2003. 'Ministerial Responsibility in the Twentieth Century'. In *The Constitution in the Twentieth Century*, ed. V. Bogdanor, pp. 281–332. Oxford: Oxford University Press.

2. Ministers as Ministries and the Logic of their Collective Action

John Wanna

As recounted in the opening chapter, ministerial responsibility is primarily understood and studied as a formal accountability process with the emphasis largely on *individual* ministerial accountability and the occasional resignation. This preoccupation with individual responsibility reflects a British obsession with the behaviour of the particular minister (Dowding and Kang 1998; Woodhouse 1994) or a scepticism of the observance of collective responsibility, especially when governments disintegrate—the so-called 'myth/fallacy' argument (see Dell 1980; Weller 1985). There is generally less attention paid to the dimensions of *collective* ministerial responsibility and the politics of maintaining cohesion, other than the seminal acknowledgment by constitutionalists of the *need* for cabinet solidarity in modern parliamentary government (Crisp 1973, 353; Dicey 1885; Jennings 1959), and the incantation of the political requirement in modern-day ministerial codes (see Australian Government, *Cabinet Handbook*, 2009, ss. 15–24). Collective ministerial responsibility is arguably a far less formal form of accountability, interpreted largely by the prime minister, and exercised through political expedience, some malleable conventions and frequent reinterpretation. Moreover, collective responsibility is defined and given expression not only in the (positive) requirements for collegial solidarity, but also in the degree of latitude shown to dissention and to breaches of the principles.

As will be explored below, ministers are political actors who are simultaneously *individual* and *collective* entities. They play out these dual but overlapping roles across a range of interactions in which they more or less engage. These interactions occur with their contemporaries at the centre of government (around cabinet and its political, symbolic and decision-making processes), in their relations with senior officials and their departments, with the public service and media and with the wider community. But, importantly, they are also played out in two other critical contexts that impact on their behaviour: first, in the context of the collaborative/competitive incentive frames they inhabit and negotiate with their fellow party colleagues; and second, *against* their political opponents or other opposing interests.

This chapter focuses on ministers acting as a ministry, as a collegial entity, expressing their 'collective responsibility'. It examines their logics of collective action—not in the narrow Olsonian sense of the 'free rider' problem, but in the sense of the compelling logic of mutual obligations and reciprocal responsibilities. Hence, the focus is on the degree of solidarity they invest with each other and especially on the role of the prime minister and other senior ministers in imposing collective conventions over the group.

Analytically, there are both *external* and *internal* dimensions to this collective endeavour. The external dimensions are where cohesion is usually a symbolic or tactical device—for instance, at ceremonial functions representing the nation, in their phalange-like behaviour in parliament, their relations with the media and interactions with lobby groups and constituents. The internal dimensions include the minister's personal relations with the prime minister, political support for the leader, the operational dynamics of cabinet and the wider ministry, factional dynamics and the degree of party support for themselves (or others) as ministers. These two dimensions constitute forms of political accountability (largely to themselves as a group) for the ministerial collective: outward accountability (accountability to the parliament, nation, the media); and inward accountability to cabinet and the party room. Senior ministers (and especially the leader) are accountable in both dimensions simultaneously and constantly. Each dimension can serve to enhance or erode the standing of the ministry depending on how ministers behave, are perceived to be performing and maintain their collegial support structures.

In Australia, there is relatively little literature on cabinet dynamics over the term(s) of the government or the operational collectivities of ministries, including the exercise of collective responsibility. A very thin literature exists, which tends to depict Australia as an essentially utilitarian and majoritarian polity, within which the individual responsibility of ministers has been to *their own party* rather than to parliament (see Encel 1962). Some constitutionalists have then gone on to reinterpret Australian practice as a political system where collective responsibility became the dominant constitutional convention (over individual responsibility) while acknowledging that this was contingent upon time and circumstance (see Finn 1990). There is even less literature on the formation of cabinets either from a qualitative (how they are formed, composed, who manages to become appointed, how coalitions are crafted) or quantitative interpretation (though see Michael Dalvean's controversial Chapter 3 in the current volume). This latter phenomenon is perhaps best explained by acknowledging that traditionally there have been few researchers who have chosen to focus on this topic, and because Australian cabinets are usually monological (single-party majoritarian governments known ahead of the election and not indeterminate multi-party coalitions negotiated in the wake of electoral outcomes).[1] The exceptions in the Australian literature are Sol Encel

---

1   The Liberal–National coalition is a standing arrangement traditionally based on a mutual recognition of territory (seats) and a non-competitive electoral stance; it is sometimes referred to as a 'coalescence' arrangement (see Sartori 1976) and is not the equivalent of party coalitions in European polities where various

(1962) who provided an earlier account of executive government; also the collected works of Patrick Weller (for example, 1985, 1989, 1990, 2007) who has both chronicled and explained the dynamics of the Fraser, Hawke and Howard cabinets; the ruminations of Neal Blewett (1999, 2006), a former academic and federal politician who recounts the machinations of the Hawke and Keating cabinets constantly searching for the epicentre of power; and Glyn Davis (1992) who mischievously treated the internal dynamics of cabinet as metaphorically akin to American 'street gangs' (paralleling the sociological works of Frederick Thrasher in *The Gang* and William Foote Whyte in *Street Corner Society*), organised by power and esteem, reputation, internal bargains, implicit deals and constant renegotiations of influence.[2]

Ministries as Both a Collegial and a Rivalling Team: The interplay of competitive and collaborative motivations and incentives

Australian ministries are invariably composites of professional *politicians*—they are composed of elected, full-time politicians, constituency-based representatives (or regional senators) and almost entirely party-aligned apparatchiks who owe their primary loyalty to their party and factional support base. These career politicians display various motivational and behavioural qualities that coexist simultaneously but may be either pronounced or latent, including: loyalties, alliances, rivalries, personal ambition, envy, jealousy or hatred, subterfuge or deception. The precise mix of these qualities on display is highly contingent depending on circumstance or exercised by political intuition and astuteness. Ministries, thus, are composed of ambitious and competitive individuals who also generally wish to convey the impression of forming a unified, collective entity of some sort. How this collective actually coheres may be *sui generis* and discrete to specific governments or prime ministers (compare the Whitlam and Hawke ministries, or those of Fraser and Howard, Rudd or Julia Gillard; see Weller 2007).

Ministers are appointed constitutionally and formally by the head of state (on advice from the prime minister) usually to fulfil dedicated portfolio or functional

---

party combinations can be formed after each election. Moreover, the coalition arrangements between the Liberal Party and The Nationals are only significant in some jurisdictions federally, in New South Wales, Victoria and Western Australia; they are not a feature in Tasmania, South Australia, the Northern Territory, the Australian Capital Territory, or now in Queensland where the two parties have formally merged.

2   There are occasional chapters in textbooks that throw light on cabinet dynamics (but usually as a clearing-house or policymaking vehicle), and occasional presentations by some of the key participants (see Codd 1990 and more generally the collection by Galligan et al. 1990). Mostly these practitioner reports merely chart current practice.

responsibilities. Importantly, they are appointed as *individuals* to their official posts—as ministers with a given title, an area of portfolio responsibility and a specific set of authorisations (often contained in statutes). They are, thus, appointed to and held responsible for specific sets of duties, compartmentalised functions, bodies of legislation and assigned organisations (departments and agencies). These ministers expect a degree of ministerial autonomy (or respected specialisation) but also expect to consult and be consulted by their ministerial colleagues. As individual ministers with compartmentalised responsibilities they enter a collective 'deal': *they* themselves look after their area of responsibility (and inform the collective of anything of major significance) and in exchange expect *other* ministers to take care of their areas (and equally inform the collective of anything significant). Hence, a functioning ministry is similar to a sporting team where each player is given specific responsibilities for a dedicated role or position, each may have to help out at stressful times, but each player performs a given role for the team (see Howard 2010, 234–8). It is their collective bargain, their collective exchange relations.

Moreover, Australian ministers are also appointed, individually and simultaneously, as members of a collective advisory committee to the Crown—as members of the executive council and advisers to the Governor-General (similar to the UK Privy Council serving the Monarch). This latter appointment is constitutional and legal in form but largely symbolic in effect (and *not* the equivalent to cabinet), but nevertheless underscores the collegial conventions of executive government. Legal authority is exercised by the 'Governor-General-in-council'. As a ministerial team there is some expectation of shared or bargained loyalty (often underscored by edicts from the prime minister at regular intervals). Under bargained loyalty, a particular minister invests and positively displays his/her loyalty to the ministerial group (or individual colleagues) and in exchange the other ministers give that particular minister their loyalty. It is a quid pro quo or a mutual insurance arrangement based on necessity, and it helps build an esprit de corps.

So, although ministers are not formally appointed as a collective, they seek to exist and operate as a collective entity, until circumstances demand some readjustment. This expression of collective responsibility (or cabinet solidarity) is a political convention rather than a constitutional requirement. Ministers in a sense form a joint commitment: individually they agree to defend each other in exchange for each of the others defending them when circumstances dictate. It is a mutual pact or protective bond. And, implicitly, they accept as part of this deal that they may be forced to tender their resignation for the collective good of the government if they are badly damaged or are unnecessarily damaging the government as a whole. One example is the vigorous defence by Prime Minister Paul Keating of his hapless Sports Minister, Ros Kelly, over the 'sports rorts' scandal (see below), where he publicly defended her to the hilt over some months until her resignation could no longer be averted, and she had to be 'culled to save the herd' (see Wanna et al. 2001, 146–9).

In Australia the notion of cabinet solidarity traditionally insisted that the 'cabinet as a whole is responsible for the advice and conduct of each of its members' and that 'cabinet should stand or fall together' (Quick and Garran 1901, 705). This is a longstanding interpretation and has regularly been codified in *Cabinet Handbook*s (Australian Government 1983–2009). In other words, *cabinet*, and predominantly the prime minister, is the primary and effective forum that controls and monitors the behaviour of ministers in real time, not the parliament; the legislature is but the final theatrical tribunal that exercises a partial prudential oversight (and usually post hoc). Moreover, it is the cabinet's responsibility, and again predominantly the prime minister's, to ensure collective solidarity is maintained. Yet the rigid imposition of these twin political doctrines (control over ministers and their solidarity as a group) has been difficult to maintain, and so various prime ministers have resorted to some creative interpretations to maintain the balance and accommodate dissent or breaches of collective responsibility (Weller 1984, 1985, 1990). Mavericks or serial dissenters in the ministry have often been permitted some latitude by prime ministers unwilling to risk public disunity—Kevin Rudd in Gillard's cabinet is a case in point.

Consequently, within the doctrine(s) of cabinet solidarity a range of interpretations exists, and each is open to the discretion of the prime minister in different circumstances.

- Hardline notions of the need for *complete unanimity* (and the avoidance of public criticism of one's colleagues) stemming from Lord Salisbury's edict on cabinet collective responsibility are often cited and paraded as 'hard rules' but, at best, these are normative aspirations and are difficult to impose especially over serious policy disputes.

- Prime ministers find it much harder *to enforce* the hardline Salisbury notion of solidarity in practice especially in relatively small parliaments (or tight parliaments); often they have to make concessions especially to powerful ministers or those with an influential powerbase.

- A more euphemistic Australian compromise, expressed by Quick and Garran (1901), is that cabinet 'should have one harmonious policy'; in other words, solidarity means *avoiding outright public dissent* by cabinet ministers (although it may be possible to challenge cabinet decisions in party forums such as parliamentary party meetings or party conferences).

- *Confidentiality* of cabinet deliberations is a crucial component of collective responsibility; cabinet's internal deliberations remain secret and its business is not leaked or canvassed in public; political or policy disagreements are meant to remain confidential; it is important not to divulge the particular policy stances or positions taken by other individual ministers or what they said on particular issues, especially those on the losing or opposing side.

- Confidentiality is an *instrument of control* for the prime minister and other senior ministers; it is also a test of loyalty of cabinet colleagues (not leaking, being trustworthy, being a confidential sounding-board, and so on).

- Increasingly, the conventions surrounding solidarity have been codified in *Cabinet Handbook*s and *ministerial guides* by prime ministers and their departments (often more by officials than the politicians); at times, these have had to be reworded to accommodate latitude, discretion and even exceptions to the 'rule'; although the most recent *Cabinet Handbook* (Australian Government 2009) presents the general principles as if they insist on absolute agreement and confidentiality (that is, no public dissent in the party room or outside to the general community); these codes pretend they do not countenance exemptions, but clearly political practice does.

Hence, while collective responsibility exists as a 'fundamental' convention (and as an aspirational ideal), it is couched in interpretation through many subordinate or 'lesser' sub-conventions that give it practical meaning. It changes in emphasis over time and according to different circumstances. For instance, while it is insisted with absolute conviction that cabinet ministers do not oppose government policy in public, some do and get away with it. In the Rudd Government, the Resources and Energy Minister, Martin Ferguson, made statements indicating he opposed the Labor Government's proposed Fuel Watch scheme on the grounds that it would increase petrol prices and hit lower-income families hardest. Ferguson's dissenting views were contained in written correspondence to his cabinet colleagues that was leaked after the decision was taken (so who leaked and why?). He ventured his defence to ABC Radio that 'as part of a Cabinet process, I am expected to actually express a view as the Minister of Resources and Energy...I made that contribution to the Cabinet processes, Cabinet decided that my views were not appropriate and Cabinet correctly decided to introduce a Fuel Watch scheme' (*ABC News*, 27 May 2008). His (leaked) correspondence and then his explanatory interview on air clearly demonstrated he opposed the decision, but he was saved by his subsequent comments reaffirming the principle of solidarity ('I am one who absolutely believes in the Cabinet process, and I accept my responsibility to argue out what is appropriate, but also to absolutely accept the outcome of Cabinet'). Ferguson was not considered to have personally leaked the letter, and the incident was covered up with a Department of the Prime Minister and Cabinet (PM&C) investigation into the leak.

Balancing the Competing Logics of Individual and Collective Responsibility

In any ministry the competing logics of *individual* and *collective* responsibility will coexist uneasily; they can operate harmoniously or in juxtaposition and on occasions collide. Arguably, the dynamics of individualism and collectivism are maintained in some sort of creative tension, but what keeps these forces in check? The following are important factors mediating these dynamics

- the political need to create the perception of collective solidarity, to appear unified and politically coherent, to be perceived to be in control of their agenda; to avoid embarrassing inconsistencies or incoherence

- leadership styles and behaviours that meld the ministry; the necessary leadership qualities to find ways to embrace the cabinet or ministry and value the input of colleagues into political or administrative decisions; strategically managing the collective

- the need to have clear lines of political demarcation over matters likely to come before the government; a clarity of roles and responsibilities within the ministry; ministers may operate with some autonomy in their own domains and be expected to take charge of a set of responsibilities yet still be required to explain their priorities to their colleagues and persuade them of their merit

- the importance of internal hierarchical principles of ranking and predictable patterns of promotion; ministerial or party seniority, known pecking orders, entitlements to office or tenure, the notion of internal queues for positions, esteem and personal standing; some collegial acceptance of the order of 'standing' (the issue here is: who is really important, who has to be treated differently, who can be discarded, and so on)

- the need to accommodate factional groups or make cross-party accommodations (including coalitional politics)

- the continual assessment of risk and the fear of a scandal or 'stuff-up'; the potential threat of individual dismissal or demotion as ministers; the likelihood of enforced resignation; or being assigned unpleasant or difficult responsibilities

- the impact of the media and public commentary on ministerial performance, and the representation of the government's 'stocks' to the wider public

- the fear of disunity and loss of public support for the government; opinion poll reactions; the comparative polling position of their political rivals: the opposition.

These factors are continually in tension and are regularly reconfigured as the government remains in power and perhaps loses momentum, records successes or weathers failures, hits crises or scandals, and either loses key personnel or gains replacements.

The Ministry as a 'Buckle' between the Leader and the Party

Cabinet is a constitutional body not mentioned in the *Australian Constitution* (or by most of the States, perhaps following the Bagehotian notion of cabinet as the 'efficient secret' of the English Constitution). Cabinet is the epicentre of executive government and public policy. It is also an ever-changing institution, run according to evolving practices and conventions that suit the prime minister of the day. In most Westminster systems, it is 'essentially an informal body; it is unsuited to formal statement in a Constitution. Practices as to its composition and operation can and do change from one government to the next; it is even possible that some system other than the present one of a "cabinet" might evolve' (Constitutional Commission 1987, 15). Yet cabinet has survived, and been continually remade. Its disciplines are sometimes tightened or relaxed, its rules made more or less informal, and some prime ministers set more store by it than others; but it continues to serve a range of useful and even indispensable political purposes for the prime minister and the government as a whole. It can be argued that the main reason for cabinet's survival is not that it has remained static, but that as an institution it has evolved and changed as the political system itself has evolved. Cabinet recalibrates itself.

Famously, Walter Bagehot once saw cabinet as the 'buckle' between the legislature and executive government. He was at the time wrestling with the (erroneous) continental European notion of the 'separation of powers' doctrine (executive policy making, legislative law making and judicial independence), promulgated by Montesquieu, against which Bagehot was arguing its empirical limitations in Westminster. He was also writing in an era before the arrival of mass-based, disciplined, adversarial political parties, which changed many of the norms and conventions of parliamentary politics.

Today, if cabinet remains an institution useful to modern party parliamentary democracies it may not be because it performs this traditional Bagehotian 'buckle'. The overlap of personnel between the executive and the legislature (the ministry which sits in parliament) no longer constitutes the cabinet's primary function or the reason for its longevity. Cabinet performs a much more important 'buckle', combining the party leader with his or her senior colleagues and with the wider party room (or caucus). Cabinet is now the buckle between the party leader (or core leadership group) and the party backbench. And, as this 'party buckle', it fulfils many important functions: it allows a confidential arena for frank discussion and deliberation; it politically hones the government's strategy; it serves as an information exchange for open debate; it arbitrates between protagonists or different policy options; it coordinates across parts of government; it determines resource allocations; it steers the government through crises; and it serves as a 'watchdog' for problematical issues or idiosyncratic decisions not advantageous to the government (see Davis 1997, 48). But cabinet also serves other important political purposes for the collectivity over time: it is the incubator of up-and-coming talent in the ministry and is useful in spotting emergent talent in the party room (the process of renewal); it functions as a sounding-board for alternative ideas or criticisms out of the public gaze; it can function as a court of appeal for those who have lost in the decision-making process (leaders, senior and junior ministers); it can act as a review body or provide a second opinion about decisions already taken (as a safety-valve function). In these important ways, the cabinet acts as a bridge between the leader and the party—operating through the 'soft' skills of communicating, persuading, listening, advising, endorsing, scoping, warning, and so on.

Party leaders and their cabinet colleagues first and foremost have to maintain the confidence of their own party. Any prime minister has to maintain the confidence of his/her cabinet and ministerial colleagues, and also the backbench and party room. Over the period 2005–07, John Howard was losing the confidence of his cabinet and party room (and famously initiated an internal review of the support for his leadership in July 2007), but he did not lose numerical support and his principal opponent, Peter Costello, never acquired the numbers to challenge and defeat him (see Howard 2010, 622–5). During Howard's last two terms (2001–07), the Liberal party room consisted of about 106–7 members and senators, of whom about 80 per cent remained loyal Howard supporters while only 20 per cent backed Costello, and this breakdown did not shift greatly over the entire life of the government. By contrast, when Kevin Rudd spectacularly lost the confidence of the Labor caucus in mid-2010 he was deposed in an overnight coup led by three or four backbench 'faceless factional leaders' who had no public visibility. Not only was Rudd challenged by the left's Julia Gillard, on whose behalf the factional leaders were accumulating the numbers for a spill, but his own numbers evaporated to the extent that he did not even contest his removal from office (Aulich and Evans 2010). At the end, it was reported that Rudd had the support of two or three cabinet ministers and a handful of loyal backbenchers out of a caucus of 107. The extraordinary deposition of a first-term prime minister by the Labor caucus was largely attributed to his inability to operate and lead as a team player (Aulich and Evans 2010).

Individual ministers themselves primarily have to maintain the confidence of the prime minister, and to a lesser extent the confidence of their other cabinet colleagues. The party backbench may express occasional internal criticisms, but is generally far less important in determining the fate of individual ministers. At various times, the retention of the confidence of the prime minister in a particular minister or the prime minister's political support in trying times is critical to the overall solidarity of the government. This is particularly important when individual ministers come under attack or are accident-prone, where the leader has to weigh up the politics of defending the minister out of collegiality or cutting the minister loose to protect the standing of the rest. Often the prime minister makes an assessment of the fate of the offending minister in terms of the seriousness of the scandal and the ways in which the minister concerned attempts to explain or defend themself in its wake.

Public Expressions of Togetherness: Creating the image or brand

Over time, in any ministry, the exercise of collective solidarity may be active or passive, genuine, cosmetic or even mythical (Dell 1980), but it is probably more important to recognise that it is usually imperative for the government to maintain the impression of collegiality and coherence—the pretence that they can work effectively as a team. To survive as a government, ministries must show they can maintain the confidence of the house, put up a credible front to their political opponents and the media, and as a working ministry find ways to deal with the business of state, much of which will involve making collective decisions and imposing collegial executive authority.

Hence, governments feel the need to invest in the impression of togetherness. In advertising parlance, ministries operate as branding devices around a leader and leadership group. They help create the image of corporate government. Collective solidarity is important in image construction and image control, as marketing strategies to convey the impression that the government remains in control of the political agenda and is effective in the dissemination of political messages. Collective solidarity is also a defensive tactic when governments need to engage in damage limitation. Accordingly, much time and effort are expended giving the impression that ministries are collective and cohesive entities (from ministerial lists and group photos at the swearing in to expressions of group solidarity in the media and parliament, the representation of each other in other chambers and refraining from speaking publicly on matters relating to another minister's portfolio).

Today, unity and cohesion are important not merely to announce and support decisions unanimously (the traditional rationale for collective responsibility), but to enable the government to operate proactively. Acting in concert reinforces the (positive) impression that the government possesses a narrative or coherent agenda, appears 'on message' in the 24/7 media cauldron, demonstrates information control and the coordination of 'spin', is coordinated in the timing and staging of public announcements, and is proficient in the tactics of whom to protect (their own besieged ministers) or whom to target for attack (shadow ministers or outside critics). Cohesion, coordination and coaching are indispensable collective strategies in the government's arsenal of weapons.

But there is a crucial asymmetry in operation in the standing of the brand. Individual ministers generally can do little to enhance the brand image (perhaps through achieving exceptional 'successes' or personal association with a popular policy), but they can easily damage the party brand or harm the particular leader's standing. Within collective responsibility individual ministerial competence is unremarkable and un-newsworthy; ministerial incompetence or scandalous behaviour achieves notoriety and saturation coverage. The brand is only as strong as its weakest link, and so over time ministers inevitably become liabilities, and when necessary are removed or demoted by the astute prime minister.

Imposing Internal Discipline: How far are ministries cohesive?

Leadership Style: When to crack the whip

Prime ministers insist on internal discipline. To them, enforcing control is the most important aspect of collective responsibility. Discipline can be enhanced (or eroded) by prime ministerial style in 'working with cabinet' and compositional factors of who comprises the ministry. As Weller has argued, the exercise of discipline by the prime minister is a 'matter of political calculation and convenience, not some immutable physical principle' (2007, 207). Thus, both Jack Curtin and Ben Chifley struggled to discipline the renegade Eddie Ward despite the fact he was a serving cabinet minister. On big issues, Ward, along with a future leader Arthur Calwell, would seek to appeal to caucus to circumvent or defeat cabinet decisions (Weller 2007, 79–83). Malcolm Fraser, anxious to restore some order to the cabinet process, once argued that cabinet needed to be a 'tight ship' based on 'contest-and-control', where debate could be lively one minute but where ultimately authority had to be imposed. He told the academic Graham Little, who was undertaking a 'psycho-social' study of his administration:

> I think there might be a difference between being a hard task-master and running a tight ship, but there is no doubt that there has got to be discipline in a team. People have got to be able to express their views strongly…they're no use if they don't. But then once a decision is made, that's got to be it for all of us. Whoever is on the winning, or whoever is on the losing side, has to accept the decision as it comes out. (Little 1989, 15)

Fraser in some instances cut some of his ministers very little slack when they disgraced themselves (for example, the sacking of Glenn Sheil in 1977 or Reg Withers in 1978), but extended considerable latitude to others including Peter Nixon, Ian Sinclair, Jim Killen and John Howard, often to the exasperation of his own party (see Hughes 1992, 141).

Bob Hawke wanted to insist on tight cabinet discipline (and codified his expectations publicly in an extensive *Cabinet Handbook*) but was tolerant of occasional dissidents (such as Stewart West), and sometimes cabinet/caucus revolts (such as over the reversal of the MX missile commitment he had reaffirmed to the US President in 1985). His successor, Paul Keating, was less interested in codified manuals, but insisted cabinet solidarity was the 'essence of our system' (Blewett 1999, 32). He went to extraordinary lengths to defend his ministers, even when their fate looked sealed. Keating adopted a political calculus of what would cause least harm to the collective. He defended the embattled Treasurer, John Dawkins, when he struck trouble over his 1993–94 budget; then he went to great lengths to protect his lightweight Sports Minister, Ros Kelly, during 1993–94 after she had presided over a funding rort to award sports facilities disproportionately to marginal Labor electorates. He refused to allow her to appear before a senate inquiry investigating the scandal, while asserting she had done nothing wrong. He was eventually forced to allow her to appear before a house committee where she effectively hanged herself by her own naive admissions that she had concocted the sports funding schemes on a whiteboard without defensible criteria. Keating, however, was far less motivated to defend his Industry Minister, Alan Griffiths, over the 'sandwich shop affair' when it appeared he had used his office (and perhaps ALP funds) to subsidise a failed local firm that was owned by a business partner of Griffiths.

John Howard talked long and hard before becoming prime minister of the need for ministerial accountability, and issued a fairly tough *Ministerial Code of Conduct* on assuming office in March 1996. Unfortunately, his ministerial colleagues (many of whom had compromising business interests or were determined to exploit their expense accounts) were not on the same wavelength. In Howard's first term, eight ministers were forced to resign, mostly over relatively minor indiscretions, expense account irregularities and a lack of documentation for expenses claimed (only one minister was forced to resign over poor performance in his first term, Senator Amanda Vanstone).[3] Howard responded by relaxing his code of conduct on pecuniary interests and instructing the Department of Finance to take over the processing of ministerial expense claims to ensure due compliance. He also did not insist that the Industry Minister, John Moore, resign after he continued to manage his share portfolio, including shares in industrial firms, well after he had become minister. After his expedient relaxation of the rules, Howard lost no more ministers to personal indiscretions until March 2007 when two went in short succession: the Human Services Minister, Senator Ian Campbell, who was compromised after dealing with disgraced former WA Premier Brian Burke, and the hapless Minister for Ageing, Senator Santo Santoro, who embroiled himself in a conflict-of-interest scandal involving medical firms and was accused of neglecting to register his current pecuniary interests. A succession of other Howard ministers resigned mid-term or at a time of their own choosing *not* because of a scandal (for example, Tim Fischer, Jocelyn Newman, John Moore, Richard Alston, John Anderson, Robert Hill, Amanda Vanstone and Rod Kemp) and others called it a day around election times (John Fahey, Peter Reith, Michael Wooldridge, Daryl Williams and David Kemp).

Kevin Rudd did not overly trust his cabinet colleagues and increasingly resorted to a kitchen cabinet of four senior ministers to decide most significant decisions (the so-called 'gang of four'—namely: Rudd, his deputy, Julia Gillard, Treasurer, Wayne Swan, and Finance Minister, Lindsay Tanner—who were all on the Strategic Budget Priorities Committee of cabinet). His penchant for what he regarded as 'efficient decision-making' led him to alienate his colleagues, who reputedly could turn up to cabinet meetings only to find predetermined decisions listed in papers tabled at the commencement of the meeting (see Tingle 2010; Wanna 2010). His cabinet was not particularly undisciplined, but Rudd's treatment of its members certainly fed into their resentment of him and his style, which eventually led to his downfall.

---

3   Amanda Vanstone was a 'wet' cabinet minister in the first Howard term, but was demoted to the outer ministry in the second term for not getting on with her department and for not making policy progress on the Liberal agendas. She re-exerted herself as Justice Minister and was reinstalled into cabinet in the third term. Kevin Rudd similarly demoted Peter Garrett (a non-aligned minister) after the 'pink batts' affair—but chose to retain him in cabinet, probably because the Prime Minister had pushed for the program despite some warnings from the minister/department.

Party and Factional Dynamics: Tension or stability?

In Coalition governments, relations between the two 'coalesced' parties are complex and occasionally fraught, with some deep-seated animosities and policy differences apparent. The Nationals' preference for regional expenditures, agricultural subsidies, family farms and opposition to issues such as deregulation and water reform have often propelled them into serious conflicts with their larger partners, the Liberal Party. The Nationals' traditional control of certain portfolios (agriculture, infrastructure, trade) often allows them to impose their priorities in these areas of strategic significance to their constituency (Botterill and Cockfield 2009). This arrangement makes it harder for the Liberals to initiate sectoral reforms (for example, the single-desk wheat-marketing arrangements). Personal cross-party allegiances can overcome some of these tensions—as occurred in Malcolm Fraser's cabinets with his close reliance on the leading Nationals (Doug Anthony, Peter Nixon and Ian Sinclair). John Howard did not have the same close personal friendships with his senior Nationals (Tim Fischer, John Anderson and Mark Vaile) but maintained a respect for their abilities. This did not prevent him from decreasing the representation of Nationals in cabinet from four in his first two cabinets (1996–2001), compared with 14 Liberals, to just three in his last two terms (2001–07) with 15 Liberals. The reduction in the Nationals' representation in cabinet was due to their declining parliamentary representation (and also because senior Liberals doubted whether the Nationals had any serious ministerial talent available).

Unlike in Labor governments, in Coalition ministries factional alliances are not as pronounced. Left–right alignments are found in centre-right cabinets but are not usually the basis of political disputes or policy differences. In a rough estimation of factional groupings, Howard's first cabinet had nine 'dries' to nine 'wets' (this 'balancing' had been a precondition of Howard's second run at the opposition leadership in 1995) and finished with 11 'dries' to seven 'wets' (although some of the original 'wets' had by then become hard 'dries'). Other internal groupings are usually aligned around personal identifications with leaders or contenders. In Howard's ministries the Costello supporters increasingly became frustrated and occasionally vocal but never managed to wrest the numbers from Howard's camp. In opposition after 2007, the leadership preferences of these two former solid blocs became problematic. The Liberal leadership was initially decided in a narrow contest between Brendan Nelson's supporters (ex-Howardites and anti-Turnbull critics) and Malcolm Turnbull's numbers; then, following internal disquiet about Nelson's own performance, Nelson was narrowly defeated by Turnbull in 2008; after which mounting right-wing opposition to Turnbull's leadership led to a three-way contest between Turnbull, Joe Hockey and Tony Abbott. Although Hockey had been expected to defeat Turnbull easily, he alienated many supporters by softening his approach to climate change and came third in the ballot; his votes then drifted to Abbott who beat Turnbull by one vote in November 2009. The leadership issue did not subside until Abbott cemented his position after his near-victory at the 2010 election.

The factional composition of the ministry and the power-base of crucial individual ministers are more important among Labor governments and can affect the coherence and internal discipline of cabinet. Discipline was arguably more difficult when caucus elected the entire composition of ministries and the leader had limited ability to determine who was in his team. Chifley, Whitlam and Hawke felt uncomfortable with some of their 'caucus-elected' ministers and would have excluded or demoted them if it had been within their discretionary powers. Since 2007 both Rudd and Gillard have exercised the right to select their own ministries (in consultation with factional leaders but with greater personal choice from the leader). Federal Labor governments have long been bifurcated between the right and left factional blocs, but with ministers largely selected on seniority and their colleagues' assessments of their abilities, with some rewarded on factional alignment or in return for dastardly deeds over, say, a leadership challenge.

Since the mid-1980s factional 'balance' in Labor governments has produced greater degrees of stability, consistency and predictability. Hawke was given a talented cabinet dominated by MPs from the right and centre-left factions, many of whom had outstanding abilities. Keating's cabinets were dominated by his own NSW right faction (with weaker performers from right factions in other States), but he also accommodated the left who provided his deputy (at the expense of the fading centre-left). Exercising greater personal choice (but also dependent on the left's numbers to secure his own elevation), Kevin Rudd's sole cabinet was the most left-aligned in Labor's history, although the representation of the right and left was relatively equal. Two members of his 'gang of four' were from the right (himself and Swan, who sometimes had tetchy relations) and two from the left (Gillard and Tanner). The factional composition of Labor's cabinets since the early 1980s is shown in Table 2.1.

Table 2.1 The Factional Composition of Four Labor Cabinets, 1980s–2010

Factional grouping	Hawke Govt 1980s (18 members)	Keating Govt 1993 (19 members)	Rudd Govt 2009–10 (18 members)	Gillard Govt 2010 (20 members)
Right Factions	8	13 (11)	8	11
Centre-left or unaligned	8	3	1	1
Left factions	2	3 (5)	9	8

Note: The drop in the right's factional numbers in the Keating cabinet was due to ministers from the right resigning and being replaced with ministers from the left.

Containing the Politics of Cabinet

Today's cabinets meet far less frequently than cabinets of yesteryear. In an era of less ideological polarisation, the fact that cabinet meets less frequently means that there is less chance of or opportunity for ministerial dissent. Cabinet can become more akin to a briefing forum, mulling through political strategies and acting as a cheer squad for the government as a whole. Weller (2007) reports that cabinets in the 1930s and 1940s met anything up to 90 times a year; by the 1950s–1970s, the number of meetings had stabilised at about 40 to 65 meetings a year with many other associated cabinet committee meetings; by the time of the Fraser Government, cabinet was meeting more than 160 times a year (more than 400 if cabinet committees were included), often with separate meetings of cabinet ministers held in quick succession. Hawke brought the pattern of cabinet meetings back to about one a week (fluctuating between 41 and 63 a year); but Howard reduced both the regularity of meetings and the business needing to be discussed (through the 10-day rule), bringing full cabinet meetings down to as low as 35 per annum (but he hived off National Security Committee meetings). Rudd did not greatly increase the regularity of meetings but invested more confidence in cabinet committees than had Howard.

Disciplining Cabinet through Orderly Retirement and Refreshment

Cabinets rely on refreshment and replacement but individual ministers may be reluctant to retire or move on unless induced to do so. Prime ministers in long-serving governments have invested some time orchestrating the orderly retirement of tired or non-performing ministers, not necessarily because they have disgraced themselves in some scandal. These regular, orderly retirements are colloquially referred to as 'taps on the shoulder'. Robert Menzies, using cricket metaphors, would say to dullard ministers who had been in parliament or in the ministry for far less time than he had that their 'innings was over'—they were sent back to the pavilion. In Keating's second ministry, John Dawkins and Brian Howe both retired to clear the way for their successors. Of the 15 cabinet members of the first Howard ministry, eight retired of their own accord without being forced out or sacked (Fischer, Anderson, Reith, Fahey, Wooldridge, Alston, Newman and Hill). But Howard gradually adopted a principle of ministerial rotation and refreshment over the downtime of the summer recess. Each year he would take a few weeks' break, using the time to consider the relative strengths of his ministry and configure his 'Christmas list' while watching cricket. On resuming official duties in late January, he would announce some resignations from his existing ministry and indicate his chosen replacements. This was a repeated and almost formalised renewal strategy undertaken in most Januaries from his second term—in 2001 four cabinet ministers and seven outer-ministers were moved; in 2002 one outer-minister; in 2006 four moves occurred in cabinet and 11 in the outer-ministry; and in 2007 three cabinet changes were made and six in the outer-ministry. All these movements occurred in January alone.

Only one minister in Kevin Rudd's ministry had to resign over a scandal (the Defence Minister, Joel Fitzgibbon, in June 2009). But in Labor's first term a number of ministers indicated they were retiring of their own accord including: John Faulkner, Bob McMullan, Bob Debus and Lindsay Tanner; and from the Gillard ministry it is likely Nick Sherry, Simon Crean, Jenny Macklin, Warren Snowden, Martin Ferguson, Robert McClelland and possibly Kevin Rudd will call it a day soon.

Conclusion

It is easy to observe that collective ministerial responsibility is a fallacy or myth from a single vantage point in history, especially when a particular government is at the time in terminal decay or wracked by successive ministerial resignations. It is much harder to draw such conclusions when one takes a longer view of parliamentary systems and government regimes. Governments new and old continually and repeatedly seek to create collective responsibility and enforce its observance to the extent they are capable. Ministerial solidarity is a recurring aspiration of governments in which they invest considerable political capital, even in its more euphemistic forms of collective purpose or collective tolerance. It is one of their principal anchors in a sea of uncertainty.

If collective responsibility is not always perfect or maximally effective, perhaps as observers we are too exacting in our standards and judgments. After all, we are observing the interactions and relations between groups of political actors (collegial rivals) in a constantly changing political context (exploited by the media and opponents), in circumstances that cannot be controlled, when routinely the business of government still has to proceed. Hence, above all else, collective responsibility is not an immutable principle (even if it can be expressed thus in codified ministerial guides) but an expedient convention enforced to greater or lesser degree by the prime minister, who has to weigh competing options and consequences. In this sense, collective responsibility as a form of accountability is less oriented externally towards parliament but more importantly internally oriented towards the leader and other senior ministers. Analytically, it may be better to think of collective responsibility as a way of ministers controlling themselves as ministers. Finally, it may be that collective responsibility is like a dog dancing on its hind legs: what is remarkable is not that it is done well, but that it is done at all.

References

Aulich, C. and M. Evans. 2010. *The Rudd Government*. Canberra: ANU E Press.

Australian Government. (various editions 1983–2009). *Cabinet Handbook*. Canberra: Department of the Prime Minister and Cabinet.

Blewett, N. 1999. *A Cabinet Diary: A Personal Record of the First Keating Government, 1991–93*. Adelaide: Wakefield Press.

Blewett, N. 2006. 'The Personal Writings of Politicians'. In *Australian Political Lives: Chronicling Political Careers and Administrative Histories*, eds T. Arklay, J. Nethercote and J. Wanna. Canberra: ANU E Press.

Botterill, L. and G. Cockfield. 2009. *The National Party*. Sydney: Allen & Unwin.

Codd, M. 1990. 'Cabinet Operations of the Australian Government'. In *The Cabinet and Budget Processes*, eds B. Galligan, J. Nethercote and C. Walsh. Canberra: Centre for Research on Federal Financial Relations, Australian National University.

Constitutional Commission. 1987. *Executive Government*. Report of Advisory Committee to the Constitutional Commission. Canberra: Commonwealth of Australia.

Crisp, L. F. 1973. *Australian National Government*. Third edition. Melbourne: Longman.

Davis, G. 1992. 'Prime Ministers and Parties'. In *Menzies to Keating: The Development of the Australian Prime Ministership*, ed. P. Weller. Melbourne: Melbourne University Press.

Davis, G. 1997. 'Executive Government: Cabinet and the Prime Minister'. In *Government, Politics, Power and Policy in Australia*, eds D. Woodward, A. Parkin and J. Summers. Sixth edition. Melbourne: Longman Cheshire.

Dell. E. 1980. 'Collective Responsibility: Fact, Fiction or Façade'. In *Policy and Practice: The Experience of Government*. London: RIPA.

Dicey, V. 1885 [1948]. *Introduction to the Study of the Law and the Constitution*. Ninth edition. London: Macmillan.

Dowding, K. and W. T. Kang. 1998. 'Ministerial Resignations 1945–97'. *Public Administration* 76(3): 411–29.

Encel, S. 1962. *Cabinet Government in Australia*. Melbourne: Melbourne University Press.

Finn, P. 1990. 'Myths of Australian Public Administration'. In *Public Administration in Australia: A Watershed*, ed. J. Power. Sydney: Hale & Iremonger.

Galligan, B., J. Nethercote and C. Walsh (eds). 1990. *The Cabinet and Budget Processes*. Canberra: Centre for Research on Federal Financial Relations, Australian National University.

Howard, J. 2010. *Lazarus Rising: A Personal and Political Autobiography*. Sydney: HarperCollins.

Hughes, C. A. 1992. 'Prime Ministers and the Electorate'. In *Menzies to Keating: The Development of the Australian Prime Ministership*, ed. P. Weller. Melbourne: Melbourne University Press.

Jennings, I. 1959. *Cabinet Government*. Third edition. Oxford: Blackwell.

Little, G. 1989. *Speaking for Myself*. Melbourne: McPhee Gribble.

Quick, J. and R. Garran. 1901. *An Annotated Constitution of the Australian Commonwealth*. Sydney: Law Books.

Sartori, G. 1976. *Party and Party Systems*. Cambridge: Cambridge University Press.

Tingle, L. 2010. 'Tensions Escalate Over Rudd's Kitchen Cabinet'. *Australian Financial Review*, 7 March.

Wanna, J. 2010. 'Political Chronicles: Commonwealth of Australia January to June 2010'. *Australian Journal of Politics and History* 56(4): 631–81.

Wanna, J., C. Ryan and C. Ng. 2001. *From Accounting to Accountability*. Sydney: Allen & Unwin.

Weller, P. 1985. 'The Hawke Cabinet: Collective or Responsible?'. *Australian Quarterly* 57(4): 319–32.

Weller, P. 1989. *Malcolm Fraser PM: A Study of Prime Ministerial Power in Australia*. Melbourne: Penguin.

Weller, P. 1990. 'Cabinet'. In *Hawke and Public Policy*, eds C. Jennett and R. Stewart. Melbourne: Macmillan.

Weller, P. 2007. *Cabinet Government in Australia 1901–2006*. Sydney: UNSW Press.

Woodhouse, D. 1994. Ministers *and Parliament: Accountability in Theory and Practice*. Oxford: Clarendon Press.

3. Predicting Cabinet Ministers: A psychological approach

Michael Dalvean

Introduction

Why did Barry Jones not become a cabinet minister while Gareth Evans did? Was it a difference in ability, social skill or political judgment? Was it inevitable that Peter McGauran, Martin Ferguson and David Kemp would become cabinet ministers while their brothers, Julian, Laurie and Rod respectively, would not? This chapter contends that there are reasons some individuals make it to cabinet and some do not, and these differences are detectable at an early stage of an individual's career and are far more important in determining who will be a cabinet minister than the often cited 'representational' factors such as factions, States or gender. The literature on the selection of cabinet ministers in the Westminster system emphasises representational factors. The more nebulous concept of talent is usually dealt with only as a secondary or unobservable factor. Thus, the probability that an individual enters the cabinet is usually thought to be determined by her party or faction, what State she represents, as well as her age and experience. The extent to which she is likely to be promoted on the basis of talent is not considered in any more than an anecdotal fashion. This chapter will address the notion of talent and argue that there are certain cognitive factors that are far more important than any other factor cited in the literature in determining who has become a federal cabinet minister in recent years.

The approach taken is to first test for the significance of the representational factors. That is to address the negative thesis first. This approach finds that only two representational factors are statistically significant. Further, these two factors explain only a small proportion of the appointments to cabinet in recent years. I then investigate cognitive/psychological factors to explain why some people become cabinet ministers while the majority does not. I mine the parliamentary record for evidence of particular ways of thinking and perceiving the world that are associated with becoming a cabinet minister. I compare a sample of parliamentarians who have succeeded in becoming cabinet ministers with a sample which has not. This comparison finds sufficient difference between the two types of individuals to predict—with an accuracy of more than 80 per cent—who is likely to become a cabinet minister using no more information than their maiden speech and their educational background. In other words, the way an individual thinks, as revealed by what he has studied and what he says in his first speech, is a better indicator of his or her probability of becoming a cabinet minister than any factor such as party/faction, gender, State of origin or age.

Representational Factors

What is a representational factor? In this chapter a representational factor is defined as one that is generally considered important to reflect the make-up of parliament. For example, when an election leads to a change in the balance of State representation of a party, there is often pressure on the leader to increase the representation in cabinet of the States whose representation in parliament has increased and to decrease the representation of those States whose parliamentary representation has decreased. Similarly, as factions grow in size, it is expected that the representation of that faction should grow in cabinet. Similar arguments are mounted for gender, house (House of Representatives [HOR] versus the Senate) and, in the Coalition, the representation of the Liberal Party vis-a-vis The Nationals. Also included in the representational calculus are the average age and experience of members of cabinet. These two differ from the other representational factors in that it is accepted that the experience and age of cabinet should not necessarily mirror the average age and experience of parliament. The leader is justified in creating a cabinet that is experienced but she may also be under pressure to ensure that there are periodic infusions of 'new blood'.

With these considerations in mind, we can create a list of representational factors that is reasonably comprehensive in terms of the issues the leader faces. They are

- age
- experience
- State/Territory
- gender
- party (Liberal Party/National Party) or faction (left, centre/unaligned, right)
- house (HOR/Senate).

One of the most direct ways of testing the influence of representational factors on the probability of any individual's being a cabinet minister (CM) is to take a cross-section of a parliamentary party at a given time and see if we can discern a relationship between the parliamentary proportions and cabinet proportions with respect to each representational factor.

Let us consider April 1996 just after the Coalition won the federal election, when Prime Minister John Howard needed to select his first cabinet. At that time there were 129 Coalition members of the Australian Parliament, of whom 15 were CMs. A breakdown of all representational factors is presented in Table 3.1.

Table 3.1 Representational Factors for the Coalition, April 1996

Senate	Female	Vic.	NSW	Qld	Tas.	SA	WA	ACT	NT	NP	Av. age	Av. exp.
35	23	27	34	29	7	16	13	1	2	23	48.6	6.6

On the face of it, the fact that more came from New South Wales (34) than Tasmania (seven) should translate into a greater number of cabinet ministers for the former; however, these data do not indicate how each of the representational factors influences the probability of any given individual's being a CM. We know that the general probability for a given member of the Coalition is $15/129 = 0.12$. But does coming from Victoria increase or decrease an individual Coalition member's probability? What about being fifty-two and having 10 years' experience? In order to answer these questions, consideration must be given to the characteristics of the entire cohort of 129 Coalition members along with all the characteristics in Table 3.1 simultaneously. But even this is not sufficient because it would only provide a snapshot for April 1996. What needs to be determined is whether there is a general trend towards rewarding particular States, parties, and so on. To do this, the study needs to evaluate several cross-sections over several periods.

I therefore take five cross-sections of the Coalition parliamentary party as it existed at the first parliamentary session for 1996, 1999, 2002 and 2005, and the start of 2007 (which reflected the reshuffle that took place in the lead-up to the November 2007 election)—a total of 192 individuals. In this way, any patterns in the way cabinet posts were awarded will be captured. To indicate the data structure that this involves, in Table 3.2 I draw out the data for two of the individuals in the cohort.

Judith Troeth is a Senator and thus scores one for this variable, while Tony Abbott is not, and receives zero. Similarly, Troeth receives a one for the variables 'Fem.' (Female) and 'Vic.' (Victoria), while Abbott receives a one for 'NSW'. Neither individual receives a scoring for National Party (NP) as they both belong to the Liberal Party. The age and parliamentary experience display the age and length of time in parliament respectively of each individual in the given years. Finally, the 'CM' column shows the CM status of the individual at the time the cross-section was taken. Abbott was promoted to CM in 2000 so he is coded as zero for 1996 and 1999 and thereafter as one. Troeth was not a CM in the years listed so receives a coding of zero for all years.

Table 3.2 Data for Logistic Regression: Abbot, A. J., and Troeth, J., 1996–2007

Year	Name	Sen.	Fem.	Vic.	NSW	Qld	Tas.	SA	WA	ACT	NT	NP	Age	Exp.	CM
1996	Abbott, A. J.	0	0	0	1	0	0	0	0	0	0	0	38.5	2.1	0
1999	Abbott, A. J.	0	0	0	1	0	0	0	0	0	0	0	41.3	4.9	0
2002	Abbott, A. J.	0	0	0	1	0	0	0	0	0	0	0	44.3	7.9	1
2005	Abbott, A. J.	0	0	0	1	0	0	0	0	0	0	0	47.3	10.9	1
2007	Abbott, A. J.	0	0	0	1	0	0	0	0	0	0	0	49.3	12.9	1
1996	Troeth, J.	1	1	1	0	0	0	0	0	0	0	0	55.8	2.8	0
1999	Troeth, J.	1	1	1	0	0	0	0	0	0	0	0	58.5	5.6	0
2002	Troeth, J.	1	1	1	0	0	0	0	0	0	0	0	61.5	8.6	0
2005	Troeth, J.	1	1	1	0	0	0	0	0	0	0	0	64.5	11.6	0
2007	Troeth, J.	1	1	1	0	0	0	0	0	0	0	0	66.5	13.6	0

Table 3.3 Coalition Representational Data from Five Cross-Sections

	n	Senate	Female	Vic.	NSW	Qld	Tas.	SA	WA	ACT	NT	NP	Av. age	Av. exp
Parliament	610	180	126	121	165	132	32	74	72	5	9	91	50.9	8.8
Non-CMs	526	158	116	102	133	123	30	57	67	5	9	76	50.8	7.9
CMs	84	22	10	19	32	9	2	17	5	0	0	15	51.7	14.0
Parl. Prop.		30%	21%	20%	27%	22%	5%	12%	12%	1%	1%	15%	n.a.	n.a.
Cab. Prop.		26%	12%	23%	38%	11%	2%	20%	6%	0%	0%	18%	n.a.	n.a.

All 192 individuals who were members of the Coalition for the period 1996–2007 were coded using these principles. Individuals who belonged to the Coalition for any part of that time were included in the analysis only for as long as they were in the Coalition. Individuals who changed party within the Coalition, State or house were coded accordingly at each point.

With the data from five cross-sections a trend emerges, explaining the long-term structure of the Parliament as well as that of the cabinet. Table 3.3 summarises the data from the five pooled cross-sections.

The pooled data involving 192 individuals provide 610 observations over the five cross-sections. Non-cabinet ministers made up 526 observations, while there were 84 cabinet minister observations. Thus, the overall probability of any individual's being a CM was 14 per cent (84/610). Taking each of the different representational factors, however, we find varying results. Over the whole period, the Senate made up 180/610 = 30 per cent of Parliament, but its cabinet proportion was only 22/84 = 26 per cent, demonstrating a slight under-representation. Females were systematically under-represented in cabinet: female representation in Parliament was 21 per cent, yet females made up only 12 per cent of cabinet. New South Wales was over-represented, with a parliamentary proportion of 27 per cent but cabinet representation of 38 per cent. Conversely, Queensland was under-represented, with a parliamentary representation of 22 per cent and a cabinet representation of 11 per cent. South Australia was significantly over-represented with a parliamentary proportion of 12 per cent and a cabinet representation of 22 per cent. Concomitantly, Western Australia had a parliamentary proportion of 12 per cent and a significantly lower cabinet representation of 6 per cent. The figures for Tasmania, the Australian Capital Territory and the Northern Territory are too small to come to firm conclusions on the basis of the raw figures.

On party representation there was close correspondence between the parliamentary proportion of The Nationals at 15 per cent and cabinet proportion at 18 per cent, reflecting the Coalition agreement that the Liberal Party will appoint NP members to cabinet at least in proportion to The Nationals' representation in Parliament. Finally, the average age of CMs (51.7 years) is almost one year older than the Parliament as a whole (50.9), reflecting the higher average experience of CMs: 14 years compared with an average of 8.8 for Parliament as a whole. The logical conclusion here is that it takes time to become experienced, hence those with more experience are older.

These figures give us a starting point for determining the influence of each representational factor on the probability of any given individual's being appointed to cabinet at any given time. The problem is that we cannot rely on them alone. Consider, for example, two phenomena that we have observed in the above descriptive data: the under-representation of females and a positive effect of having more experience. On the face of it there is a rather straightforward case for saying that these phenomena are independent; however, let us consider that they may be linked. The women have an average experience of 7.7 years—less than the non-CM average of 7.9 and much less than the CM average of fourteen. Therefore, in addition to any bias against women based on their gender, we must also take into account the fact that there was only a small pool of experienced women to draw from. So a certain proportion of the under-representation of women observed is due to women being relatively inexperienced in comparison with men. That is, a proportion of the under-representation of women did not occur because of their gender but because of their lack of experience. Of course, the low number of women in Parliament might be caused by gender and hence their lack of experience by gender, but once in Parliament gender does not seem to be a further factor. It is only by 'controlling' for experience that this fact emerges. Similarly, the under-representation of one State may be due to some other factor such as under-representation of members from the Senate or NP. To tease out these complex possibilities, we need to take into account all the variables that are presented in Table 3.3 simultaneously rather than individually. The way to do this is to use logistic regression with a repeated measures design.

The details of the Coalition representation factors logistic regression model is presented in Appendix 3.1A. In the Coalition model, New South Wales (the largest State) is the excluded category so the coefficients for the other States are calculated in respect of New South Wales. It should be noted that, as no ministers were drawn from the Australian Capital Territory or the Northern Territory over the period under consideration, these Territories were not included in the analysis. The following discussion summarises the results.

In the Coalition representational factors model there is no statistically significant effect of being female, a member of the NP, a senator or coming from any State other than Queensland. There is a significant ($p < 0.05$) negative effect of coming from Queensland, indicating that CMs were preferentially chosen from New South Wales as opposed to Queensland. Age is significantly ($p < 0.01$) positively associated with CM while age squared is negatively associated with CM. This means there is a negative quadratic relationship between age and CM. The probability of appointment to cabinet increases up to the age of forty-seven, after which it decreases. In both models experience is significantly ($p < 0.01$) positively associated with CMs, while experience squared is borderline significantly ($p < 0.1$) negatively associated with CM. This provides some evidence that there is a negative quadratic relationship between experience and age with the probability of appointment to cabinet rising until 31 years' experience, after which the probability of appointment falls.

The conclusion from the model is that there is evidence for a negative quadratic relationship between age and CM, experience and CM, and a negative association between Queensland and CM indicating that there was a negative effect of coming from Queensland in comparison with New South Wales. None of the other variables is significant. Thus, the majority of the representational variables is not significant.

As well as there being few variables with statistical significance, the classification accuracy of the model using representational factors is quite low. The classification accuracy is 87 per cent, which seems impressive until we realise that the baseline accuracy is 84 per cent. This represents a small improvement. The specificity of the Coalition model—that is, its ability to detect those who will be cabinet ministers—is only 26 per cent. In other words, of the 84 CM observations only 12 actual appointments to cabinet are explicable, leaving 72 unexplained by the representational factors. The conclusion is that the Coalition models, which include all the representational factors usually cited in the literature, do not explain the bulk of cabinet appointments.

A second study was undertaken with data from the Australian Labor Party (ALP) in opposition. The problem with these data is that for most of the period the shadow ministry was not divided into a shadow cabinet and a shadow outer ministry. This division, however, was made for the period 2005–06, enabling a cross-sectional analysis for the ALP for these two years. It should be noted that this provides a sample size of 175, which is lower than that usually required for a regression analysis of this nature. The results, thus, should be interpreted with some caution. Details of the models are provided in Appendix 3.2. The results are similar to those for the Coalition. In the ALP representational model, New South Wales is the excluded category for the geographical variables and the right faction is the excluded category for the three factions (left, right and centre/independents).

Experience is significantly ($p < 0.01$) positively associated with CM and experience squared is significantly negatively associated with CM. Thus, there is evidence for a negative quadratic relationship between CM and experience as in the Coalition model. Furthermore, Western Australia has a significant ($p < 0.05$) positive coefficient and South Australia has a borderline significant ($p < 0.1$) positive coefficient, indicating that there was a positive effect on CM of coming from these States in comparison with New South Wales. Thus, the only representational factors that were significant are experience, experience squared (borderline), Western Australia and South Australia (borderline). None of the other representational factors is significant.

Furthermore, the ALP models explain very few of the actual shadow cabinet appointments. The representational ALP model has a classification accuracy of 79 per cent—equal to the baseline. The specificity is 25 per cent for ALP, indicating, as with the Coalition models, that these representational factors account for few actual appointments to cabinet.

Before continuing it is worth diverging from the main argument to explain how the coefficients for most of the representational factors in both parties could be non-significant when the qualitative accounts state that representational factors affect cabinet appointments. Much commentary has been devoted to the influence of factions on ALP parliamentarians' careers; intense rivalry between the States has been cited as the reason for many cabinet appointments or lack thereof; commentators accuse both the Coalition and the ALP of not adequately representing gender in Parliament. Yet the regression analysis tells a different story. It shows that the influence of most representational factors is not significant and that the effect on actual appointments is weak. How can we reconcile these two opposing viewpoints?

The best way to conceptualise the situation is to consider the effect of perfect representation. Consider a parliamentary party with 120 members from which the leader has to select a cabinet of twelve. The probability of being a CM for any individual is 1/10. We will now divide the party into three factions (we could use States, gender or any other representational factor—the concept is exactly the same). Faction A has 30 members, Faction B has 20 and Faction C has seventy. The leader needs to maintain factional balance so she must ensure that the 12 members of cabinet are drawn from each faction in proportion to the faction's numbers. Thus three members are drawn from Faction A, two from Faction B and seven from Faction C. What is an individual's probability of being a CM if he or she is from Faction A? The answer is $3/30 = 1/10$, for Faction B the probability is $2/20 = 1/10$, and for Faction C the probability is $7/70 = 1/10$. For all factions, the probability of being selected to become a member of cabinet is 1/10—exactly the same as the probability for a member of the parliamentary party without taking factions into account. In other words, if the leader draws CMs from the factions in the same proportion as their numerical representation, being a member of any faction does not alter the probability of being a CM no matter how numerous its members or how 'powerful' it is relative to the other factions.

What this indicates is that, in a parliament where the leader draws cabinet members from the representational factors in perfect proportion to their representation in parliament, there is no statistical effect of the representational factor. There is only a statistical effect where there is bias in the leader's choice. Let us consider how this explains the results in the Coalition model. The coefficients for the majority of representational factors except age, experience and Queensland are not significant because leaders tend to draw CMs instantiating the various representational factors (excluding age, experience and

Queensland) in close proportion to their numerical representation in Parliament. There is a statistically significant negative effect of coming from Queensland (in comparison with New South Wales). This indicates that perfect representational practices were not observed in relation to these States. There is also a statistically significant negative quadratic effect of age and experience, indicating that the leader did not draw CMs from Parliament in such a way as to mirror in cabinet the age and experience structures of Parliament.

The same is largely true for the ALP in opposition. There is good evidence for a negative quadratic relationship between experience and CM. There is also evidence for a positive association bias towards drawing CMs from South Australia and Western Australia in comparison with New South Wales. These statistical effects indicate bias in that the leader is departing from perfect representation.

Summary

I have examined the factors that are usually cited as important for explaining cabinet appointments. I found that in both the ALP and the Coalition there was some evidence for a quadratic relationship between experience and CM and, in the case of the Coalition, between age and CM. There was also a statistically significant negative effect in the Coalition model of coming from Queensland. In the case of the ALP in opposition, there was some statistical evidence that coming from Western Australia and South Australia was positively associated with CM in comparison with coming from New South Wales. Beyond these effects, no statistical effect was observed. In other words, the majority of the representational factors were not significantly associated with CM. Furthermore, in both the ALP and the Coalition models the explanatory power was small.

In order to explain these counterintuitive findings, I explained that the statistical effect of the representational factors occurs only if there is a bias. Thus, where the leader draws cabinet members from the representational factors in Parliament in proportion to their representation in Parliament, there will be no statistical effect of the representational factors. The fact that there is a statistical effect of some of the States, age and experience indicates that the leader is exhibiting some bias in relation to these factors; however, as the classification accuracy shows, even though there is some statistical bias in respect of some representational factors, the overall explanatory effect of these factors is not great. In short, the representational factors do not explain the majority of appointments to cabinet.

So, there being very little evidence for the explanatory power of representational factors, we must seek an entirely different method of determining who becomes a cabinet minister.

The Sample

The cohort from which the model was created consists of all ALP and Coalition parliamentarians who were in Parliament at any stage between the federal elections of April 1996 and November 2007.

The modelling process was conducted separately for the Coalition and the ALP. The reason for this was that the accuracy achieved by splitting the analysis in this way was substantially higher than the accuracy achieved by undertaking a combined analysis. This is good evidence that, despite some similarities in the qualities that lead to cabinet appointments in the Coalition and the ALP, there are also significant differences.

Individuals were divided into CMs and non-CMs. The group of non-CMs was made up of backbenchers (BBs), junior ministers (JMs) and parliamentary secretaries (PSs). Individuals were coded as BB, PS, JM and CM according to the highest executive level each achieved in government. For example, Coalition member Malcolm Turnbull had been both a PS and a CM; he was defined as a CM because this was the highest executive level he had achieved while the Coalition was in power.

For the Coalition there were 192 subjects. Of these, 34 reached the position of CM at some stage in their career. The remaining 158 comprised 33 JMs, 25 PSs and 100 BBs. For the ALP sample there were 147 subjects. Of these, 34 were CMs, 17 JMs, 10 PSs and 86 BBs.

In order to create logistic regression models, parliamentarians were divided into two categories: the case group, which consisted of the CMs; and the control group, the non-CMs. Details of the potential case and control groups for both the Liberal-National Party Coalition (LNPC) and the ALP are presented below.

	LNPC	ALP
Case group (cabinet ministers)		
CMs	34	34
Total in case group	34	34
Control group (non-cabinet ministers)		
JMs	33	17
PSs	25	10
BBs	100	86
Total in control group	158	113

There is, however, a problem with this study design. Many of the BBs were not in Parliament for long enough to demonstrate executive potential. In general, there is a lag time before an individual is appointed to a CM position. For members of the Coalition who entered Parliament at the 1996 election, those who became CMs took an average time of approximately 5.5 years with a standard deviation of 2.5 years. By including all the BBs in the groups outlined above, we would be including members who were in Parliament for terms considerably shorter than this. These people might have been appointed to CM positions had they had the time in Parliament to demonstrate their ministerial ability. This problem was addressed by excluding individuals who were BBs and who were in Parliament for less than 10 years. The idea here is that an individual who was a BB who had been in Parliament for more than 10 years was by now clearly unlikely to be appointed to a CM position.

A related problem is that where a BB's party may have been in opposition during the bulk of his or her parliamentary career it is possible that, had that party been in government, the BB might have achieved an executive position. In order to reduce the probability of this type of error, those BBs who held any kind of shadow ministerial position in opposition were also excluded. This leaves a cohort of BBs who are truly BBs in that they were not considered to have any executive potential in either a government or a shadow ministry.

The restriction on the definition of BBs therefore reduces the number of BBs in the models to 36 in the LNPC model and 21 in the ALP model. Thus, the final figures for the control groups are as follows.

	LNPC	ALP
JMs	33	17
PSs	25	10
BBs	36	21
Total in control group	94	48

The control groups thus represent a good spectrum of ministerial ability to compare with the case groups. The BBs represent those who have demonstrated no ability to function in any kind of executive role; PSs have demonstrated a bare minimum of ministerial potential; JMs have demonstrated ministerial potential but not sufficient to warrant a promotion to cabinet.

The Independent Variables

The basic variable used in this exercise consists of a dummy variable for legal education as well as a number of linguistic variables derived from the maiden speech.

It makes sense that an individual's cognitive style and way of looking at the world are influenced by his or her education and therefore it was considered important to account for education in the model. Initially, several dummy variables for various types of education were tried in the model. These included dummies for having a tertiary education of any kind, having a technical/scientific/medical education, having an arts or law degree and having a postgraduate degree.

The linguistic variables were derived from a computer-aided text analysis of the maiden speech of each individual parliamentarian in the samples. The idea of using maiden speeches is based on the assumption that there is a quality that leads to cabinet membership that can be extracted from the speech acts of members and that the maiden speeches of members are a good source for these speech acts because they all occur in a similar manner, format and context. Another benefit of maiden speeches is that they tend to cover general topic areas. Most include a biographical sketch of the member and reference to the characteristics of her electorate. They tend to contain discussion of general economic questions as well as specific issues that affect the member's electorate and particular subjects that interest the member. Finally, many speeches include thanks to people who have helped the member get into Parliament.

It is important to compare members' speaking on a broad spectrum of topics. Let us consider what might occur if we did not do this. Consider a speech by a member representing her party's position on a concrete area such as taxation policy and a speech by another member representing her party's position on a more abstract area such as human rights. If we were to compare these we might conclude that the first member was more concrete in outlook while the latter was more abstract. In fact, it is the subject matter that is leading to the distinction not the cognitive style of the member. In order to avoid this problem we need wide-ranging speeches, and the maiden speech is ideal for obtaining a speech sample that shows how the member addresses a relatively broad spectrum of subjects.

It should be stated at this point that I do not suggest there is a causal connection between the speech and the subsequent career trajectory. Rather, the maiden speech is a marker of particular cognitive characteristics. Because it is essentially on topics the member chooses, the maiden speech is likely to be highly indicative of what she or he considers important. As such it is likely to be indicative of what the member thinks about and, more importantly, how the member thinks. The maiden speech instantiates a general set of psychological/cognitive characteristics of the individual; it is contended that these characteristics are what lead to cabinet appointment. Thus it makes no sense to say that a member might change the content of their maiden speech in an attempt to change their career trajectory. A good analogy here is that of a blood test that is used to assess the risk of a heart attack. The presence in high proportions of low-density lipoprotein does not cause a heart attack; however, it is a marker indicative of a syndrome, the presence of which increases the risk of having a heart attack. I do not contend that the presence of certain verbal characteristics as revealed in maiden speeches causes selection for cabinet; however, they may be related to a cognitive 'syndrome', the presence of which significantly increases the 'risk' of being chosen as a CM.

One other issue of importance is whether the maiden speech consists of the member's own thoughts. This can be answered by pointing out that maiden speeches are highly likely to be written by the members themselves. Neophytes are less likely to have the resources of those members, such as ministers, who regularly have their speeches written by others; however, in rare cases where a speech is written by another, it is highly likely to reflect the thinking style of the member, and the member will vet the content and style before delivery. The 'ghost writer' problem has been given careful consideration in text-analysis literature. Suedfeld and Rank (1976) found that the spontaneous speech utterances of a selection of 19 revolutionary leaders had the same level of linguistic complexity as prepared speeches, indicating that both the individual's actual speaking style and the speeches they had had prepared for them reflected the same underlying cognitive style. This indicates that the vetting by the speaker of the style and content of prepared speeches is highly likely to ensure that the verbal characteristics in the prepared speech closely mirror those of the speaker's actual verbal characteristics. Winter (1987) explained why presidential inaugural addresses, usually written by a speechwriter, could nevertheless be reliably used to derive 'motive scores' of individual presidents:

> When formal prepared speeches are scored, it is natural to ask whether the results reflect the motives of the president or those of the speech writers. There are, however, several reasons for believing that this is not an important problem. First, any good speech writer knows how to produce words and images that feel appropriate and comfortable to the presidential client. Second, before a speech as important as the first inaugural address, presidents spend a good deal of time reviewing and changing the text, paying special attention to the kinds of images that are coded in the motive-scoring systems. For example, the various drafts of President Kennedy's inaugural address show insertions and deletions of scorable imagery, in Kennedy's own handwriting. Many speeches in the Eisenhower Library archives show the same. Thus, although the words may have originated from many sources, in the end an inaugural address probably says almost exactly what the president wants it to say. (Winter 1987, 198)

There is no reason to think that these considerations do not apply to the maiden speech of Australian parliamentarians. After all, maiden speeches provide the first opportunity for Australian parliamentarians to introduce themselves to Parliament. Hence, it seems reasonable that, if it were written by a 'ghost' the parliamentarian would still spend considerable time and effort to ensure that it represented what she wanted to say or wanted to project in terms of message and persona.

It should be stressed that, for the purposes of the construction of the models, a maiden speech is defined as the first speech given by the individual in Federal Parliament. Thus, for those parliamentarians who had experience in State parliaments, the maiden speech in the Federal Parliament was used. For those parliamentarians who had lost their seats and then were later re-elected the maiden speech was taken as the first speech given in the first period in Parliament.

The most technically demanding aspect of the model-building process is the transformation of the maiden speeches into linguistic variables. This was done with the text-analysis program Linguistic Inquiry and Word Count (LIWC). Pennebaker and King (1999, 1296) state that 'one of the most daunting problems in assessing linguistic styles is in deciding on the appropriate dimensions of language and, once selected, determining the best unit of analysis'. Their solution is to concentrate on the 'how' rather than the 'what' of discourse. The idea here is that the way people express themselves provides data about them. This is the basis of the LIWC approach.

The problem with many attempts to use text data to create a profile of the speaker is that a theoretical stance is taken about underlying constructs such as personality traits or motives and it is assumed that these constructs are manifested in the speaker's narratives. This is essentially the approach taken by Emrich et al. (2001) and House et al. (1991). To avoid having to rely on theoretical constructs, Pennebaker and King developed the Linguistic Inquiry and Word Count program. The difference between LIWC and other text-analysis methods is that the categories were determined empirically based on how words are actually used. This is quite different from most other word-count strategies, which make assumptions about the relationship between word categories and what they reveal about underlying psychological characteristics. For example, Martindale's (West et al. 1983) regressive image method breaks a large sample of common words into 'concept' words as opposed to sensory words, and holds that those who use concept words are less aligned with the primordial impulses than those who use sensory words. Thus, to 'travel' involves a concept because it does not mention the means of locomotion. In contrast, to 'walk' is a sensory word because we can imagine the sensations associated with walking. Martindale and Dailey (1996) used this method to show that there is a link between high creativity and higher use of sensory words. Another theoretical approach is that of Herman (2003), which holds that the use of words high in certainty is associated with the construct of conceptual complexity. The theoretical approaches to text analysis are similar in that they posit an underlying psychological construct and use text analyses based on word-count strategies to tap the construct. In a CM selection problem we have little idea as to what is important.

In contrast with the theoretical approaches, LIWC is based on the empirical analysis of language use. The starting point with LIWC is the dictionary and its division into sub-dictionaries or categories. The original categories were chosen because the program's originators wanted to develop a list of words associated with common behavioural and cognitive processes and activities. These processes and activities became the 72 basic categories used in LIWC. They included 'negative emotion', 'affect', 'leisure', 'work', 'family', 'social activities' and 'psychological processes'. For each of these basic categories the developers sought a list of associated words. For example, the psychological processes category words were developed from the Positive Affect Negative Affect Scale (Watson et al. 1988, cited in Pennebaker et al. 2007), *Roget's Thesaurus* and standard English dictionaries. From these sources the list of words associated with 'psychological processes' was developed. The initial set of words was then assigned to other categories according to their cognitive content. Thus, the word 'angry', as well as going into the 'psychological processes' category, went into the 'anger', 'negative emotion' and 'affect' categories. An important aspect of the 72 basic categories is that there is a hierarchical structure. In determining the basic cognitive and behavioural categories it was necessary to account for different levels at which each word could be categorised. For example, it would not be sufficient to categorise the word 'offensive' as 'affect'. A separate, more detailed category was required to capture the negative connotations of the word. Thus, hierarchical categories were added so that each word could be categorised at a high order and one or more lower-order specific categories. 'Offensive', for example, is categorised as 'affect', at the highest order and, at progressively lower orders, as 'negative emotion' and 'anger'.

It should be noted that there was no more theory involved in the process of creating the LIWC word categories than knowledge of how the words are used in Standard English. The lack of any theoretical structure in the process is evident in that the procedures used to vet the words included in each category were entirely empirical. To determine which words should be included in each category, an agreement of at least two out of a panel of three judges was required; otherwise the word was dropped. The resulting categorisations were then subjected to the same process by a panel of three different judges.

Since the first version of LIWC came out in 2001 there have been modifications. The 2007 version has 80 categories. Sixty-eight of these are word categories while the remaining are structural and include such measures as words per sentence, commas and long words (greater than six letters). Parts of speech have appropriate categories, enabling words to be classified according to person, tense, and so on, as well as by cognitive content. The total number of words recognised by the 2007 version is approximately 4500 including word stems. From a large sample of written and spoken language across multiple genres, Pennebaker et al. (2007, 10) found that 82 per cent of the words used were included in the 2001 LIWC dictionary. Thus, there is good evidence that the LIWC dictionary captures a large proportion of words used in spoken and written English.

The running of LIWC is straightforward. LIWC works by comparing the words in the target text with the words in the various pre-established category dictionaries. If a word in the target text is one of the words or word stems in one of the category dictionaries, the appropriate word categories are incremented. The word 'family', for example, falls into the categories of 'social', 'family', 'leisure' and 'home'. If 'family' occurred twice in a text of 200 words, each of the 'family', 'leisure' and 'home' categories would be incremented by $2/200 = 1/100$. Final output for all variables except the 'word count' variable is expressed as a percentage of the total number of words in the text.

The utility of LIWC in text analysis has been demonstrated across a substantial number of domains. Tausczik and Pennebaker (2010) list 121 studies using LIWC for text analysis since 2001 when the first version became commercially available. These include applications to political discourse. LIWC was used to analyse television interviews with Democrat presidential candidates in the 2000 and 2004 US elections. It was found that John Kerry and John Edwards used similar rates of 'positive emotion' words whereas Kerry used higher rates of 'negative emotion' words. A comparison between Kerry and Al Gore found that they had very similar linguistic styles. In particular, they had very similar levels of pronoun usage and insight and cognitive words. Edwards' interviews were statistically significantly different from both Kerry's and Gore's on these measures. Hirst et al. (2010) analysed the Hansard of the Canadian Parliament in two periods over which the government had changed. They found that the party in government uses more 'positive emotion' words while the party in opposition uses more 'negative emotion' words. Yu et al. (2008) used LIWC to determine whether it was possible to use text analysis to classify opinions on topics in US congressional debates as 'for' or 'against'. The idea of such applications is that it should be possible to determine whether a speaker supports or opposes a topic under discussion on the basis of markers such as positive and negative emotion. They found that most congressional debate involves very low levels of sentiment and concluded therefore that using sentiment-laden adjectives was not sufficient for opinion classification in political speech. Niederhoffer and Pennebaker (2002) used LIWC to analyse the official transcripts of the Watergate tapes. They were looking for evidence that in dyadic conversation the words of one speaker will co-vary with the words of the other. The idea behind this is that the words used by the first speaker prime the second speaker to use particular words. This 'synchrony' is the verbal equivalent of physical synchrony in which interlocutors will mirror each other's body language. They found support for the language-synchrony hypothesis at both the turn-by-turn level and the overall conversational level.

The LIWC approach constitutes the majority of the linguistic variables in both the ALP and the Coalition models; however, it was found in preliminary modelling that the accuracy of one of the models could be improved by including another set of variables from the maiden speeches. As only one of these variables was significant in the model-building process, this analysis and discussion are confined to this variable. The variable comes from the results of Paivio et al. (1968) (hereinafter PYM). In this study a selection of 925 concrete and abstract English nouns was measured on a number of linguistic scales. One of the scales was the ease of definitions. For each word in the sample, subjects were asked how easy it was to define on a scale of one to seven, with seven being easiest to define. Out of the sample of 925 words the word that was easiest to define was 'baby' (score = 6.79) while the hardest was 'gadfly' (score = 1.92). Paivio et al. (1968) found that the number of definitions a word has is correlated with other linguistic variables such as the concreteness of a word, the age at which it is acquired and the 'imagability' of the word—that is, how hard it is to imagine the object depicted, the idea being that abstract nouns are harder to imagine than concrete nouns.

The PYM scores on 925 common nouns were used to create a proxy for the average number of definitions of the words used in maiden speeches. The procedure was as follows. The first step was to identify, for each speech, which of the 925 words in the PYM sample were present. The average for these was then calculated. Consider, for example, the sentence 'The baby ridiculed the gadfly's umbrella'. In this sentence the words 'the' and 'ridiculed' are not in the PYM sample, so they are ignored. The words 'baby', 'gadfly' and 'umbrella' are in the sample with scores of 6.79, 1.92 and 6.04 respectively. As the sentence contains three words from the PYM sample, the 'def' score for the sentence is calculated as follows: (6.79 + 1.92 + 6.04)/3 = 4.92. If 'baby' appeared twice—as in the sentence 'The baby ridiculed the baby gadfly's umbrella'—its score would be included twice, so the calculation is: (6.79 + 6.79 + 1.92 + 6.04)/4 = 5.39. In this way we get a proxy for the average number of definitions of words used in each speech. It is only a proxy because it is based on a 925-word sample; however, as we shall see, this variable is useful in the modelling process.

The Modelling Process

As the problem is essentially one of classification, two traditional modelling processes were considered: logistic regression and discriminant analysis. Inspection of the data revealed that some of the variables were not normally distributed. Furthermore, there was evidence of some nonlinearity between the dependent and independent variables. Discriminant analysis assumes a normal distribution of variables and linear association between independent and dependent variables while logistic regression does not. Thus, logistic regression was deemed more appropriate than discriminant analysis.

In order to fit the best possible model, forward stepwise regression was used. This procedure involves using an algorithm that selects the independent variables from a large selection of possible independent variables. The algorithm selects those variables that are best at predicting the dependent variable. All 80 LIWC variables were initially considered for inclusion, as were linguistic variables based on the Paivio et al. (1968) study and the education variables. Several LIWC variables, such as 'swearing' and 'parentheses', were excluded from the analysis. Swearing was excluded because of problems with the recognition of words in context (this is a problem with the word-count strategy in general). For example, the software was unable to distinguish between the use of the word 'bloody' in the context of a description of a battle and its use as an expletive. The punctuation category 'parentheses' was excluded because Hansard changed its style on parentheses during the period over which the sample was taken. The earliest speech in the sample is from Ian Sinclair, who delivered his maiden speech in 1961. At that time, if the member mentioned another member by his title, the Hansard transcribers did not insert the name of the mentioned member's constituency in parentheses. This practice was adopted significantly later, meaning that the use of parentheses is not consistent across the sample of speeches.

Untransformed independent variable data were used in the initial stages of model development. The preliminary models created using these data had high predictive power but, due to the non-normal distribution of the data, the confidence intervals of several of the variables were very wide. To remedy this problem, highly non-normal variables were transformed into quintiles. Thus, cases falling in the first quintile were designated one, those falling in the second quintile were designated two, and so on up to the fifth quintile. Variables transformed in this way are designated with a terminal 'Q'. Finally, all variables were standardised to make interpretation of the coefficients easier. This had no substantive influence on the model or its interpretation.

The Coalition Model

Variables that were significant in the Coalition model were as follows.

- Dummy variable for *legal education*: this denotes individuals who have had a legal education, which academically entitles them to practise law. It is significantly positively associated with CM.

- *Spatial words*: this is the rate of use of spatial terms such as 'over', 'up' and 'around'. This variable is significantly positively associated with CM.

- *Certainty words*: this is the rate of use of words denoting certainty such as 'absolute', 'never' and 'exact'. This variable is significantly positively associated with CM.

- *Apostrophe occurrence*: this variable measures the rate of occurrence of apostrophes. As we will see below, the use of apostrophes in Hansard is a proxy for references to third parties. This variable is significantly positively associated with CM.

- *Feeling words*: these are words that denote sensations associated with touch such as 'hand', 'flexibility' and 'rough'. These terms are significantly positively associated with CM.

- *Second-person pronoun* (you): this is an index of the use of the second-person pronoun. It is significantly negatively associated with CM.

- *Colon occurrence*: this is the rate of occurrence of colons in the texts of speeches. There are several situations in which colons are used in Hansard. One of these is when recording an elaborate quotation and this usage constitutes the majority of occurrences in the maiden speech sample.

Two of the variables in the Coalition model are not significant

- *all punctuation*: this is an index of the amount of punctuation used in a speech and can be seen as a proxy for linguistic complexity; this is negatively associated with CM but is not significant (p = 0.139)

- *definitions*: this, as we saw above, is a proxy for the average number of definitions of the words used in speeches and can be taken as being some indication of the sophistication of the vocabulary used; this variable is negatively associated with CM but is of borderline significance (p = 0.068); however, its inclusion added to the predictive accuracy of the model.

Parameter estimates for all variables in the Coalition model are presented in Table 3.4.

Table 3.4 Parameter Estimates for the Coalition CM Model

	B	S.E.	Wald	df	Sig.	Exp(B)
spaceQ	−0.807	0.352	5.264	1	0.022	0.446
feelQ	0.941	0.340	7.654	1	0.006	2.561
certainQ	−0.864	0.338	6.519	1	0.011	0.422
AllPct	−0.475	0.321	2.185	1	0.139	0.622
DefQ	−0.556	0.305	3.325	1	0.068	0.574
youQ	−1.018	0.364	7.823	1	0.005	0.361
ColonQ	−0.880	0.326	7.271	1	0.007	0.415
ApostroQ	0.596	0.316	3.551	1	0.059	1.815
Law	1.110	0.294	14.209	1	0.000	3.034
Constant	−1.903	0.379	25.269	1	0.000	0.149

The model explains between 39 per cent and 57 per cent of the variance in CM (Cox and Snell $R^2 = 0.39$; Nagelkerke $R^2 = 0.57$). The Chi square of 63.89 with df = 9 is significant (p = 0.000), indicating that the independent variables have a significant effect on the dependent variable. The estimation sample classification accuracy is 88 per cent (baseline = 73 per cent). Tenfold cross-validation was used to test the model. The results for all tenfolds were summed and yielded a classification accuracy of 82 per cent (sensitivity = 0.85, specificity = 0.73, Kappa = 0.55). Thus, on measures of classification accuracy the model is efficient. Variance inflation factors were between 1.38 (AllPct) and 1.09 (feelQ), with an average for all nine variables of 1.17, indicating that there was no evidence of multi-collinearity.

From the above summary it is clear that the model is efficient at classifying members of the Coalition cohort and that all the variables are likely to be very useful in explaining why some people become CMs while others do not. In particular, the specificity—that is, the ability of the model to predict who is likely to become a CM—is 0.73. The specificities of the Coalition representational models in the first section above were 0.25 for Coalition model one and 0.26 for Coalition model two. Thus, the ability of the cognitive model to predict who will be a CM is approximately three times greater than that of the model based on representational factors. To sum up the predictive accuracy of the model, using their maiden speech and information about an individual's legal training is enough to determine whether a new entrant to Parliament will or will not become a CM with approximately 80 per cent accuracy.

The ALP Model

Several of the variables in the ALP model are also in the Coalition model.

*   *Legal education*: in the ALP model, as in the Coalition model, this variable is significantly positively associated with CM. Also in common with the Coalition model is that fact that, of all the variables in the model, this has the strongest influence on CM.
*   *Spatial words*: in the ALP model spatial term use is positively associated with CM. It is interesting to note that this is the opposite of the sign for the same variable in the Coalition model.
*   *Certainty words*: in the ALP model, the use of certainty terms is positively associated with CM. Interestingly, this variable, like spatial term use, has the opposite sign in the Coalition model.
*   *Apostrophe occurrence*: in the ALP model, as with the Coalition model, this variable is significantly positively associated with CM.

Table 3.5 Parameter Estimates for Variables in the ALP Cabinet Logistic Regression Model

	B	S.E.	Wald	df	Sig.	Exp(B)
Legal	1.737	0.501	12.035	1	0.001	5.680
adverb	1.572	0.517	9.240	1	0.002	4.815
conj	−1.465	0.501	8.538	1	0.003	0.231
space	1.590	0.560	8.067	1	0.005	4.902
certainQ	1.137	0.453	6.312	1	0.012	3.118
ApostroQ	1.317	0.489	7.245	1	0.007	3.733
Constant	−0.753	0.383	3.864	1	0.049	0.471

Notes: All variables are significant at the $p < 0.01$ level, except certainQ, which is significant at the $p < 0.05$ level. All variables are positively associated with CM except conj.

The model explains between 51 per cent and 69 per cent of the variance in CM (Cox and Snell $R^2 = 0.51$; Nagelkerke $R^2 = 0.69$). The Chi square of 58.6 with df = 6 is significant ($p = 0.000$), indicating that the independent variables have a significant effect on the dependent variable. The estimation sample classification accuracy is 89 per cent (baseline = 58.5 per cent). Tenfold cross-validation was used to test the model. The results for all tenfolds were summed and yielded a classification accuracy of 80 per cent (sensitivity = 0.83, specificity = 0.76, Kappa = 0.59). Thus, on measures of classification accuracy the model is efficient. Variance inflation factors were between 1.35 (conj) and 1.04 (apostroQ), with an average for all six variables of 1.22, indicating that there was no evidence of multi-collinearity.

From the above summary it is clear that the model is efficient at classifying members of the ALP cohort and that all variables are likely to be very useful in explaining why some people become CMs while others do not. In particular, the sensitivity of 0.76 demonstrates that the cognitive model is significantly more accurate at detecting who will be a CM than the representational models (ALP model one sensitivity = 0.19; ALP model two sensitivity = 0.25). Again, with this approach we can determine whether a new entrant to Parliament will or will not become a CM with approximately 80 per cent accuracy.

How Do We Explain These Results?

The cognitive model provides a very convincing argument for the proposition that the individual cognitive characteristics of parliamentarians are what determine who will and who will not be appointed to cabinet. There has always been speculation that this was the case. Commentators often refer to 'talent' as being important but this is the first time anything akin to talent has been used to try to predict who will become a CM.

Although it is not an objective of this chapter to explain the specific influence of each of these variables on the dependent variable, it is worthwhile to briefly consider what may be going on. There are 11 different variables in the two models. Rather than attempting to account for all these variables, I give some general indications of the kind of influences that cognitive variables can have on cabinet appointments. Accordingly, I focus on the variables that are common to both models.

Legal Education

The positive influence of a legal education on the odds of an individual being appointed to cabinet has been noted in both parties. One can speculate as to why those with a legal education think differently from those without. One plausible explanation is that the mode of thinking that lawyers need to learn is akin to the mode of thinking involved in the work undertaken by a CM. There is some evidence that the mind-set of lawyers is something that is learnt. Christensen (2006) describes how high-achieving individuals who enrol in the law find it very difficult at first to adapt to the kind of thinking required to understand legal argument. These students in general perform well on verbal ability tests and yet have considerable difficulty in their early encounters with legal reasoning. By the end of their first year, most students have acquired the skill.

Miller (1995) has gathered a significant body of evidence indicating that lawyers in the US Congress are different from non-lawyers. As might be expected, one area in which lawyers have an advantage is the drafting of legislation (Miller 1995, 77). Legally trained members of the legislature are particularly useful in detecting technical defects in bills. Non-lawyers are more likely to defer to the judgment of their lawyer colleagues on such legal matters (Blaustein and Porter 1954, 99–100, cited in Miller 1995, 77). Non-lawyers are more likely to leave the consideration of constitutional issues to the courts. Furthermore, the technical aspects of law-making are more likely to be attended to by lawyers than non-lawyers (Morgan 1966, 156–57, 343–44, 366, cited in Miller 1995, 77). According to Miller, '[t]hese differences are subtle, but extremely important' (Miller 1995, 77).

Spatial Terms

The use of spatial terms was significant in both the Coalition and the ALP models although the effect was negative in the former and positive in the latter. The use of spatial terms has been found to be correlated with a propensity for expressing thought as opposed to affect (Marsh et al. 2005). What this implies is that members of the Coalition who express affect are more likely to become CMs while members of the ALP who express thought are more likely to become CMs. This is consistent with some of the research on the differences in ideological outlook. Skitka and Tetlock (1993), for example, find that liberals are more likely to want to help all claimants for welfare assistance whereas conservatives tend to want to withhold assistance from claimants who are responsible for their plight. In the case of the liberals, the decision is arrived at via a relatively sophisticated realisation that it is difficult to trade off the value of welfare in monetary terms. Thus it is a 'thoughtful moral judgment' rather than an 'ideological reflex' (Skitka and Tetlock 1993, 1212). In the case of the conservatives it is a more punitive—that is, affect-laden—process. What this indicates is that the strongly factual and analytical aspects of liberal thinking are valued in the ALP. The more affective characteristics are valued in the Coalition. These characteristics aid the promotion of individuals in their respective parties.

Certainty Words

We saw that in the ALP those who use more certainty words are more likely to become CMs while those in the Coalition who used certainty words are less likely to become CMs. What cognitive or behavioural characteristic is detected by certainty words? Fast and Funder (2008) found in a laboratory setting that subjects who use comparatively more certainty words are more likely to be judged by themselves, acquaintances and third parties unknown to the subjects as being more verbally and gesturally fluent and more socially adept than those who use fewer certainty words. The study used assessments by the subject and two of the subject's acquaintances on numerous 'micro-level' personality and behavioural characteristics such as 'is introspective', 'engages with the conversational partner' and 'is aloof'. Thus we have good evidence that certainty word use is associated with some aspect of personality linked to gestural and verbal fluency, which facilitates social interaction. The interesting question is why this characteristic should be advantageous for the ALP parliamentarian and disadvantageous for the Coalition parliamentarian. One possibility is that persuasion is acceptable in a traditionally working-class party whereas in a conservative party it could be seen as an attempt to subvert the existing hierarchy. The plausibility of this account is strengthened if we consider the number of leaders of conservative parties who have been considered uncharismatic speakers: John Gorton, Billy McMahon, Joh Bjelke-Petersen and Tim Fischer. John Howard merited the dismissive verdict: 'There is little to remember him by in his public utterances' (Errington and Onselen 2007, i); while another commentator observed that Howard's speech contains 'no cadence, no poetry, no elegance of language' (Adams 2000, 15). It is difficult to imagine such individuals becoming leaders in the ALP where a premium is placed on charisma. Gough Whitlam, Paul Keating and Bob Hawke were reported to be highly charismatic speakers. It is possible that, given the fundamental cognitive differences between conservatives and liberals (Carney et al. 2008) that seem to have a neuro-cognitive basis (Amodio et al. 2007), being charismatic is an advantage for the aspiring ALP CM but disadvantageous to their Coalition counterpart because conservatives see charisma as impolite.

Apostrophe Occurrence

Apostrophe occurrence (AO) is positively associated with CM in both models. In the text samples the majority of apostrophes is used either as the genitive marker or to indicate quotations. Inspection of the texts indicates that significantly fewer apostrophes are used to mark contractions. The apostrophe is therefore a proxy for references to and recognition of the authority of third parties. The positive association between apostrophe occurrence and being a CM is therefore somehow related to the focus of CMs on third parties. One only quotes another if one considers the other as being more authoritative. Thus, it is possible that AO taps into some measure of humility. The idea here is that the central notion of humility is exemplified by an individual's realisation that she has both strengths and weaknesses, can learn from others and that there is something greater than the self (Morris et al. 2005, 1331). Such an individual is very likely to be deferential to others, as she is aware that they have information and attitudes that she can use to improve her understanding of the world. Humble 'individuals appreciate that they do not have all the answers and, as a result, actively seek out the contributions of others as a means of overcoming their individual limitations' (Morris et al. 2005, 1332).

There is clearly a role for humility in any group situation given that a leader has to be receptive to information and adapt to it. Those who have high opinions of themselves tend to be unable to adapt to information that does not support their self-view (Bushman and Baumeister 1998; Heatherton and Vohs 2000). Furthermore, there is evidence that those with high self-esteem are likely to be more irritating and belligerent towards others (Colvin et al. 1995).

Humility seems to be the antithesis of narcissism. The essential difference between the humble and the narcissistic person is that the former is involved in a process of comparing himself with the larger context whereas the latter is locked into a 'what about me' framework (Coutou 2004, cited in Morris et al. 2005, 1335). Typically, the narcissist is only interested in activities that outwardly promote their own glorification, and is therefore less adept at completing mundane tasks (Wallis and Baumeister 2002, cited in Morris et al. 2005, 1334).

This general overview of the variables common to each model demonstrates that there are highly plausible explanations as to why cognitive variables might have predictive power. It is likely that the predictive power of the variables I have not discussed is because they tap into some cognitive characteristic that is beneficial in a parliamentarian's attempt to become a CM.

Conclusion

The purpose of this chapter has been to demonstrate the efficacy of the cognitive model of CM selection. It began by demonstrating that the standard explanation for CM selection was highly inefficient. It then demonstrated with a cross-sectional model of the Coalition involving five cross-sections and 610 observations that only 25–26 per cent of cabinet appointments could be explained by using the standard representational variables. Similar results were found for a cross-section of the ALP in opposition.

Having concluded that the representational model is inadequate, a model was developed that focused on the cognitive characteristics of parliamentarians. Using one educational and eight linguistic variables, we can predict who would become a CM with an accuracy of approximately 80 per cent. Similar results were found for an ALP model based on one educational and five linguistic variables. This indicates very strongly that cognitive measures are highly predictive of the likelihood of being appointed to cabinet. I have not attempted to explain in detail the reasons for the relationships between the variables and the outcome; further research is likely to cast light on the precise nature of the processes at work.

References

Adams, D. 2000. 'John Howard: Never Great, Always Adequate'. In *The Howard Government: Australian Commonwealth Administration 1996–1998*, ed. G. Singleton, pp. 13–25. Sydney: UNSW Press.

Amodio, D. M., J. T. Jost, S. L. Master and C. M. Yee. 2007. 'Neurocognitive Correlates of Liberalism and Conservatism'. *Nature Neuroscience* 10(10): 1246–7.

Blaustein, A. P. and C. O. Porter. 1954. *The American Lawyer: A Summary of the Survey of the Legal Profession*. Chicago: University of Chicago Press.

Bushman, B. and R. Baumeister. 1998. 'Threatened Egotism, Narcissism, Self-Esteem, and Direct and Displaced Aggression: Does Self-Love or Self-Hate Lead to Violence?'. *Journal of Personality and Social Psychology* 75(1): 219–29.

Carney, D. R., J. T. Jost, S. D. Gosling and J. Potter. 2008. 'The Secret Lives of Liberals and Conservatives: Personality Profiles, Interaction Styles, and the Things They Leave Behind'. *Political Psychology* 29(6): 807–40.

Christensen, L. M. 2006. 'The Psychology behind Case Briefing: A Powerful Cognitive Schema'. *Campbell Law Review* 29(1): 303–23.

Clark, J. M. and A. Paivio. 2004. 'Extensions of the Paivio, Yuille, and Madigan (1968) Norms'. *Behavior Research Methods, Instruments, and Computers* 36(3): 371–83.

Colvin, C. R., J. Block and D. C. Funder. 1995. 'Overly Positive Self-Evaluations and Personality: Negative Implications for Mental Health'. *Journal of Personality and Social Psychology* 68(6): 1152–62.

Coutou, D. 2004. 'Putting Leaders on the Couch. A Conversation with Manfred F. R. Kets de Vries'. *Harvard Business Review* 82(1): 65–71.

Emrich, C., H. Brower, J. Feldman and H. Garner. 2001. 'Images in Words: Presidential Rhetoric, Charisma, and Greatness'. *Administrative Science Quarterly* 46(3): 527–57.

Errington, W. and P. van Onselen. 2007. *John Winston Howard: The Biography*. Melbourne: Melbourne University Press.

Fast, L. A. and D. C. Funder. 2008. 'Personality as Manifest in Word Use: Correlations with Self-Report, Acquaintance Report, and Behavior'. *Journal of Personality and Social Psychology* 94(2): 334–46.

Heatherton, T. F. and K. D. Vohs. 2000. 'Interpersonal Evaluations Following Threats to Self: Role of Self-Esteem, Personality Processes and Individual Differences'. *Journal of Personality and Social Psychology* 78(4): 725–36.

Herman, M. 2003. 'Saddam Hussein's Leadership Style'. In *The Psychological Assessment of Political Leaders: With Profiles of Saddam Hussein*, ed. J. M. Post, pp. 375–86. Ann Arbor, Mich.: University of Michigan Press.

Hirst, G., Y. Riabinin and J. Graham. 2010. 'Party Status as a Confound in the Automatic Classification of Political Speech by Ideology'. In *Proceedings of 10th International Conference Journées d'Analyse Statistique des Données Textuelles, 9–11 June 2010*, eds S. B. Isabella and C. L. Giuliano, pp. 731–42. Rome: Sapienza University of Rome.

House, R. J., W. D. Spangler and J. Woycke. 1991. 'Personality and Charisma in the US Presidency: A Psychological Theory of Leader Effectiveness'. *Administrative Science Quarterly* 36(3): 364–96.

Marsh, E. J., B. Tversky and M. Hutson. 2005. 'How Eyewitnesses Talk about Events: Implications for Memory'. *Applied Cognitive Psychology* 19(5): 531–44.

Martindale, C. and A. Dailey. 1996. 'Creativity, Primary Process Cognition and Personality'. *Personality and Individual Differences* 20(4): 409–14.

Miller, M. C. 1995. *The High Priests of American Politics: The Role of Lawyers in American Political Institutions*. Knoxville: University of Tennessee Press.

Morgan, D. 1966. *Congress and the Constitution: A Study of Responsibility*. Cambridge, Mass.: Belknap Press of Harvard University Press.

Morris, J., C. M. Brotheridge and J. C. Urbanski. 2005. 'Bringing Humility to Leadership: Antecedents and Consequences of Leader Humility'. *Human Relations* 58(10): 1323–50.

Niederhoffer, K. G. and J. W. Pennebaker. 2002. 'Linguistic Style Matching in Social Interaction'. *Journal of Language and Social Psychology* 21(4): 337–60.

Paivio, A., J. C. Yuille and S. A. Madigan. 1968. 'Concreteness, Imagery and Meaningfulness Values for 925 Words'. *Journal of Experimental Psychology* 76(1): 1–25.

Pennebaker, J. W. and L. A. King. 1999. 'Linguistic Styles: Language Use as an Individual Difference'. *Journal of Personality and Social Psychology* 77(6): 1296–312.

Pennebaker, J. W., C. K. Chung, M. Ireland, A. Gonzales and R. J. Booth. 2007. *The Development and Psychometric Properties of LIWC 2007*. Austin, Tex.: LIWC.net.

Skitka, L. J. and P. E. Tetlock. 1993. 'Providing Public Assistance: Cognitive and Motivational Processes Underlying Liberal and Conservative Policy Preferences'. *Journal of Personality and Social Psychology* 65(6): 1205–23.

Suedfeld, P. and A. D. Rank. 1976. 'Revolutionary Leaders: Long-Term Success as a Function of Changes in Conceptual Complexity'. *Journal of Personality and Social Psychology* 34(2): 169–78.

Tausczik, Y. R. and J. W. Pennebaker. 2010. 'The Psychological Meaning of Words: LIWC and Computerized Text Analysis Methods'. *Journal of Language and Social Psychology* 29(1): 24–54.

Wallis, H. M. and R. F. Baumeister. 2002. 'The Performance of Narcissists Rises and Falls with Perceived Opportunity for Glory'. *Journal of Personality and Social Psychology* 82(5): 819–34.

Watson, D., L. A. Clark and A. Tellegen. 1988. 'Development and Validation of Brief Measures of Positive and Negative Affect: The PANAS Scales'. *Journal of Personality and Social Psychology* 54(6): 1063–70.

West, A., C. Martindale, D. Hines and W. T. Roth. 1983. 'Marijuana-Induced Primary Process Content in the TAT'. *Journal of Personality Assessment* 47(5): 466–7.

Winter, D. G. 1987. 'Leader Appeal, Leader Performance, and the Motives Profile of Leaders and Followers: A Study of American Presidents and Elections'. *Journal of Personality and Social Psychology* 52(1): 96–202.

Yu, B., S. Kaufman and D. Diermeier. 2008. 'Classifying Party Affiliation from Political Speech'. *Journal of Information Technology & Politics* 5(1): 33–48.

Appendix 3.1

Coalition Representational Model

The model discussed in Appendix 3.1 was created using a repeated measures design with the individual as the subject effect and the cross-section year as the within-subject effect.

The variables included were

- age
- age squared
- experience
- experience squared
- States (Victoria, Queensland, South Australia, Western Australia, Tasmania); New South Wales is the reference category
- gender
- party (Liberal Party/National Party)
- house (HOR/Senate).

The Territories Australian Capital Territory and Northern Territory were excluded because no ministers were drawn from these locations and they are therefore redundant levels in the model.

Table A3.1 Coalition Representational Model Parameter Estimates

| Parameter | B | Std error | Confidence interval | | Hypothesis test | | |
			Lower	Upper	Wald Chi-square	df	Sig.
(Intercept)	−21.579	5.8029	−32.953	−10.206	13.829	1	0.000
[NP = 1]	−0.265	0.5559	−1.354	0.824	0.227	1	0.634
[NP = 0]	0[a]	.	.	.	.	.	.
[Senate = 1]	−0.403	−0.4927	−1.369	0.562	0.670	1	0.413
[Senate = 0]	0[a]	.	.	.	.	.	.
[Female = 1]	−0.688	0.5410	−1.748	0.373	1.615	1	0.204
[Female = 0]	0[a]	.	.	.	.	.	.
[Vic. = 1]	−0.728	0.5674	−1.840	0.384	1.645	1	0.200
[Vic. = 0]	0[a]	.	.	.	.	.	.
[Qld = 1]	−1.423	0.6950	−2.785	−0.061	4.193	1	0.041
[Qld = 0]	0[a]	.	.	.	.	.	.
[Tas. = 1]	−1.139	1.3174	−3.721	1.443	0.747	1	0.387
[Tas. = 0]	0[a]	.	.	.	.	.	.

| Parameter | B | Std error | Confidence interval | | Hypothesis test | | |
			Lower	Upper	Wald Chi-square	df	Sig.
[SA = 1]	−0.443	0.6605	−1.738	0.851	0.451	1	0.502
[SA = 0]	0[a]	.	.	.	.	.	.
[WA = 1]	−1.241	0.8007	−2.810	0.329	2.400	1	0.121
[WA = 0]	0[a]	.	.	.	.	.	.
Age	0.798	0.2343	0.339	1.257	11.595	1	0.001
Age^2	−0.008	0.0023	−0.013	−0.004	13.910	1	0.000
Exp.	0.314	0.0845	0.148	0.479	13.774	1	0.000
Exp.^{2}	−0.005	0.0029	−0.011	0.001	3.011	1	0.083

Appendix 3.2

ALP Representational Model

The model discussed in Appendix 3.2 was created using a repeated measures design with the individual as the subject effect and the cross-section year as the within-subject effect.

The Territories Australian Capital Territory and Northern Territory were excluded because no ministers were drawn from these locations and they are therefore redundant levels in the model.

ALP Representational Model

Variables included

- age
- age squared
- experience
- experience squared
- States (Victoria, Queensland, South Australia, Western Australia, Tasmania); New South Wales is the reference category
- gender
- house (HOR/Senate).

Table A3.2 ALP Representational Model Parameter Estimates

| Parameter | B | Std error | Confidence interval | | Hypothesis test | | |
			Lower	Upper	Wald Chi-square	df	Sig.
(Intercept)	−23.947	17.6200	−58.481	10.588	1.847	1	0.174
[Senate = 1]	−0.585	0.6234	−1.807	0.636	0.882	1	0.348
[Senate = 0]	0[a]	.	.	.	.	.	.
[Female = 1]	0.177	0.8169	−1.424	1.778	0.047	1	0.828
[Female = 0]	0[a]	.	.	.	.	.	.
[Vic. = 1]	1.092	0.7694	−0.416	2.600	2.016	1	0.156
[Vic. = 0]	0[a]	.	.	.	.	.	.
[Qld = 1]	0.304	1.1772	−2.003	2.612	0.067	1	0.796
[Qld = 0]	0[a]	.	.	.	.	.	.
[Tas. = 1]	0.281	1.0534	−1.784	2.345	0.071	1	0.790
[Tas. = 0]	0[a]	.	.	.	.	.	.
[SA = 1]	2.613	1.5388	−0.403	5.629	2.882	1	0.090
[SA = 0]	0[a]	.	.	.	.	.	.
[WA = 1]	1.727	0.8712	0.019	3.434	3.929	1	0.047
[WA = 0]	0[a]	.	.	.	.	.	.
[L = 1]	−0.529	0.6691	−1.840	0.782	0.625	1	0.429
[L = 0]	0[a]	.	.	.	.	.	.
[CI = 1]	−0.606	1.0306	−2.626	1.414	0.346	1	0.556
[CI = 0]	0[a]	.	.	.	.	.	.
Age	0.932	0.7268	−0.492	2.357	1.645	1	0.200
Age^2	−0.012	0.0075	−0.026	0.003	2.379	1	0.123
Exp.	0.768	0.2498	0.279	1.258	9.462	1	0.002
Exp.^{2}	−0.022	0.0108	−0.043	−0.001	4.112	1	0.043

4. Democratic Ambivalence? Ministerial attitudes to party and parliamentary scrutiny

James Walter

Introduction

This chapter draws upon research into the working lives of a particular cohort of Australian federal politicians—those elected on 10 December 1977.[1] They were interviewed twice in 1978—on arrival in Canberra and again at the end of that year—for a monograph on their experience of acculturation to parliament and to representative politics (Walter 1979). All but two were interviewed again between 2005 and 2009 when their parliamentary careers were over. The sequence provides an unusual opportunity for longitudinal comparison of attitudes, aspirations and beliefs of a cohort at the beginning of their political careers, and again in retrospect as they look back on their achievements.[2]

Not all of the new parliamentarians of 1977 participated in the initial study; of the 27 new backbenchers that year,[3] four were excluded because of past federal parliamentary experience and one refused to participate. When it came to the follow-up interviews about 30 years later, of the initial group of 22, one (former Senator Janine Haines) was deceased and one (former Senator Allan Rocher) could not be located. The resulting subject group (now numbering 20, and all male) was as shown in Table 4.1.

In following the fortunes of a single cohort, we are reminded of the contingencies of politics. It is not a 'representative' group that can be drawn upon for statistical purposes, but rather one whose membership is entirely fortuitous. Yet its collective biography gives us a snapshot of the experience of politics at a historically important juncture in Australian history, as the policy regime that had prevailed since the late 1940s faltered and a new orthodoxy was ascendant.

---

1   The longest-serving member of the cohort, Senator John Watson, completed his final term in Parliament at the 2007 federal election.
2   Recent research was funded by an Australian Research Council Discovery Grant, 2005–2007 [DP0557983]. The transcripts of the original 1978 interviews are held in the National Library: see James Walter, Papers 1976–1986, NLA MS 7846.
3   There were 24 elected on 10 December 1977—14 MHRs and 10 senators—with two senators appointed during the course of the year and one further MHR joining as the result of a by-election.

Table 4.1

Name	DOB	Party	Age at entry/exit	Years in parliament	Ministry	Cabinet
Neil Blewett	24.10.33	ALP [Reps]	44/60	1977–94 (17)	Yes	Yes
John Brown	19.12.31	ALP [Reps]	46/59	1977–90 (13)	Yes	Yes (not long term)
Ewen Cameron	12.1.30	Lib. [Reps]	47/63	1977–93 (16)	No	
Jim Carlton	13.5.35	Lib. [Reps]	42/59	1977–94 (17)	Yes (plus shadow ministries)	No
John Dawkins	2.3.47	ALP [Reps]	[27] 30/47	1974–75; 1977–94 (c.18)	Yes	Yes
G. Dean	13.6.42	Lib. [Reps]	35/41	1977–83 (6)	No	
Ron Elstob	29.11.24	ALP [Sen.]	53/63	1977–87 (10)	No	
Gareth Evans	5.9.44	ALP [Sen.]	33/55	1977–99 (22)	Yes	Yes
Clyde Holding	27.4.31	ALP [Reps]	46/67	1977–98 (21)	Yes	Yes (very briefly)
Brian Howe	28.1.36	ALP [Reps]	41/60	1977–96 (19)	Yes	Yes
Ben Humphreys	17.8.34	ALP [Reps]	43/62	1977–96 (19)	Yes	Yes (not long term)
James Johnston	18.6.30	Lib. [Reps]	47/50	1977–80 (3)	No	
Barry Jones	11.10.32	ALP [Reps]	45/66	1977–98 (21)	Yes	No
David MacGibbon	13.5.34	Lib. [Sen.]	43/64	1977–98 (21)	No (Shadow)	
Colin Mason	28.10.26	Dem. [Sen.]	51/61	1977–87 (10)	n.a.	
Chris Puplick	13.5.48	Lib. [Sen.]	29/42	1977–90 (13)	No (Shadow)	
Peter Shack	20.6.53	Lib. [Reps]	24/40	1977–83; 1984–93 (c. 15)	No (Shadow)	
Michael Tate	6.7.45	ALP [Sen.]	32/48	1977–93 (16)	Yes	No
Baden Teague	18.9.44	Lib. [Sen.]	33/52	1977–96 (19)	No (Shadow briefly)	
John Watson	25.1.37	Lib. [Sen.]	40/70	1977–2007 (30)	No (Shadow briefly)	

Although there was roughly equal representation of the major political parties within the cohort, the experiences of the party subgroups were to be significantly different. The nine Liberals, entering Parliament at a point when their party had almost repeated the landslide it achieved under Malcolm Fraser in 1975, could scarcely have expected that their opportunities to make a mark in government were limited: only one of their number (Jim Carlton) would achieve ministerial status before 1983; none would sit in cabinet;[4] and only two would survive the long years of Labor's hegemony (1983–96) to experience the return of Coalition government under John Howard—and neither of these would attain a high profile in the Howard years.

The Labor members, on the other hand, were to reap the benefit of a change in the political tide: nine out of 10 would gain ministerial appointments (the exception was Senator Ron Elstob); seven would sit in cabinet (although three of these only briefly); but four (Gareth Evans, John Dawkins, Brian Howe and Neil Blewett) were more or less continuously in the Hawke and Keating cabinets,[5] holding at different times such important portfolios—among others— as the treasury, finance, trade, attorney-general, foreign affairs and the deputy prime ministership. When assessing attitudes of this cohort to party and parliamentary scrutiny of executive government, then, one must acknowledge the disproportion in relative experience, with the Labor members having vastly more direct executive experience, and Liberals looking in from the outside. Yet what were their starting points?

At the Beginning

A series of broad generalisations was more or less true of the entire cohort in 1978.[6] They acknowledged the importance of the legislative function and spoke in highly conventional terms of Parliament's significance as a forum, but they did not subscribe to the myth that real decisions were made in Parliament: 'the general governing of the country is really an executive–civil servant, or political executive–civil servant operation, and in most cases those are only marginally affected by what goes on in Parliament' (Labor MP). Important decisions were made within the building, but not in the public domain or through debate

---

4   Six would hold shadow ministries at various points in opposition, but only four appeared serious contenders.

5   Evans and Dawkins were in cabinet from the first; Howe and Blewett were initially in the outer ministry, with Howe first appointed to a cabinet post in December 1984, and Blewett in July 1987. Blewett and Dawkins resigned from Parliament in 1994, Howe in 1996 and Evans in 1999.

6   For more detailed elaboration of the points below, see Walter (1979, 21–31).

in the public chambers. 'What happens in the House itself on the surface has less effect than what happens behind the scenes. But it happens within the institution of Parliament, nonetheless' (Liberal MP).

> Whatever source [sparks a policy issue]...it then comes through the sifting process of public service activity, government backbench committee work, and then it goes into the legislative committee and into cabinet and then the party room...by the time it reaches the public eye in the House of Representatives, most of the battle's over. (Liberal MP)

The locus for influence was the party room, the possibility of scrutiny was primarily in party backbench committees, and the forum for decision was the executive.

Many ascribed importance to parliament's role in disseminating information, airing positions and facilitating opinion aggregation:

> I don't believe that debate in Parliament has much effect on the other side, or on changing any of its policies and attitudes. I do however believe that there is a percolation effect on the general pattern of debate out to the community...and perhaps more importantly I think the things you say in the House, if you say them well enough or the speech is good enough in content, will be picked up. (Labor MP)

For one or two, Parliament's publicising potential was essential—'a bigger, better class-room than you've ever had before' (Labor MP). But in most cases, their actions were at odds with this assertion: they did not pay attention to what was said outside the party or committee room; they confessed to rarely listening to their backbench peers; few felt they gained significant information from parliamentary debate; and none felt that intervention in the chamber was effective as 'by the time it reaches parliament, you've heard it all before', and 'it became clear to me that unless you had got in and put your case to the minister before the subject had ever arisen there was little chance that you were going to have much of a say in the matter' (Liberal MP). In any case, Labor members were not the only ones bound by their caucus: regardless of party (and despite protestations by some Liberals that they would cross the floor if conscience demanded), the backbenchers—at least at this early stage of their careers—were realists who would limit dispute and contention to their own party committee or party room rather than the parliamentary chamber.

These views were not surprising: more experienced backbenchers at that time had put 'what we do in parliament' at the bottom of their list of functions (Ruddock 1978, 243); and contemporary surveys of parliamentarians in Britain and Italy showed that they also rated their institutions modestly (Putnam 1973). Nonetheless, for opposition backbenchers, this was immensely frustrating:

> I've never felt quite so peripheral or quite so marginal or quite so lacking
> in any influence over the course of what happened in something I've
> spent so many hours doing…Really just a question of sitting around
> a lot and listening to other people and…I don't find that an especially
> productive sort of an exercise. (Labor senator)

Even government backbenchers cavilled at the constraints on their capacity
publicly to have an effect on anything:

> The work up in parliament, it always had to be party demands to a large
> extent but you liked to feel that you had input…You worked to see that
> the area was covered and you put out a report that was worthwhile even
> if mostly they weren't read…it was…frustrating, but you realise that's
> part of the way things are done. (Liberal MP)

Predictably, then, there was a tendency to support parliamentary reform of
the sort that would enhance parliamentary power in relation to the executive
and, again, this was more or less general: 'one of the great weaknesses of our
parliamentary system is that the Parliament itself does not play a greater role in
relation to regular executive and civil service action than it does…I'd certainly
like to see that strengthened' (Labor MP). Common themes were improved
physical conditions and better facilities, improvement in the investigative
function (particularly through a better committee system in the lower house),
more opportunities for private members' business and general backbench
participation, more staff, and removal of ministers from the Senate to make it
a genuine house of review. There were some different emphases according to
party affiliation: government backbenchers wanted stronger overview of the
bureaucracy; opposition backbenchers advocated strengthening parliamentary
oversight of the executive and more stringent application of processes to prevent
'ministerial waffle', abuse of Question Time and 'oppressive use of the gag'.

In reality, most were well aware that the executive held the legislative reins and
because of stringent party discipline was able to control the legislature. Thus,
the continual resort to the party room—only there could argument or dissent
conceivably influence one's own frontbench colleagues: 'a backbencher can
influence, or a group of backbenchers can influence, party decisions in the party
room. I think that's probably the most significant influence [they can have]'
(Labor MP). For opposition backbenchers there was something else at stake in
parliamentary action: speeches there would not influence government policy
but were seen as potentially swaying public opinion and changing attitudes:

> In so far as one is trying to create ultimately a climate of public opinion
> which will bring your party, your views, to power, then the…debates

and what you say, you hope, will have some effect. Key phrases sometimes get picked up, you find that organizations that are interested…have read your speech, and that creates dialogue. (Labor MP)

What did this mean for democratic accountability? In most cases, backbenchers saw themselves as primarily accountable to their party: they would not be in Parliament at all were it not for their party affiliation, and it was the party that would be held to account at the next election. Some, but not all, acknowledged a responsibility to their constituents; the view that 'my primary obligation is to the people who voted for me' (Liberal senator) was rare. And as for the transparency that would facilitate informed citizen judgment? Here, views were more varied, including an implication that a general understanding of party positions (parliament's educative function) rather than the detail of decisions was what counted, with a minority suggesting that since what really mattered happened outside parliamentary chambers, the operations of committees and even the party room should be opened to public scrutiny:

[O]ne of my main concerns is to try to exhibit to the public the sort of things that go on behind the scenes, the sort of debate and discussion that goes on in non-public places—in the party room, between members, or between members and ministers. The Australian public is not sufficiently aware of the hard work behind the scenes. (Liberal senator)

Views on this matter were also linked to attitudes to how constituents understood the political role. Some felt that, inevitably, the role was not understood:

It's my job as a representative…to be informed, and even the best informed of my constituents have very little idea of even that concept… It's also my job to have a view of my role that is more highly developed than others [except perhaps] political scientists or whoever in my electorate might have happened to study the subject…it's important for me to have a much more creative view about my role, which they may never understand. (Liberal MP)

Others, in contrast, saw their job as channelling the community: 'I think that [a backbencher]…can reflect the mood of the community more accurately than those who are in, say, the higher ranks, or in cabinet, because they are so much more out of touch.'

This sort of variability on the question of accountability encourages a deeper probing of responses on Parliament, the executive and indeed what the backbencher is there for. And here one can see the beginnings of differential patterns, a move away from what at first seemed common responses. The drivers seem to be the importance ascribed to policy activism, Parliament itself and 'the people' one represents.

Policy Activists

Aspiring policy activists described their purposes directly, sometimes with great precision: 'What I would really like to see…is for this government to come to grips with a genuine, effective national science and technology policy for Australia' (Liberal senator). More broadly, they spoke of engaging with change:

> I've always approached the question on the basis of being interested in changing the course of Australia's development, including the way we do things, the way we look after people, the way we appear to the rest of the world…The political process is just one way of influencing that… but…it's the way I think I'm better suited to. (Labor MP)

> I'm ultimately more interested in policy than in political tactics…I'm myself in a safe seat and the role of a member in a safe seat is…to improve the quality of the policy decision. (Liberal MP)

They linked career advancement with their policy orientation: 'taking an intelligent interest in policy…[is] the best way of preparing yourself if you're given anything else to do, and also bringing yourself to the attention of those who might be making that decision' (Liberal MP). They were in little doubt what they were there for, and this linked to views of the role of government itself as the driver of development. Party was, for them, more important than Parliament in shaping government:

> [Parliament] could control the executive if it wanted to. But it doesn't because…it can't because of the influence of the political parties. Now I don't see that as a bad thing, by the way. I think it's very much more important for government to be controlled by political parties than…by parliament itself. (Labor MP)

> The order of effectiveness of control over the executive [is] one the party room, two the Senate, three the House of Representatives through its procedures, in that order. But I don't think control of the executive is as big a problem as control of the bureaucracy. (Liberal MP)

They rated executive direction highly: 'Complex problems are best resolved in the first instance by technocrats and bureaucrats at the administrative level, and by executive direction, in order to establish priorities and get programmes running' (Labor senator). Not surprisingly, then, they were less concerned with the 'encroachment' of the executive on Parliament, making such comments as: 'The executive is reasonably well controlled. In fact…they're controlled to the extent of destroying a lot of their potential initiative' (Liberal MP); and 'above all else [Parliament] is simply the institutional vehicle for determining who is the Executive at any given time' (Labor senator). And of course, this tied in with their ambitions: achieving a ministry was everything, since only then would direct engagement with policy deliberation be possible:

> The prospect of being in Parliament as such has only got a reasonably limited appeal...But the whole point about Parliament of course is that being here is the precondition for being anything else...[I] would not put any time limit on reaching the ministry, but obviously that's where the real action is, and obviously that's where I'd ultimately like to be. (Labor senator)

> I'm used to occupying positions of greater responsibility than I have now...and I don't think I'd be satisfied with staying on the backbench for ever. But I'd...expect to stay on the backbench for the length of this parliament because there are a hell of a lot of people in the queue. (Liberal MP)

Finally, one's obligation to the people was abstract and subordinate to other considerations:

> [I]f there's a mistake which the Labor Party made in government it was that it tended to respond too quickly, and too generously, to the various demands of...interest groups...The government probably thought it could expect support from those groups, which wasn't always forthcoming...It would have been better for the government to say, well, we are the ones who are best able to interpret what to do in a community. We are not going to take all that much notice of you people, because you are not elected—we are...

> [*And later in this interview*] Many people misconstrue what they would call the interest of their constituency. What they really mean is the view of those people who are most vocal and most influential in their constituency and I always tend to keep that in proportion...I would be...more interested in pursuing what was in the interest of the party in general rather than what the most influential people in the electorate were saying. (Labor MP)

In all cases, this group held safe seats.

Parliamentarians

A second subset could be designated parliamentarians. For them, even if decisions were made in domains not accessible to the public, Parliament remained important as a forum within which there can be public scrutiny of government—that's the first and major point as I see it. It's a forum in which opposition is formally recognized, which I think is absolutely the key to the democratic system...I think it's extremely important and effective in influencing events. Partly I suppose simply because of its tremendous propaganda power. (Labor senator)

Parliament can be one step ahead of public opinion, public demand. And I think that changes can be brought about through the parliamentary system...For a person who's psychologically disposed to being involved in public activities, the parliament is still the best place...If it's not parliament and one is going to operate in the public arena...I mean it's almost got to be parliament or the street. (Liberal senator)

Sharing the general view of the limitations of the institution, they nonetheless thought it could be improved, typically focusing on both changes to formal procedures and improvements to the committee system as means of enhancing legislative scrutiny and executive accountability. It was one of this number who thought transparency relating to what was decided in 'non-public' spaces a useful reform: 'some sort of public exhibition of how the place works is important' (Liberal senator). In most cases, there was reference to the hope of an executive role, but this was not, even at the outset, the sole criterion of success:

I suppose that anybody who wants to come into the parliament and didn't have the ambition to advance shouldn't be here, and he wouldn't have exhibited the sufficient ambition to come in the first place...The front bench is only another step forward. But I certainly won't see it as an example of mass failure or a matter of great frustration if I don't make the front bench. (Labor MP)

I don't see my Senate career in terms of a ministerial appointment...[or ministerial appointment as] the badge of success or failure of my career. (Liberal senator)

For the parliamentarians, however, what they did in Canberra, what could be done potentially on the national stage and 'for the country', rated more highly than what they did back in the constituency: 'Nobody here in federal parliament has a higher responsibility than his responsibility to the nation...And if the interests of his particular electorate are not coincidental with the interests of the nation...then he is in a very difficult position, but I think his responsibility is to the nation first' (Liberal senator).

Delegates[7]

The final group can be designated delegates of the people. They might well be proactive: 'I think', said one, 'that you only put a point of view in the chamber [rather than really influencing policy]...I think that a Senator's work...is done in the electorate convincing a lot of people in the electorate. I think that you help to bring certain pressures on parliament by that work' (Labor senator). But more typical were views such as these:

> I think essentially you're really trying to relate to your electorate...that is of primary importance...You have to let them know that you're active and doing the job as their representative...More broadly you do see your role as being part of a team, part of a decision making process...but that flows from the somewhat narrower start that I've just defined...The narrow start is the important one: you are elected by a certain number of electors in your electorate, and I think you have to satisfy them that you are doing their job for them. (Liberal MP)

> You've got to be in your electorate assisting your constituents more so than here in Canberra...the main job of a politician the way I see it today is, being political, if you want to stay alive and stay in politics you've got to show that you're doing a job in your electorate...It's how you fire back in your electorate that makes you a good politician. (Labor MP)

Their executive aspirations were qualified:

> I came in not with any particularly blue-eyed ideal, but pragmatically attempting to do a job, to contribute to doing a job to the best of my ability...There is no single goal or ambition that you can say I have, and I quite frankly don't understand anybody who does. (Liberal MP)

While advancement would be appreciated, their ambitions were not precisely articulated: 'I'll remain in parliament until I feel it's time for a change' (Liberal MP). They were critical, but had a realistic view, of executive power and did not expect reform to change this. In some cases they advanced principled views of their responsibility to the people, but for most it was conceived as necessity: 'I'll only stay there if I work hard and am a good member...There's a good chance of staying there if you work hard enough' (Liberal MP); 'Any politician who doesn't put his electorate first is mad. There's enough backstabbing and factional operations going on [in] any political party' (Labor MP). They were preoccupied with insecurity and with shoring up the home base—constituency responsibilities and local branch activity rated highly. Often it was for good

---

7   Here and throughout the chapter, I draw on one of the most familiar typologies of representation: the delegate/trustee distinction (see Eulau and Wahlke 1978; Sawer and Zappala 2001).

reason—some (but, interestingly, not all) occupied marginal seats. Two of their number would be short term, but some would survive as long as the high achievers.

Where would the differential conceptions of these subsets of the 1977 cohort lead?

Looking Back

Looking at the career trajectories of our cohort, there was a remarkable congruence between the initial attitudes of the three subgroups and the degree of later political success. All of those whose attitudes fitted the pattern designated above as 'policy activist' achieved ministerial or shadow ministerial status. In hindsight, it is fitting now to reclassify these as 'executive/achievers'. Some of the 'parliamentarians' also reached the ministry or shadow ministry, although they were less likely to reach cabinet proper and were more ambivalent about executive experience. But those most trenchant about their parliamentary identity, or the value of the institution, usually reached only the margins of influence, though they sometimes offered cogent retrospective arguments about their political success—usually in terms very different from those used by the 'executive/achievers'. The third group, however—those who were constantly looking back to the constituency, who interpreted their role as 'delegate of the people'—would not reach the inner circle. David Riesman's (1950) distinction between inner and other-directed characters serves well to highlight the dynamic in play. The executive/achievers were inner directed, driven by their own sense of what mattered and acknowledging accountability only to their own conscience—which, said one, 'ought to be more demanding' than party, Parliament or electorate (Liberal minister). The delegates of the people were other directed, taking their cues from elsewhere, but, it was ruefully reflected, though they struggled to keep in touch and to reflect their community, 'the pressure from that direction wasn't great' (Liberal senator). How did these factors translate into retrospective attitudes to government and democracy?

Executive/Achievers

Most of the executive/achievers, reflecting on their experience, found confirmation of their initial views of the importance of executive direction and a relatively modest role for parliamentary scrutiny. Their views, in other words, had not changed as a result of experience: success had confirmed what they always knew, and to some extent their views had hardened. 'My expectation', said one, 'was from day one purely instrumental. It was all about winning government and then it was about using government…to do good policy things…I've only ever regarded parliament as a means to acquire the capacity to do things in executive government' (Cabinet minister 1).

> I always felt that a lot of politicians were policy people and I always felt that I was a policy [person]—I mean I was never really interested in the parliament as such. I never felt I was going to become a parliamentarian, I felt I was there to do something else and the parliament was a means to that end. So I wouldn't ever think I achieved a great deal as a parliamentarian as such, but as a policy person I think I probably achieved some things, yes. (Cabinet minister 2)

They looked around them and saw that all who mattered were of the same ilk:

> [O]ne of the things I think that struck me about the Keating and Hawke government was that the policy concerns they had were striking. I mean Evans, [John] Button, Don Grimes, Peter Walsh, Dawkins…A lot of them were very much driven by policy concerns and they wanted to make these sorts of changes, that's what drove them along. I doubt whether that was true of Hawke in the same way…he was very detached and he was a very good manager because of that detachment. But Keating… again, I would have said that most of my cabinet colleagues were in it primarily to bring about changes. That is not to neglect the fact that achieving those changes would be good for them (politically). (Cabinet minister 3)

The consequence was a fairly careful calibration of the prerogatives of the Parliament and the executive:

> From my point of view the most important forum was not the parliament but the cabinet room. It is useful to be effective in parliament as well but it's not as important, when you're in government, as being effective in the cabinet room…

> [*And later*] It's the executive that matters…[W]hat the New Zealanders have done is really very peculiar…[T]he theory of it was that you wanted parliament running the government, not the executive, but I think that's a nice theory but I don't think it works terribly well. What you lose in that is a kind of authority and an ability to get things done in difficult circumstances…I mean the parliament is useful for keeping the government honest and that's a key role…that level of accountability is very important in terms of preventing corrupt practices or having secret things going on…But the most important part of it is having a strong but nevertheless accountable executive. Not being pushed around by the parliament though too much! (Cabinet minister 4)

Within the cabinet, however, it was not a competition of equals; the Expenditure Review Committee (ERC) was in the box seat: 'The policy agenda was determined largely by the ERC, not by the cabinet. The usual inner-party "democracy" there, the inner group' (Cabinet minister 2).

> [By] the time I came to cabinet the ERC was really in charge of [the] funding of the government and that's where the arguments took place between the economic makers and occasionally poor characters like me hauled in to justify our heavy expenditures. But there's a lot of policy making there by the cabinet leadership…none of the major issues I was involved with was ever contested in the cabinet. It was really getting the money that was the issue, I mean; my toughest times were never in cabinet, they were always in the ERC. (Cabinet minister 3)

Cabinet colleagues loomed large, the party had to be considered, experts were attended to—but public opinion was of less interest:

> I will be sensitive to the views of the chief colleagues in the government… Also I took general heed of the party, and especially of the [relevant] caucus…committee and I went out of my way to duchess people in that committee, keep them informed. The leading figures on that committee are the ones you knew had influence, because provided your stuff got through there you were unlikely to have any problems in caucus. So I think those two kinds of awareness were given a fairly high priority. I'm not sure I took much notice of public opinion…the other thing you pulled in, expert knowledge. I think I took a lot on from expert knowledge, if the experts convinced me. (Cabinet minister 3)

> I was able for years to basically be indifferent to, to ignore the currents and the things that were running in the community…you just can't do that if you're in the Rep seat; you just have to be attuned to what people are saying. (Cabinet minister 1, Senate based)

Indeed, for the high-achiever circle, even the party came to be of less significance:

> Hawke's usual [forays] into caucus I thought were pretty lacklustre because he never put the effort into caucus that he put into cabinet. He prepared himself superbly for cabinet, but you got the feeling that he never made that kind of effort with caucus except, as I say, when he was under pressure, and on the whole he had a very easy laid-back relationship with caucus. (Cabinet minister 3)

Yet there were some in the high-achiever group who were uneasy, who had some residual concern for what they were doing to Parliament:

Well I think the executive gets more and more powerful and I think that was probably less so when I was first in parliament. I think there was the sense in which individual opinions counted much more...I think the whole show has become much narrower as the society has become much more complex and I think that's a huge worry in the long run. The executive became more and more powerful all the time and I think we're responsible for a lot of that. (Cabinet minister 2)

I would have thought that if you want to make a condemnation of the Hawke/Keating government it was their almost total failure of attention to constitutional parliamentary and party reform...The one thing the cabinet did to my amazement was that they killed off estimates committees in the lower house, which in opposition we in the lower house had enjoyed as one of the few places where backbenchers could have a go at the government, get to the public officials. But on the grounds of efficiency, one of the first acts of the Hawke government was that it was ended, on the grounds that it was being done well enough by the Senate. I think it was typical of their attitude, or our attitude I suppose, that those sorts of issues never got any real attention or enthusiasm from the government...I think the constitutional efforts we made were ham-fisted and poorly planned and I suspect not very enthusiastically supported by many members of the cabinet. (Cabinet minister 3)

One of these critics had shown an affinity with 'parliamentary' values in 1978 (though his 'policy activist' traits were pre-eminent); the other had always disavowed an interest in Parliament as such. Both critics in a sense represent figures moving towards the 'parliamentary' end of the spectrum as the oligarchic nature of their enterprise became more apparent. Yet, not surprisingly, while less fulsome than others of the inner circle (who would argue 'if you look at what are the basic parameters that give this country its institutional strength, its economic strength and such reputation as it has internationally just about every single element in the equation was a function of that period', Cabinet minister 1), they were pleased with what had been achieved, and proud to have been involved:

I felt in the '80s that it was a very strong government. I can't...believe I was there really, there were a lot of people with much more ability than I had. I felt that I was surrounded by people of some substance and arguments were very rigorous. That's why I had to learn to convert what I would regard as a moral argument into an argument that was much more empirical. (Cabinet minister 2)

Parliamentarians

The self-descriptions of the parliamentarians may well be partially shaped by retrospective self-justification, but the interesting consistency between their initial views and where they ended up suggests an element of principle is also at work. They described themselves in 1978, and even more strongly in recent interviews, as parliamentarians first:

> I suppose the central thing is you see…yourself in the role of a member of the parliament and I was…I've always been a life-long Liberal but I never saw my role primarily…I would never have put my party position…or my party feelings in a dominant role. (Liberal shadow minister 1, Senate)

> I've been pretty much a person of the parliament. (Liberal senator, briefly Shadow minister 4)

They saw themselves as speaking for issues and ideas, the national interest, whatever the cost:

> If you do [what I did], which is to try and speak the truth and to believe in something, and I believed in a number of things, not least relating to social justice and education let alone a whole lot of other things like shaping Australia, my priority was to work for them. Now, I'm not going to be made prime minister doing that…coming from that Liberal tradition where we speak the truth and I love it and I believe the people love it. The only people who don't love it is governments who want everyone to do what they say. (Liberal senator, briefly Shadow minister 5)

> I see myself to some extent as a public intellectual and the result is… it's been a common element of simply raving on about things and trying to excite people about ideas or excite people about experiences. (Labor minister 3)

They held strong views about what could be achieved through Parliament:

> [Y]ou achieve a lot of things that don't ever make the headlines. If you develop interests in various areas and you speak responsibly on them, not in parliamentary debates necessarily…But to work through the committee system and to talk in the party room, and you get up to speak about something and…people listen to you because you're respected and when policies come up and you go and talk to a minister or a shadow minister and say look there's some elements here that need development or you haven't thought about or could be done in a better

way...and you're known to know what you're talking about, then you have an influence. But no one ever gives you a headline for that. (Liberal shadow minister 1, Senate)

What you learn is the art of waiting and building coalitions within the party room and across the chamber when you're in the minority in the Senate. And so whilst there may be some disappointment in not getting something this year or this session, your gaining credibility over time is just part of the art of politics, and the disappointment can sometimes be turned into quite a satisfying result. (Labor minister 2, Senate)

They did not evince the indifference towards electorate or constituency voices that was manifest among the executive/achievers:

[Constituency work is] very important in that it keeps you in touch with real people. It keeps your feet on the ground...It's a rarefied atmosphere. It's 'Yes, sir. No, sir. Three bags full, sir.' Cars and staff and offices and meals on tap, I mean it is a rarefied life...To go and judge [the] best-dressed bike competition at the local primary school fete, it keeps your feet on the ground, and to get to meet people and hear what they have to say and what their concerns are. (Liberal shadow minister 2)

Still, in keeping with their parliamentary preoccupation, they held to a trustee (rather than a delegate) view of representation: 'it's up to me to make a judgment at the time as to what I think [is] best. And if people don't agree with me, then they've got recourse to it later on' (Liberal shadow minister 1, Senate, speaking in 1978). Yet those who achieved ministerial office encountered the grind of satisfying cabinet, getting through the institutional process and yet pursuing their policy objectives:

[T]he toughest part about politics and in the...junior ministry...[is] that if you want to do something...you've got to take it through into cabinet and then...you have to take it through to the caucus committee and then you've got to take it through the caucus and then once that's all approved, then you've got to get it into the parliament...But the thing is you have to wait...Because you've got Treasury and basically all the senior ministers and, you know, money and all this sort of stuff, that's really important. So you might think, well you know, I'm the minister I'm not going to do all this, but it's very frustrating because you can't do it as quick as you'd like to be able to do it. (Labor minister 1)

In consequence, their views about what is was realistic to expect shifted—from idealism towards Realpolitik:

> [W]hen you get there you think, you know, I'm a member of parliament, I'm going to do what I can for the country and for the people in the electorate and all that sort of stuff and thanks very much for voting for me and I'm going to serve you and all that. And I did that to a pretty big degree but then…after you've been in there a while, it can't always happen like you thought it would happen. (Labor minister 1)

Typically, they came to think cynically that success depended on relations with the leader:

> [B]eing friends of the leader is the first prerogative for advancement, if you're looking at success in terms of a ministerial appointment…I'd have defined success as someone who had a broad relationship with the community and was aware of the broad interests and was able to work to promote those interests through that career. (Liberal shadow minister 1, Senate)

Those parliamentarians who became ministers or shadow ministers remained all too aware that key decisions were made in an inner circle to which they had not gained admission:

> [D]ecision-making was very much top down and what would happen would be that decisions were made by the ERC, they'd then commit to cabinet, the cabinet will then commit to the ministry. And the ministry really just let the caucus then…tag along. Everything, all the decisive factors were contained in the budget…When the budget was presented to the caucus you might be looking at a process that only took ten minutes literally. Somebody would move, Keating would move the budget to be endorsed, yes, vote, bang and it was all over…The caucus debate was not significant…[As for the broader ministry] I remember the government had agreed on something which everyone was unhappy about, so I remember walking out with [Michael] Duffy and I said how did that happen? And he said well it's all a matter of numbers. He said there's three of them and there's only 24 of us. (Labor minister 3)

> [I]n any party the legislation really flows out of the ministry and you're presented with it often at a stage where it's very late in the day and very hard to negotiate a change. (Liberal shadow minister 1, Senate)

They were also markedly more wary of the competition from colleagues than had been the executive/achievers (who acknowledged the battles but were not threatened by them).

> [Maintaining good relations with caucus] is hugely important because if they're not happy with what you do and when you come up for the

ministry again…someone will run against you if they're not happy with what you're doing…You know, because when you run into problems… they aspire…they take your job. And one thing…I told Kevin Rudd, I said, 'Now listen Kevin your mates of today can be enemies of tomorrow', you know. And I was meaning months on, because you're all aspiring. (Labor minister 1)

[Y]ou're sitting there at question time and the second question comes out of the blue to the fellow sitting next to you, Minister for x, and you can immediately whiff the smell of an attack…and you think thank God it's not me and you sit there and whilst you feel some personal sympathy you're quite pleased that you are not the object of attack. And when the time comes when you are, you know they're thinking exactly the same…I mean to go from the caucus into the ministry is to achieve the reason why you went to the parliament and you're suddenly part of the elite group and there is a camaraderie, but if it means your fate as opposed to their fate then they prefer to see you swinging than themselves obviously. (Labor minister 2, Senate)

The real personal enmity is, I think, in the same side. It's not across the parties. You know that Winston Churchill story where the young member of the House of Commons is looking over and Churchill is on the front bench and this young fellow says, 'Oh look at the enemy', and Churchill turns around to him and says, 'No, my boy, that's not the enemy. That's just the opposition.' (Liberal shadow minister 2)

[T]here's a very large number of people in there, particularly, not only opposition, but a lot of people in your own side that are hoping that you can make a fool of yourself. It's actually not in their interests for you to do that well. (Liberal shadow minister 3, Senate)

Indeed, their experience encouraged not only an accommodation with Realpolitik in some cases (see above), but also a degree of bitterness as their party took a direction other than that for which they had signed on:

The point is that because government was doing all the driving, you see, the party had gone out of policy making. One of the issues I've talked about [is] policy anorexia…between 1986…or 1983 and 1996, the engines of policy generation were the cabinet and the bureaucracy. (Labor minister 3)

[T]he great swing from protected industries to the market forces, the user pays concept…I think has gone far too far now, it needs to be re-evaluated…we were in the stage where we not only had huge tariff barriers but quotas as well, we did have inefficiencies [but]…I think we dismantled it all far too quickly. I think if we hadn't been driven by the ideal types in Treasury and Treasury really governs Australia. It doesn't matter what conceit parliamentarians have, Treasury have the whip hand and I think, you know, if we'd taken a more sober approach to [the] reform of the whole of the protection issue…a number of industries that disappeared and will never be re-established may well have adapted and survived…I think we went through a very unfortunate period in the Liberal Party with…I think it was that guy from West Australia, John [Hyde]…I don't think he had much background in economics, although that was his favourite topic, and he unfortunately introduced this wet and dry thing, which, I thought was enormously divisive and totally irrelevant too…it was a bowdlerised, patronised view of wets and dries. It was very uncomfortable and some of us had some pretty big fights about that. (Liberal shadow minister 1, Senate)

If the Liberal Party was soundly beaten, but I think it is going to take two beatings, they might reinvent themselves as a genuinely liberal party. (Liberal senator, briefly Shadow minister 5)

Yet they continued to salvage some sense of the importance of their contribution to the 'national conversation':

[T]he *ex post facto* satisfaction I get out of it would be to say that I never cease to be amazed by people I run into in the street or people I meet on a plane who said you've had a tremendous influence on my thinking, had a tremendous influence on me and I've never met you before, but I want to express gratitude. (Labor minister 3)

There's a hell of a lot of work in the parliament itself, as opposed to politics in general and somebody's got to do that work…And you have a number of backbenchers, not too many, but you've got a number who work very hard at those things and they never get any recognition, reward or acknowledgement for what they do. But they actually keep frying the fish. (Liberal shadow minister 1, Senate)

[K]eeping the Liberal Party within cooee of the public's sense of justice. I'd been helping to do that…[I] was constantly listening to the people I represented…but to some extent Australia…The whole debate in Australia, I would listen to it, participate in it and so it was fascinating. I loved it. It was much better than academic work. It was very real because the government does it or it doesn't do it, and when it doesn't do it eventually it catches up and they've got to do it. So I'm usually about three or five years ahead. (Liberal senator, briefly Shadow minister 5)

> Fred Chaney said, [I'm a] shining example, if a person specialises, [of]
> how you can really be effective as a backbencher...I've never been
> really [prominent], apart from [on] superannuation and tax and the
> accountability issues...and I've got much more satisfaction out of that
> than if I'm happily being a Minister of Veterans Affairs or Electoral
> Affairs or something like that. (Liberal senator, briefly Shadow minister
> 4)

Delegates

The third group—those who persisted in identifying as 'delegates of the
people'—did not attain positions of influence. Thus, if their views developed,
it was not as a result of executive experience. The contrast between their views
and those of the high achievers is illuminating. More than the other two groups,
they were overwhelmingly Coalition backbenchers, tempting the conclusion that
their attitudes were a product of opposition, and of the attempt to understand
their position, rather than experiential learning or persisting principle. And yet
some of the Liberal cohort gained frontbench roles as shadow ministers and had
clear affinities with executive/achievers or parliamentarians; the delegates did
not. The consistency between their initial views and retrospection prompts the
question: to what extent was their attention to the constituency an impediment
to advancement in Canberra?

> [T]he first and foremost thing in my opinion is not to neglect the people
> who put you there. You must maintain contact and listen to their
> problems...And I think the second thing is you use common sense and
> balance. And don't think you were born to be king, you just do the best
> you can...[T]he constituency was number one for me...I enjoyed getting
> around. It was a bit of a pain having to do it but once you got out there
> and started meeting people it was great, and they appreciated it. (Liberal
> MP 1)

The emphasis on commonsense, balance and *not thinking you were born to be
king* (this last in marked contrast with the executive/achievers) recurs. Others
would explicitly eschew ambition:

> Most of us in my experience were in there doing a job, which we felt had
> to be done. To a great or lesser degree we did it to the best of our abilities.
> There were those who were as well motivated by a very rich ambition,
> which I didn't have. I had some ambition but I certainly wasn't in there
> to feather my nest or to further my career as it were, I was just happy to
> stay along and do the best I could. (Liberal MP 2)

It is interesting, briefly, to review their views on policy processes and executive government. For them, party and committee work remained important: 'the backbenchers can play a role and they do play a role. Well they serve on committees and that sort of thing and they bring that up into the caucus, all their ideas and that sort of thing' (Labor senator). While some were convinced they had an impact through such means, others did not evince great confidence in the traction gained:

> I did a fair bit of work on the backbench committee for industry. I remember I was part with Jim Carlton actually of a group who were lobbying for lower tariffs, that was one of our things at one stage. But I can't sit here and now and say here because of that something happened. It was just part of the mix of ideas and debate that was going on at a party level. (Liberal MP 2)

> The backbench committee often was the outlet if you were involved with any of the backbench committees. If you could put your case hard enough, maybe the leader of that committee would take it up strongly with the minister involved and occasionally the ministers used to come down and talk to the backbench committees and I think you could get a little bit, but as I said at the beginning I felt that if you didn't get to these ministers before they had spoken, your chances of getting it… they didn't like to ever go back and…change their mind. It's very hard to do that, very hard to get them to change. (Liberal MP 3)

They maintained a realist view of the executive:

> I think the executive has always been dominant…you've got to have a group of people who will sit down and work out policy and present the policy and then if you agree with them you go with them, if you don't you don't. You can't have policy-making formulation with…70 or 80 people who are quite convinced that they were born to be prime minister… you'd get nowhere. So that's why you have executive government and I think it's the only way to make the democracy work. (Liberal MP 1)

In several cases, their view of what it took to gain executive appointment emphasised contingency rather than merit:

> [B]ecoming a minister is not an easy thing…I don't know, but it depends on the state you come from and then the number of contenders in the party in that state and the balance between Senate and House of Reps, because there's got to be some Reps and some Senate. The easiest way to become a minister in a coalition government is to be a member of the

National Party from a state that has few representatives in the National Party, and have ability, some ability anyway, you don't have to be brilliant. (Liberal MP 1)

It was understandable that, while reiterating their commitment to matters of concern to their own electorate, some would rate their role in modest terms:

[A]part from particular issues of concern to their own electorates I'm not sure just how important in the general run of things is the contribution the members make in the party room etc, etc, etc. I don't know about that. Because I have a feeling often that on many issues the executive already has its expert advice from its own departments and officials and no matter what we say this is the way we're going to go. Such and such is the way we're going to go. So I'm not sure about that. It is important I think that both through committee work and in the party room points of view are made known and stands are taken and I think that is important and to that extent, yes, we have a role, backbenchers have a role. But is it any better a role than being a foot soldier? (Liberal MP 2)

Others, however, felt they had been effective:

I came here with no pretensions to lead the country or to be a minister, just to represent people, and so while a lot of people might say, 'Well, you've been here 27 years and not being a minister in government', you know, 'it's all very well to say you've been in opposition,' or been on the executive opposition, but during those years, I achieved quite a lot in terms of amendments…So, it's been very satisfying…And I've really been able to stand up for causes. (Liberal senator 1)

[I]t would have been nice to have achieved a ministry somewhere along the line but I wasn't there long enough to get there. Otherwise, no I was happy with what I was doing. I served on one parliamentary committee… and that was very interesting. Backbench work was interesting. (Liberal MP 2)

[Y]ou've got to have pin prickers. You know, populist ministers, even leaders of any party, you've got to pin prick it because they're full of balloons…all these guys, they have got to be reminded when they go outside their credibility area. (Liberal senator 2)

Conclusion

When this cohort entered Parliament it appeared at first glance that there were common attitudes: election was as a party representative, so accountability was primarily to the party; significant decisions were not reached in the public chambers of Parliament, but happened within the building and could be influenced by backbench activity in the party room and in committees; Parliament was a useful forum for influencing the climate of public opinion through the 'percolation effect' of debate; there should be reform to increase parliamentary efficiency and to enhance the power of Parliament in relation to the executive. Yet closer examination showed that even then there were different emphases within the cohort, patterns that would subsequently correlate with success in gaining executive appointment.

One group—the policy activists—had significant 'big picture' aspirations to affect the course of Australian development; couched their objectives in policy terms; spoke of their ambitions wholly in terms of attaining a cabinet position (as the way to put policy into effect); believed it was the role of the party rather than Parliament to control the executive; rated executive direction highly (and was not overly concerned about executive 'encroachment' on Parliament); and was comparatively indifferent to public opinion. This group was to be the most successful: they were to be the executive/achievers of their day. Its members' views changed little as a result of experience. Rather, on looking back, their instrumental approach to Parliament was confirmed; they measured success in terms of policy outcomes; they acknowledged accountability to Parliament and to the public, but were led to a careful calibration of parliamentary power in relation to the executive—'Not being pushed around by parliament too much'; and, in a descending hierarchy of importance (the ERC, then cabinet, then party), public opinion came last. Yet some of their number showed a residual concern for the adverse effects of what they had done to Parliament and its processes; these had spun out from the centre towards the parliamentarians.

The second group—the parliamentarians—had set out with the conviction that Parliament's importance was underrated; it was a means of promoting 'the national conversation' and in this its members could be one step ahead of public opinion. This group saw the improvement of parliamentary processes to enhance the quality of legislation and to enhance executive accountability as important. Its members did not see gaining a ministerial role as a necessary measure of success, and had a trustee interpretation of their representative role (they would do what was best for 'the nation' rather than a particular electorate). Some of them would attain ministerial/frontbench roles, a couple even entering cabinet, but none would reach the inner circle. Looking back, they persisted in rating their parliamentary role as more important than party affiliation, arguing that what had been achieved often depended on work behind the scenes through parliamentary processes and 'building coalitions' across Parliament. They admired those who had been prepared to speak out, whatever the cost. They were critical of inner-circle decision making and often frustrated by more powerful 'executive achievers' in pursuing their objectives. But they had tempered their idealism—'it can't always happen like you thought it would happen'—and it was this group which had modified its views of ministerial/frontbench roles, with a Realpolitik interpretation of what was needed to succeed. In tandem, they expressed higher levels of insecurity than had the executive/achievers— there was always someone out to get your job, since 'you're all aspiring'. A few, from both parties, ended with bitter reflections on party change, but most confirmed a sense of satisfaction with what they had managed to contribute to 'the national conversation'.

The tailenders were the delegates. They set out believing that their task was to 'do a job for the electorate' and that initially they should concentrate on addressing the problems of their constituents rather than the work in Canberra. They were hesitant about articulating objectives and ambivalent about ambition. The best qualities were 'balance', 'commonsense' and not believing 'you were born to be king'. None would reach the front bench. A couple of them were to be short-termers, battling in marginal seats, but some remained in Parliament for lengthy terms. And these still spoke in the end of 'the first and foremost thing' being 'not to neglect the people who put you there'. Modest in their own ambitions, they emphasised the importance of being guardians of the people's interests and pin-prickers of the inflated egos of their more ambitious peers—'70 or 80 people who are quite convinced that they were born to be prime minister'. Some would argue in detail about how effective they had been, most would attest to some satisfaction in the role, but one gave voice to what one suspects was a more common conclusion: 'is it any better a role than being a foot soldier?'

The self-belief of the executive achievers was remarkable: they were inner directed, driven by their own sense of what mattered, and acknowledging accountability only to their own conscience. They did not disavow ambition and were always intent on policy impact, more dismissive of parliamentary constraint and less attentive to public opinion (which was there to be shaped rather than responded to) than those of their peers who identified themselves as either what I have called 'parliamentarians' or 'delegates of the people'. One is drawn to the conclusion that they were 'intent on pushing and pulling the world into shape, forcing us to take notice of [them] whether we like it or not... [giving] us the big picture, its size and splendour presumably a measure of the [men] who put it in place'.[8] They had not come to an accommodation with 'the iron law of oligarchy' (Michels 1911) through experience; a belief in the necessity of political elites was where they started: 'we are the ones who are best able to interpret what to do in a community.' It is a position with a long history: in Australia, the need for steering by an elite political class had been vigorously argued by 'new liberals' from early in the twentieth century (see Walter and

---

8   I am paraphrasing Little (1997, 25) here—he was speaking of Paul Keating.

Moore 2002). Arguably, it is an attitude of ambivalence towards democracy, if by democracy is meant a concern for dispersed leadership, institutional checks and balances, respect for institutional norms and public responsiveness. Yet those who were more attentive to the conventional indicators of democratic accountability, their institutional obligations and their representative roles— the parliamentarians and the delegates—were the ones disadvantaged in the competition for influence. In fact the parliamentarians, at least those who gained the front bench, were the ones who were obliged to temper their idealism— to accept a sort of oligarchic incorporation—in the interests of gaining policy traction.

Can we draw any conclusions about contemporary politics from a cohort whose service, in the main, spanned 20 years from 1977 until the late 1990s? If one compares the attitudes of this group with political biographies from earlier periods (Walter 2009), though this can hardly be conclusive, one's impression is that the ambition of the policy activists is perhaps more overt than was evident among earlier generations; is this a cultural shift, or were politicians of the past more willing to remain parliamentarians or delegates, less driven to 'change the course of Australia's development'?

On the other hand, comparing this cohort with subsequent generations provokes three observations. First, there has been a 'younging' (Weller and Fraser 1987) and professionalising (Jones 2003) of politics in succeeding cohorts. While the embourgeoisement of the political elite was certainly evident by the late 1970s (Encel 1981; McAllister 1992, Ch. 9), this was a group that was still more occupationally diverse than those who were to follow (for details, see Jones 2003; Pickering 1998; Walter 1979; and compare Weller and Fraser 1987). Second, the corollary is that this cohort had, with only one exception, taken up politics following an earlier career (or careers). Not for them the route of employment in a politician's office, or within the party organisation or a party-affiliated entity, which has increasingly characterised the novice politicians of the late twentieth and early twenty-first centuries. This group therefore had both life experience and work skills (including, in some instances, substantial administrative experience) that would stand them in good stead in governance, and that may be less common in those whose lives have been given entirely to politics as a first career. The extent to which this may have engendered different attitudes is yet to be explored. One might hypothesise that with professionalisation there has been yet further skewing towards activists and away from parliamentarians and delegates. Who, then, is to sustain sufficient of the parliamentarian's scepticism about the '70 or 80 people who are quite convinced they were born to be prime minister' to demand reality checks?

These observations notwithstanding, it is not my intention to lament the 'undemocratic' nature of the policy innovators of the past 20 years or the activists of the present. While, as I have argued elsewhere, they may sometimes go 'too far' (Walter 2005, 2008; Walter and Strangio 2007), we cannot prosper without their drive, imagination and innovation. I suspect that in the long term the range of character types drawn to politics is relatively unchanging; this cohort shows again that we are fated to see our circumstances dictated by people whose interest in policy change and 'power chances' trumps conventional concerns with democratic accountability. Political elites are inevitable; the task is not to attempt the futile enterprise of encouraging 'the democratic personality' (which, in this cohort, was most manifest amongst the parliamentarians and the delegates), but instead to build political frameworks that acknowledge policy activists as catalysts yet ensure 'democratic elitism' (Higley and Burton 2006) and decision processes that encourage 'deliberative democracy'. These are tasks for another day.

References

Encel, S. 1981. 'The Political Class: The Called and the Chosen'. In *Class Inequality in Australia*, ed. P. Hiller. Sydney: Harcourt Brace Jovanovich.

Eulau, H. and J. Wahlke. 1978. *The Politics of Representation: Continuities in Theory and Research*. Beverley Hills, Calif.: Sage.

Higley, J. and M. Burton. 2006. *Elite Foundations of Liberal Democracy*. Lanham, Mass.: Rowman & Littlefield.

Jones, C. 2003. Working in Politics: Australian Parliamentarians and Professionalism. PhD Thesis, School of Social Sciences, La Trobe University, Melbourne.

Little, G. 1997. 'The Two Narcissisms: Comparing Hawke and Keating'. In *Political Lives*, ed. J. Brett, pp. 16–27. Sydney: Allen & Unwin.

McAllister, I. 1992. *Political Behaviour: Citizens, Parties and Elites in Australia*. Melbourne: Longman Cheshire.

Michels, R. 1911 [1968]. *Political Parties: A Sociological Study of the Oligarchical Tendencies of Modern Democracy*. New York: Free Press.

Pickering, P. 1998. 'The Class of '96: A Biographical Analysis of New Government Members of the House of Representatives'. *Australian Journal of Politics and History* 44(1): 95–112.

Putnam, R. D. 1973. *The Beliefs of Politicians: Ideology, Conflict, and Democracy in Britain and Italy*. New Haven, Conn.: Yale University Press.

Riesman, D. in collaboration with R. Denney and N. Glazer. 1950. *The Lonely Crowd: A Study of the Changing American Character*. New Haven, Conn.: Yale University Press.

Ruddock, P. 1978. 'Remarks'. *Fourth Australian Parliamentary Seminar: Transcript of Proceedings*, p. 243 ff. Canberra: Parliament of Australia.

Sawer, M. and G. Zappala (eds). 2001. *Speaking for the People: Representation in Australian Politics*. Melbourne: Melbourne University Press.

Walter, J. 1979. *The Acculturation to Political Work: New Members of the Federal Backbench*. Canberra: Australasian Political Studies Association and Parliament of Australia.

Walter, J. 2005. 'Why Prime Ministers Go Too Far'. In *Australian Security after 9/11: New and Old Agendas*, eds D. McDougall and P. Shearman, pp. 189–206. London: Ashgate.

Walter, J. 2008. 'Is There a Command Culture in Politics? The Canberra Case'. In *Public Leadership: Perspectives and Practices*, eds P. 't Hart and J. Uhr, pp. 189–201. Canberra: ANU E Press.

Walter, J. 2009. 'Political Biography'. In *The Australian Study of Politics*, ed. R. A. W. Rhodes, pp. 97–106. Basingstoke, UK: Palgrave Macmillan.

Walter, J. and T. Moore. 2002. The New Social Order? Australia's Contribution to 'New Liberal' Thinking in the Interwar Period. Presented to Jubilee Conference of the Australasian Political Studies Association, Australian National University, Canberra, 2–4 October.

Walter, J. and P. Strangio. 2007. *No, Prime Minister: Reclaiming Politics from Leaders*. Sydney: UNSW Press.

Weller, P. and S. Fraser. 1987. 'The Younging of Australian Politics or Politics as First Career'. *Politics* 22(2): 76–83.

5. Ministerial Accountability to Parliament

Phil Larkin

Introduction: The decline of parliament?

For many commentators, parliament's role in holding governments to account is the subject of laments for a better past and a central element in claims of a decline of parliament and of a democratic deficit (for a recent review, see the discussion in Flinders and Kelso 2011). The claim that parliament's role has been undermined has a number of dimensions. The primary one centres on the rise of organised and disciplined parties. In the parliamentary 'golden age' of the nineteenth century, with little in the way of disciplined parties, the executive could only maintain parliament's confidence by being constantly accountable to the legislature's wishes. With the emergence of organised parties, however, the executive effectively gained control over the legislature: the party leadership was able to use its control of promotion from the backbenches to ministerial positions or to committee chairs to enforce discipline on its members and, commanding a majority of members of the lower chamber, parliamentary government became a byword for executive dominance of the legislature, with parliamentarians reduced to 'lobby fodder' and executive accountability achieved only through the ballot box at election time. Flinders and Kelso (2011) note that by the early decades of the twentieth century the decline narrative had become dominant. It still—an academic backlash notwithstanding—holds considerable sway in the popular imagination: the Power report was an exemplar of the tradition, concluding that 'the Executive in Britain is now more powerful in relation to parliament than it has been probably since the time of Walpole' (Power Inquiry 2006, 128). It is, of course, important to note that the decline-of-parliament thesis relates only to some functions; parliament's role in, for instance, forming the executive has not declined in any way. But it is claimed that its role in forming governments has damaged its role in subsequently holding them to account; in Wheare's terms, its role in 'making the government' overshadows and compromises its role in 'making the government behave' (1963).

Of course, it should be noted that the decline-of-parliament thesis was primarily developed in the context of the United Kingdom (though see, for example, Elgie and Stapleton 2006 on Ireland; and the discussion relating to Australia in Halligan et al. 2007, 2–4). In Australia, where political parties' discipline in

Parliament is pronounced, even by high, Westminster standards, a case could be made that its Parliament would have declined more than any other were it not for an unusually powerful second chamber composed via a voting system that ensures that it is usually outside government control. The roles of 'making the government' and 'making the government behave' have been divided between the two chambers of the Australian Parliament, whereas in the United Kingdom they remain, to a large degree, merged, with the House of Commons taking on both the government-formation role and the main scrutiny and accountability functions as well.

But the claim that the rise of the party has caused a decline of parliament has been supplemented by more recent developments. The mass media's focus on leadership and the resulting 'presidentialisation' of politics reinforce the role of the executive at the expense of parliament. The increased volume of legislation and its increased specialisation have seen the key nexus of policy making shift from the executive and parliament to the executive and the bureaucracy and even, if one accepts the claims of the network governance theorists, to a variety of key sectoral groups (Rhodes 1996). And then there is the tendency to outsource policy delivery to providers in the private sector, with accountability no longer a matter of hierarchical relationships but of horizontal, contractual ones (Bovens 2005, 199). Parliament, it is claimed, remains ill equipped to cope. The associated 'agencification' of government, with important policy work devised and implemented by public bodies at arm's length from government and outside direct ministerial control, has contributed to the feeling of the diminished importance of traditional, hierarchical accountability relationships. And the nation-state is now only one level at which 'governance' happens and policy is determined. The extent to which there has been an emergence of 'global governance' might be debated, as well as its impact on the sovereignty of national governments (has sovereignty been diminished?). Yet what cannot be disputed is that parliaments are firmly tied to the national level, leading to fears that key decisions have somehow escaped them.

The claims of the decline-of-parliament thesis have, of course, been strongly denied (see Cowley 2002; Flinders and Kelso 2011). What is true though is that there has been a rise to prominence of a variety of other organisations focused on accountability such as auditors-general, ombudsmen and various watchdogs and inspectorates. These bodies exist outside the traditional, hierarchical model of accountability running through the minister to parliament (Bovens labels them 'diagonal'; 2005, 196). Furthermore, they generally have at their disposal greater resources and specialist expertise with which to scrutinise government than has parliament.

It would be easy to conclude, under such circumstances, that parliament is ill equipped to perform its traditional role of holding the executive to account or that it is something of an irrelevance, undermined by its role in forming governments. Yet it remains the central plank of the government accountability framework for a number of reasons. First, from a legitimacy perspective, parliament is the only accountability institution directly elected by the citizenry and directly accountable to it through the ballot box. In a principal–agent formulation, parliamentary democracy sees the citizenry delegate its law-making powers to their parliamentarians who, in turn, delegate that power to a subset of their number who form the government in a 'chain of delegation' (Strøm 2003). In return, there is a chain of accountability running from agent to principal in the opposite direction: from government, through the rest of parliament, to the citizenry—the ultimate principals. It is for legitimacy reasons that at least some of the extra-parliamentary accountability sector works through parliament to some extent: the Australian National Audit Office (ANAO), for example, provides advisory support for the senate estimates process and the Joint Committee of Public Accounts and Audit (JCPAA), parliament's primary public accounts committee. Whilst not directly part of the hierarchical accountability relationship, its primary role has often been to better inform parliament.

Furthermore, accountability is not a single act and ministerial accountability to parliament has a number of dimensions. First, parliament has to have some means by which it can establish what decisions have been taken and with what effect. Second, it needs a means to extract from the minister some form of explanation (or 'account') of why decisions were taken and the effects of the outcomes while judgment is made about the adequacy of such explanations. And third, in the light of these, is the potential to impose some form of sanction or retribution: to be accountable, '[a]gents must not only be "called" to account but also be "held" to "account"' (Mulgan 2003, 9; see also Bovens 2005, 184–6). This accountability industry is generally limited in its capacity to sanction. If ministers have broken laws then they may be held to account and punished by the courts but, for the most part, ministerial performance is not primarily a matter of adherence to the laws of the land but of judgments (considered or otherwise) about governing competence. There is little scope for these unelected scrutineers of government to do more than make recommendations. If ministers are agents, it is ultimately to parliament as the principal that the task of sanctioning falls.

It should also be noted that the concept of 'accountability to parliament' is, in practice, a slight misnomer. Certainly, executive authority is derived from parliament and ministers remain answerable to it. But it suggests that parliament acts as a single, unified actor whereas in reality it is a forum in which ministerial accountability takes place (or is actively evaded). As King (1976) notes in relation to the British House of Commons, there is a series of relationships within parliament that determines the relative strength of the legislature vis-a-vis the executive and affects the capacity of parliament to hold government to account. The key relationships are between the government and the opposition, between the government and its own backbench, and between the government and the backbenches as a whole. As we shall see, these relationships impact upon different aspects of the accountability process. Moreover, the Australian Parliament comprises two chambers that usually have significantly different party compositions; those parties have different stakes in the accountability process. In this respect, opposition and minor parties carry out most of the heavy lifting of ministerial accountability. As the government-in-waiting, the opposition has a clear interest in highlighting poor performance and focusing on apparent misjudgments or evidence of maladministration. The party of government, on the other hand, will have a clear incentive to rebut accusations of poor performance, avoid its discovery or, where this is not possible, apportion blame elsewhere. They are also likely to have an incentive to minimise the opportunities through which they can be held to account (though this might be tempered by the knowledge that, once in opposition, the roles will change and their interest will be in maximising the capacity for executive scrutiny).

This picture of ministerial accountability to parliament is, then, highly politically charged and subjective; surely it must be possible to establish in a more objective fashion the extent of ministerial competence? Certainly governments have sought to put accountability on a less fluid and contingent footing. Ministerial codes have been devised that specify what it is that ministers should be accountable for, particularly in relation to the actions of the bureaucrats in their department (Special Minister of State 2008). Whilst the opposition might call for the resignation of the minister when a public servant in their department has made some costly error or misjudgment, the code states that the issue is whether the minister could reasonably have known about this or, once becoming aware of it, did not take adequate steps to remedy the situation. Instead of a purely rhetorical activity, blame apportionment becomes to some extent grounded by the standards set out in the code. There have also been attempts to change the focus of ministerial accountability to parliament away from inputs and process towards outputs (Mulgan 2008, 457–60).

Nevertheless, ministerial competence is not something that can be objectively defined according to common standards over which there is universal agreement. Policy rarely fails unambiguously and beyond dispute, and even in the case of the most apparently egregious errors of policy design and implementation, the label of ministerial incompetence, like that of policy 'failure' or 'fiasco', is contingent. When a policy fails, that failure will need to be discovered; it will be subject to explanation, which will attempt to show how there really has not been a failure at all or that the carefully designed policy has been undermined by a change in circumstances that could not possibly have been foreseen; and counterarguments that the results are worse than could have been expected or that changed circumstances should have been foreseen, or even that the policy was wrong-headed and should not have been introduced at all. For the minister responsible to be held to account (rather than simply called to account), the case for the prosecution will have to be seen publicly to have prevailed and the 'failure' label made to stick. Inevitably, ministerial competence is the product of the political process and will be defined by it.

In the principal–agent formulation, the delegation of decision making by the principal comes with the risk of agency loss: the possibility that the interests of the principal and agent diverge and the agent acts according to their own interests rather than those of their principal. In the context of parliaments, there are *ex ante* and *ex post* means of minimising agency loss. *Ex ante* means might include the selection of candidates for ministerial posts or the requirement that policy is approved by the parliamentary party, the wider party membership or by parliament itself. Alternatively, the principal may monitor the actions of their agent and require them to report back *ex post*.

Questions With and Without Notice

The best-known, most public and most infamous example of *ex post* monitoring is Question Time in the House of Representatives, when 'Questions Without Notice' are put to government members in the House. It is undoubtedly the most high-profile aspect of the parliamentary sitting period and attracts much media attention. This media attention has meant that its usefulness as a means of obtaining information has been overshadowed by its role as a set-piece confrontation between the government and the opposition: broadcast live and with all the lobby correspondents looking for stories, it becomes less an exercise in information gathering and more an opportunity for partisan point-scoring and a forum where leadership credentials are tested. Question Time ordinarily takes place every sitting day for a minimum of 45 minutes and usually for more than an hour. This is only a convention, however, and the prime minister can curtail it, choosing to take questions 'on notice' instead (Harris et al. 2005, 529). It ordinarily opens with the leader of the opposition asking a question of the prime minister, followed by a government backbencher, with the parties then alternating in this manner; on average, 18 questions are asked (Harris et al. 2005, 530). Question Time's historical roots in Westminster in the pre-mass-democracy era are evident, maintaining as it does that the central divide in parliament is between the government and the backbenches rather than between the government and opposition (hence the equal prominence accorded to government and non-government backbenchers). The high public and media profiles of Question Time ensure that questions from the opposition are primarily designed to embarrass the government, while those from the government backbenches are generally designed to publicise its achievements and to present it in the best possible light. Many of the questions from the government side are planned (the infamous 'Dorothy Dixer' tactic).

With Question Time in the House of Representatives so readily dismissed as party political theatre, it has attracted limited systematic study. Rasiah (2006) conducted an analysis of a sample of Questions Without Notice on the subject of Australia's military involvement in Iraq. She found it lacking as an accountability mechanism, with Dorothy Dixers predominant amongst questions from the government backbenches (and long-winded answers to them using up the allotted time) and ministers evading questions from the opposition. In a similar vein, whilst maintaining that even a Dorothy Dixer could be useful in accountability terms as it provides the minister to whom it is directed the opportunity to explain their position, McGowan (2008) regards Question Time as significantly less effective than the equivalent process in the United Kingdom, Canada or New Zealand. He analysed a sample of questions and answers from each parliament, concluding that relatively fewer questions are asked in the Australian House of Representatives than in other parliaments, and, of those asked by opposition MPs, fewer than half are likely to be given a proper or even partial answer (McGowan 2008, 75). Both studies were limited in scope, but nonetheless support the widely held view that Questions Without Notice are a largely ineffective means of ministerial accountability. One experienced parliamentarian concluded that 'question time is essentially an electioneering exercise, and is not usually a source of factual information. Indeed, new opposition members are warned never to ask a question without knowing the answer, for an unexpected answer might be very embarrassing' (Hamer 2004, 237–8).

Of course, extracting information from ministers is only one element of their accountability to Parliament. Extracting an explanation is also significant and Question Time could be said to fulfil this function. But given that answers can diverge significantly from the question, the duration is limited and members' questions offer only a 'single shot' with no opportunity to follow up, its usefulness in this respect is also limited. In terms of blame apportionment and the public testing of ministerial explanation, however, Question Time may play a role. If a minister appears to be too blatantly evading questions on a topic on an ongoing basis, there is the possibility that their credibility will be damaged, given the public nature of the occasion. In this sense, the media attention becomes a key component of accountability rather than a factor undermining it.

There are several modest reforms that seem to have the potential to redress the balance between 'making the government' and 'making the government behave'. The introduction of tighter rules on what constitute questions and answers would be a first step. Allowing the questioner to follow up with a supplementary question after the answer from the minister would simply bring Australian Question Time in line with many other comparable parliaments. A properly independent speaker would enforce these rules. In 1996, amidst promises of more independence, the Speaker did allow supplementary questions, providing they were from the member who had asked the original question and arose directly from the minister's answer. It was a short-lived experiment that irritated the Prime Minister sufficiently for the Speaker to be forced to resign from office.

If the furore surrounding Question Time limits its use as a means of extracting information from ministers, written 'Questions On Notice', where questions are tabled and answers given publicly but away from intense media scrutiny, would seem to have greater potential as a way of scrutinising government. There are, however, a number of factors that limit the usefulness of written questions in the accountability process. First, and most significantly, a minister is under no obligation to answer a question. Whilst this is the case for Questions Without Notice as well, the relative obscurity of written questions, buried in the *Notice Paper*, away from media and public attention, means that ministerial refusal to provide an answer to a question is unlikely to attract much publicity. Figure 5.1 shows how the numbers of both Questions On and Without Notice vary widely from year to year. And the number of Questions On Notice receiving an answer varies. For example, in the 2005–06 session, some 60 per cent of Questions On Notice received an answer. In the 2007–08 session (an election year), only 41 per cent of written questions were answered. But in 2009–10, the figure was 78 per cent (albeit of a smaller total). Refusal to answer may be justified on the grounds of the cost of providing an answer; however, this does not have to be demonstrated, providing a convenient way for ministers to avoid publicly giving information. And the time taken to produce an answer can be considerable—90 days or more—which has the effect of reducing the relevance of the question and the information provided (if it is answered). There is also the limitation, inherent in the non-discursive format of written questions, of their scope. They can form a useful tool for a parliamentarian to extract specific bits of information on an issue that they are actively investigating. They are less useful in trying to explore an issue more broadly or as part of a 'fishing trip' to establish whether an issue is worth investigating further. This is a constraint not faced by, for instance, committee investigations.

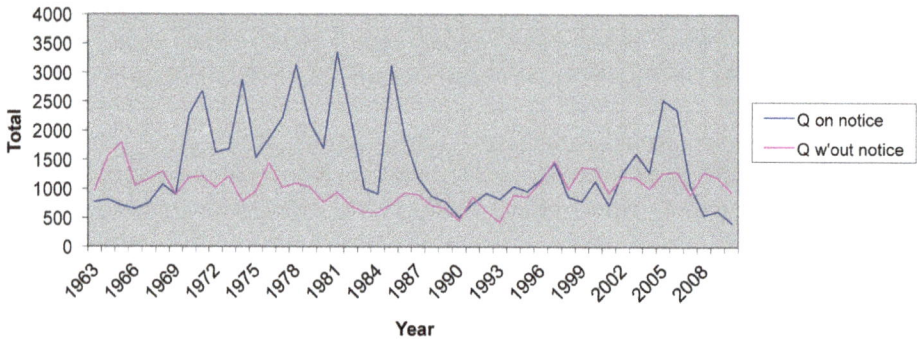

Figure 5.1 Questions to Government, 1963–2010

Source: Annual reports of the House of Representatives and the Senate.

Committees

If Question Time is the most high-profile means, parliamentary committees are seen as an increasingly important vehicle of ministerial accountability. Parliamentary committees have a number of advantages over Questions On or Without Notice, and they can give a rather broader and fuller account of ministerial performance. First, because they work through inquiries, they can more thoroughly investigate policy and administration in a particular area and the role of the minister therein. Second, in receiving written submissions and holding hearings with stakeholders, a more rounded picture of the role and performance of ministers and their departments can be gained. As accountability revolves around explanation and interrogation of that explanation, the more deliberative committee process allows this more directly. Third, it has been claimed that properly functioning committees develop internal modes of working that overcome the partisan divisions of other areas of parliamentary life. Working in a small, focused group, committees can develop a certain esprit de corps that breaks down party divisions and sees them develop a degree of independence and willingness to defy their party leaderships and dissent from established party positions (Sartori 1982). Moreover, because committees are expected to base their findings on the evidence they receive in the course of their inquiries rather than on the basis of the predetermined positions of their political parties, again they have the potential to provide a more objective, or at least bipartisan, perspective on ministerial performance. And last, where the committees specialise by subject area, they have the capacity to acquire expertise and experience over time and are consequently better placed to scrutinise the executive and hold it to account. But these are generic advantages of parliamentary committees and the extent to which committees in the Australian Parliament actually develop them needs closer investigation.

There are three systems of standing committee, specialising by policy area (and allied to specific government departments and agencies)—house, joint and senate—with the Senate dividing the legislative and investigative roles between a system of paired committees.[1] In addition there are select committees, established by the parent chamber to investigate a specific matter, ceasing to exist when they have reported (though they are rarely used in the House). Whilst all have nominally the same remit—that of investigating the policy, administration, finances and legislation of the ministries within their competency (with the Senate legislative standing committees responsible for scrutinising bills and draft bills, estimates, annual reports and 'performance', and reference committees responsible for investigating other matters; Senate Standing Order 25[2])—the differences in the way their parent chamber operates have seen an informal division of labour emerge between them. Because committees do not generally have the power to initiate their own inquiries, they are reliant on references from the parent chamber.[2] With the government by definition holding a majority in the House and party lines largely adhered to, house committees have tended to focus on prospective policy issues, perhaps in cooperation with the minister. Matters potentially embarrassing to the government are unlikely to be investigated. But the government rarely has a majority in the Senate, and therefore cannot block references of bills or matters for investigation to committees for inquiry. Consequently, the bulk of the legislative scrutiny and scrutiny of ministers and departments takes place in the Senate. To illustrate, the House Procedure Committee reported in 2010 that, at the time of writing, 90 per cent of house standing committee inquiries were policy investigations and 10 per cent government scrutiny. By contrast, inquiries by senate committees were approximately 30 per cent for policy and scrutiny combined, with the remaining 60 per cent legislative inquiries (Standing Committee on Procedure 2010, 111–13).[3] The JCPAA is the main vehicle for budgetary scrutiny, though the senate estimates process is also tied to investigating departmental finances (and in fact ranges rather more widely).

Such is the perceived centrality of the senate committee system to the holding of the ministry to account that when the Howard Government won a rare and narrow senate majority, serious concerns were raised about Parliament's

---

1   The system of paired committees was abolished under the Howard Government's senate majority (ensuring all committees had a government chair) but reinstated under Labor, when the Senate was again under no single-party control.

2   They do have ongoing references to examine annual reports though these are little utilised.

3   In comparison, the proportion for scrutiny in the British House of Commons was approximately 60 per cent.

continued capacity to hold the executive to account in any meaningful way (see, for example, Sawer 2005). Senate committees require a matter to be referred by the Senate as a whole, meaning a government majority in the Senate had the capacity to block all senate scrutiny of bills and government policy. As it turned out, it seemed that the Government accepted the principle that the senate committees should continue to review significant bills and these continued to be referred (albeit with sometimes ridiculously short time frames for reporting). The principle of executive scrutiny was, it seems, less engrained. References to committees were blocked. Evans (2008b) compares the success rate of motions for references to senate committees before and during the period of government senate control.

Table 5.1 Sources of Committee Motions

Date	Total motions	Total negatived	Non-govt motions	Non-govt motions negatived
2001–04	63	10	60	10
1.7.05 – 20.9.07	63	38	52	38

Source: Evans (2008b).

Table 5.1 reiterates the significance of the party political element of executive accountability and the inevitable, adversarial component that that entails. It clearly shows how the Opposition and minor parties were the major source of motions referring matters to committees for consideration. Prior to 2005, with no party controlling a majority in the Senate, most of these motions were approved. Once the Government gained control of the Senate, it vetoed the majority of the potential committee inquiries, including high-profile and controversial 'policy fiascos' such as the Australian Wheat Board's involvement in Iraq; consequently, accountability was reduced.

Sartori (1982) argues that committees overcome established partisan positions by maintaining unanimity—achieved by committee members operating 'give and take' or the principle of 'deferred reciprocal compensation'. Where a committee works on the basis of majority rather than unanimous decision making, it could arguably be said not to be a functioning committee at all (Sartori 1982, 230). The reality is that party lines are largely adhered to in senate committees and investigations rarely proceed unanimously; there are few significant or controversial inquiries that do not result in dissenting reports. Where the Senate is not under government control, the Opposition and perhaps the minor parties will agree to the report, with the government members composing a minority report largely rejecting the criticisms contained in the main one. Under the Government's period of senate control, it was, predictably, the Opposition and minor parties that contributed the dissenting report or reports. The contrast with, for instance, the British House of Commons select committees, where unanimity and cross-party agreement in reports are prioritised, is marked.

It would seem then that, in this respect at least, the benefit of committees does not apply in the Senate. Sartori, of course, privileges the deliberative process through which committees work rather than their outputs. An alternative view would be that rather than the single perspective that dominates a unanimous report and the compromises and fudges that maintaining cross-party consensus entail, allowing minority reports enables a wider range of viewpoints to be represented (Mattson and Strøm 1995, 283–4). The difficulty here is that, if the dissenting reports are merely a vehicle for existing party positions then there is no wider range of views represented and it is easier for any criticisms to be dismissed as partisan point-scoring. Moreover, governments are only expected to respond to the main report: where the government controls the Senate, government would escape responding to criticism from other parties' senators.

Given the accountability process conventionally revolves around interrogation of ministers and their explanation, the government response is an important part of the accountability process. Part of the appeal of committees in the accountability process is that they have a deliberative dimension: in the course of an inquiry, government can make a written submission and ministers may appear at hearings (though they cannot be forced to and, with the majority of the ministry in the House, the minister responsible is more likely to be represented by a 'proxy' senate representative). And, following the committee's final report, government should provide a written response to it. Where minority reports exist then any issues raised are unlikely to be addressed, of course. Moreover, the thoroughness of the response is likely to vary and to be contingent on the circumstances of the minister: they are under no obligation to comprehensively address any criticisms and, at times, are likely to find it more politically expedient to ignore them altogether. Whilst the government is expected to provide responses within three months, they are frequently late and at times never materialise at all. The Senate lacks the mechanisms to force a government formed in the House to act so, in the absence of action taken in the House against the government (by definition, by its own backbench), there is little that can be done directly. The only retribution would be through indirect collateral damage from any impact on the government's popularity (and it should be noted that reports from house committees, which are not as hostile to government, also go without responses).

It was the failure of government to respond to committee inquiries that led to accusations that 'democracy' was being 'denied' (Ryle and Pryor 2005); certainly, the Howard Government, at which these accusations were levelled, evidently did not accord any great priority to committee reports or to the convention that they be replied to relatively promptly. Attempts to measure the 'effectiveness' of parliamentary committee reports have focused on the report recommendations and their subsequent treatment by government (for example, Hindmoor et al. 2009; Russell and Benton 2011) as one dimension of measuring the strength of Parliament vis-a-vis the executive. But from an accountability perspective, the impact of the committee's recommendations on policy is less important than the evaluation contained in the report and the government's subsequent explanation and justification of its record and future course of action. Yet governments consistently fail to respond to committee reports in a timely fashion (currently the 'agreed' deadline for a response is three months in the House and six in the Senate).

The most recent update of the number of committee reports that have not received a response within the agreed time frame is 133 in the Senate and 61 in the House. There are often legitimate reasons for failing to meet the deadline: the department may be waiting for the outcome of a review or new results of some sort to be made available before responding, for example. Clearly, though, some governments have simply decided not to respond to particular committee reports: the Howard Government left office in 2007 without ever providing a proper response to the Senate Select Committee report on the 'children overboard affair', *A Certain Maritime Incident* (Select Committee on a Certain Maritime Incident 2002), simply reporting that the 'government response may be considered in due course' (Abetz 2007, 110). On taking office in 2007, the Labor Government committed to responding to committee reports more promptly than its predecessor (Faulkner 2008), yet the total number currently outstanding is higher than at the change of government. (The figures were then 106 for the Senate and 72 for the House).

One aspect of the senate committee process that requires no reference and over which non-government parties have a free hand is senate estimates. The thrice-yearly estimates process (main, supplementary and additional) allows the most sustained scrutiny of the minister (or their senate delegate) and their department. The starting point is the estimates of expenditure to be included in the government's appropriation bills, with the Senate's thematic committees taking responsibility for scrutinising the departments within their remit. Whilst nominally focused on the narrow scrutiny of proposed expenditure, the estimates process has evolved into a very much broader-ranging scrutiny of government policy and administration. Previous governments have been frustrated by this and have attempted to narrow the scope of estimates hearings to focus not on what is being done—the merit of the government's legislative program—but on how it is being done: the efficiency with which it is being implemented. Such attempts have been denied: the appropriation bills are a claim on the public purse and anything that relates to or influences that claim is legitimate for the committee to investigate (Evans 2008a, 368): 'as an essential part of [the] appropriations process, the estimates committees evaluate the appropriateness of programs' (Uhr 1989, 6).

Estimates might appear the closest to clear, apolitical accountability that Parliament achieves. It is, after all, focused on the activities and record of the individual minister and their officials rather than the whole of the government and has a clear evidence base in estimates of expenditure, departmental reports, ANAO reports and other official publications. Explicit attempts have been made by governments to steer the estimates process away from a perceived obsession with the inputs and the process and towards the success of specified policy in achieving specified outputs; from the politically contentious issue of policy formulation to how successfully it has achieved its goals (Mulgan 2008).

It is, however, still an essentially political activity. In order to maximise media coverage for each one, no more than four committees will conduct their estimates hearings at the same time, again highlighting the role of the media in the whole process of accountability. Questioning will be conducted almost exclusively by non-government senators and aimed at uncovering evidence of poor administration, flawed assumptions or partisan motives, for instance. Ministers or, in the more frequent instances where the minister is based in the House, their senate spokespersons are questioned directly, but much of the interrogation will be directed at their departmental officials and is generally far more focused on operational details (the decision-making process, the details of policy design and implementation, and so on) than parliamentary questions, for example; it has been speculated that this might have increased over time, as service delivery is shifted out of direct state control (Brenton 2010). Nonetheless, and in keeping with the political nature of parliamentary accountability, even questions directed to officials could be seen as a proxy attack on the minister and their managerial competence.

Even so, either in spite of this political contestation or because of it, or due to the apparent inadequacies of other parliamentary means for holding ministers to account, the public prominence of senate estimates has seemingly continued to rise, as has the priority given to it by the senators themselves. The amount of parliamentary time spent on estimates has grown steadily and the number of column inches in Hansard it generates has grown as well (Mulgan 2008, 62).

Establishing how well committees perform in holding the government to account is difficult (see Larkin 2010). Looking at the formal powers of committees says nothing about how those powers are used. One can count the number of inquiries held, hearings held or reports published, but these only measure activity and not 'effectiveness'; a lack of activity *might* indicate a lack of effectiveness but the inverse—that activity equals effectiveness—clearly does not hold. The number of times a committee caused a change or reversal in government policy would be one measure but, even if one could identify the committee as the sole cause of this, there is also the possibility that government policy may change in anticipation of committee objections. And of course there are no agreed standards: governments might well object that a committee is interfering in the policy process, whilst the committee (or the non-government members of it) complains that the government is ignoring the will of Parliament. But what can be established is the extent to which the government fails to provide information to committees, refuses to appear (or prevents staff from doing so, on which there is more discussion below) or fails to deliver a response to a committee report on time or at all. The lack of commonly held and enforceable minimum standards of government cooperation with the senate committees clearly limits their potential effectiveness. The government, of course, has to remain free to reject committee conclusions or recommendations, but should be obliged to explain itself and its reasons for doing so. Doing so would, again, merely bring Australia's Parliament into line with its counterparts.

Ministerial Staff and the 'Accountability Vacuum'

A characteristic of Westminster-derived models of administration has been a clear dividing line between the political executive and a 'neutral' bureaucracy— neutral insofar as it serves governments of any political persuasion equally. Of course it has long been observed that the bureaucracy has interests of its own that it may try to advance, be they budget-maximising or bureau-shaping or something else entirely, as well as a suspicion by government ministers that the Public Service is predominantly staffed by sympathisers with political parties other than their own. In order to more closely align the interests of the bureaucracy with those of the executive, various measures have been introduced in Australia to increase its 'political responsiveness' (see MacDermott 2008). This has led to fears of bureaucratic politicisation; however, the lines of accountability are still relatively clear and the distinction between departmental and more political work defined in codes of conduct (Special Minister for State 2008).

Around the edges of ministerial accountability, however, is a regiment of special advisors. They are directly employed by ministers and answer directly to them. With special advisor roles having developed in a largely ad-hoc manner and the role of each differing in each ministerial office and each appointment (for example, an advisor taken on secondment from the Public Service may well have a very different role from one drawn from the party), there has been little in the way of regulation of their behaviour or formalising of their lines of accountability; such regulation as there is appears in the *Members of Parliament (Staff) Act 1984* (the '*MOP(S) Act*') but is largely directed at ensuring no conflicts of interest exist on entering the minister's office. But what is clear is that special advisors have acquired a substantial policy development role and 'enjoy a level of autonomous executive authority separable from that to which they have customarily been entitled as the immediate agents of the minister' (Select Committee on a Certain Maritime Incident 2002, para 7.107). Yet, unlike ministers or officials, they are largely immune from direct scrutiny by Parliament, and accountable only through their minister. Opinion on whether they are entitled to immunity has been divided; however, the Parliament's inability to put into force its power to compel individuals without immunity from appearing before committees has seemingly rendered this somewhat academic (Select Committee on a Certain Maritime Incident 2002, paras 7.137–43).

Parliament's inability to scrutinise ministerial staff as well as ministers creates the clear potential for an accountability 'vacuum' (Keating 2003). Where ministerial staff are working to the minister's direct instruction, the chain of accountability running through the minister to Parliament may hold. But if they are operating with a degree of delegated authority and autonomy, it breaks down. A minister can claim ignorance of their activities and decline responsibility for the actions of their staff whilst, at the same time, the advisor can escape being held to account by Parliament. Given the established preference for blame avoidance on the part of elected representatives (see Weaver 1986), the potential for ministers to blame staff—safe in the knowledge that there is likely to be little scrutiny of their respective roles—is clear.

Indeed, events such as the 'certain maritime incident' would suggest that this accountability gap is not simply potential or hypothetical but very real, and that it has indeed been used by ministers to dodge accountability. In this instance, the minister claimed information had been passed to his advisors but they had not then informed him. But the veracity of this was never investigated because the minister was able to prevent the advisors appearing before the senate inquiry into the matter. Keating sums up the accountability vacuum thus:

> The government is maintaining: first, that key advisers failed to provide critical information to ministers. Second, because ministers were not properly informed, ministers can now avoid taking responsibility for the actions (or lack of action) of their personal advisers, while denying the right of parliament to question those advisers. Furthermore, the government itself has taken no action on its own behalf to bring the relevant advisers to account. (Keating 2003, 92–3)

The Rudd Government introduced a code of conduct for ministerial staff to supplement the *MOP(S) Act* in 2008. It includes, amongst other things, clauses governing disclosure of gifts, divestment of outside business interests where a potential conflict of interest exists, and the importance of honesty. In the light of the 'children overboard' saga (under the Howard Government), it also includes an obligation to '[fa]cilitate direct and effective communication between their minister's department and their minister' (Special Minister of State 2008). But it makes no provisions for accountability to Parliament, instead limiting advisors' executive role on the basis that if they have no executive role, they need have no direct accountability to Parliament. Moreover, there are no clear sanctions. Any punishment for a breach of the code of conduct will be determined by the prime minister's chief of staff and the relevant minister, leaving the accountability vacuum largely untouched and ensuring the minister's capacity for blame avoidance remains intact (Maiden 2008).

Conclusions

We have considered some of the means through which parliaments hold ministers to account. In doing so, we have primarily focused on parliament's capacity to extract information from ministers and to compel them to explain their actions. But, as Mulgan emphasises, accountability is not confined to scrutiny and for ministerial accountability to parliament to be properly realised there needs to be some scope for rectification and sanction: ministers need to be held to account as well as being called to account (2003, 9).

It is in relation to parliament's capacity to sanction that the implications of King's (1976) observation about the multiple relationships involved in executive–legislative relations become apparent. In the investigative or scrutinising aspects of the accountability process—the extraction of information and explanation—the key relationship is between the executive and the opposition front and backbenches. Ministers will attempt to avoid blame for any disappointments or controversies and to justify their actions and outcomes through contextual explanation. The opposition will be engaged in a process of apportioning blame and attempting to label the minister incompetent (and, by association, calling into question the governing competence of the entire government). The non-government parties, however, have no direct capacity to sanction ministers for poor performance. They can investigate ministerial performance and can label the minister a failure by interrogating and casting doubt on explanations for their performance. Instead, the Senate may express its displeasure through passing a censure motion, but that is little more than a public display of disapproval: 'If the Senate chooses to censure a minister...ministers shrug and continue in their post' (Weller 2007, 204). The issue of sanction is a product of relationships within the governing party.

The ultimate sanction for ministerial failure is removal from post, either to a less prestigious ministerial post or back to the backbenches. The prime minister is responsible for the allocation of ministerial portfolios and so it is the relationship between an individual minister and the prime minister that is pre-eminent in terms of this element of accountability.[4] The prime minister is in turn dependent on the continued confidence of the parliamentary party or the 'party room'—described by Weller as 'the gatekeepers to office and the sentinels protecting and scrutinising cabinet' (2007, 200)—for continued survival. In this respect, the opposition and minor parties are not without the power of sanction but it is a power that can only be applied indirectly, acting as 'inducer rather than an enforcer' (Mulgan 2003, 62).

In order to 'induce' real rectification or sanction, the non-governing parties must use parliament to attract media and public attention to ministerial shortcomings and generate sufficient public outrage to put sufficient pressure on the governing party to force a minister from office or engineer a policy reversal. Weller (2007, 213) argues that '[a]ccountability to the party is the only immediate means that makes sense under existing practices', dismissing accountability through parliament as 'essentially rhetorical'. For Weller, accountability to the party room is generated through ambition and rivalry and disputes over policy within the party itself. But the reality is that the sanction aspect of ministerial accountability operates 'through' the party room rather than 'to' it. Unless parliament can properly scrutinise ministerial activity by accessing information, by asking questions and receiving proper answers, and by requiring ministers to provide an explanation of their decisions and interrogating those decisions thoroughly, and without the pressure on ministers that this can generate, the pressure on the governing party is lessened and accountability to the party room is weakened. This is why any scope for ministers to evade scrutiny is a cause for concern.

References

Abetz, E. 2007. Senate Hansard, 21 June. Canberra: Parliament of Australia.

Bovens, M. 2005. 'Public Accountability'. In *The Oxford Handbook of Public Management*, eds E. Ferlie, L. E. Lynn jr and C. Pollitt. Oxford: Oxford University Press.

---

4   The prime minister may not be entirely free to appoint who they choose; there may be the 'big beasts' of the party to placate and balance between different wings or factions to maintain (the factions have formalised this within the Labor Party). But the allocation of specific portfolios is the gift of the prime minister and it is the prime minister who ultimately has the power to sanction ministers.

Brenton, S. 2010. Ministers or Managers: Changing Conceptions of Accountability through Financial Management. Paper presented to the Australasian Political Studies Association Conference, Melbourne, 28 September.

Cowley, P. 2002. *Revolts and Rebellions: Parliamentary Voting under Blair*. London: Politico's.

Elgie, R. and J. Stapleton. 2006. 'Testing the Decline of Parliament Thesis: Ireland, 1923–2002'. *Political Studies* 54(3): 465–85.

Evans, H. (ed.). 2008a. *Odgers' Australian Senate Practice*. Twelfth edition. Canberra: Department of the Senate.

Evans, H. 2008b. *The Senate, Accountability and Government Control*. Parliamentary Studies Paper no. 4. Canberra: Crawford School of Economics and Government, Australian National University.

Faulkner, J. 2008. Restoring Integrity to Government. Ministerial Statement, 4 December, Parliament House, Canberra, <http://www.senatorjohnfaulkner. com.au/file.php?file=/news/VAYCKHXIYU/index.html>

Flinders, M. and A. Kelso. 2011. 'Minding the Gap: Political Analysis, Public Expectations and the Parliamentary Decline Thesis'. *British Journal of Politics and International Relations* 13(2): 249–68.

Halligan, J., R. Miller and J. Power. 2007. *Parliament in the Twenty-First Century: Institutional Reform and Emerging Roles*. Melbourne: Melbourne University Press.

Hamer, D. 2004. *Can Responsible Government Survive in Australia?* Second edition. Canberra: Department of the Senate.

Harris, I. C., B. Wright and P. E. Fowler (eds). 2005. *House of Representatives Practice*. Fifth edition. Canberra: Department of the House of Representatives.

Hindmoor, A., P. Larkin and A. Kennon. 2009. 'Assessing the Influence of Select Committees in the UK: The Education and Skills Committee, 1997–2005'. *Journal of Legislative Studies* 15(1): 71–89.

Keating, M. 2003. 'In the Wake of "A Certain Maritime Incident": Ministerial Advisors, Departments and Accountability'. *Australian Journal of Public Administration* 62(3): 92–7.

King, A. 1976. 'Modes of Executive–Legislative Relations: Great Britain, France, and West Germany'. *Legislative Studies Quarterly* 1(1): 11–36.

Larkin, P., 2010, *Can Committee Performance Be Measured?* Papers on Parliament no. 54. Canberra: Department of the Senate.

MacDermott, K. 2008. *Whatever Happened to Frank and Fearless? The Impact of New Public Management on the Australian Public Service.* Canberra: ANU E Press.

McGowan, A. 2008. 'Accountability or Inability? To What Extent Does House of Representatives Question Time Deliver Executive Accountability Comparative to Other Parliamentary Chambers? Is There a Need for Reform?'. *Australasian Parliamentary Review* 23(2): 66–85.

Maiden, S. 2008. 'Staffers' Conduct Code "Sanction Free"'. *The Australian*, 26 June.

Mattson, I. and K. Strøm. 1995. 'Parliamentary Committees'. In *Parliaments and Majority Rule in Western Europe*, ed. H. Doring. New York: St Martin's.

Mulgan, R. 2003. *Holding Power to Account: Accountability in Modern Democracies.* Basingstoke, UK: Palgrave Macmillan.

Mulgan, R. 2008. 'The Accountability Priorities of Australian Parliamentarians'. *Australian Journal of Public Administration* 67(4): 457–69.

Power Inquiry. 2006. *Power to the People*, <http://www.powerinquiry.org>

Rasiah, P. 2006. *Does Question Time Fulfil its Role of Ensuring Accountability?* Discussion Paper 12/06. Canberra: Democratic Audit of Australia. <http://democratic.audit.anu.edu.au/papers/20060424_rasiah_qt.pdf>

Rhodes, R. A. W. 1996. 'The New Governance: Governing without Government'. *Political Studies* 19: 652–67.

Russell, M. and M. Benton. 2011. *Selective Influence: The Policy Impact of House of Commons Select Committees.* London: The Constitution Unit.

Ryle, G. and L. Pryor. 2005. 'Democracy Denied'. *Sydney Morning Herald*, 20 June.

Sartori, G. 1982. *The Theory of Democracy Revisited.* Chatham, NJ: Chatham House.

Sawer, M. 2005. *The Senate Changeover—Implications for Democracy.* Paper. Canberra: Democratic Audit of Australia. <democratic.audit.anu.edu.au/papers/200507_sawer_senate.pdf>

Select Committee on a Certain Maritime Incident. 2002. *A Certain Maritime Incident.* Canberra: Senate.

Special Minister of State. 2008. *Code of Conduct for Ministerial Staff.* Canberra: Australian Government. <http://www.smos.gov.au/media/code_of_conduct.html>

Standing Committee on Procedure. 2010. *Building a Modern Committee System: An Inquiry into the Effectiveness of the House Committee System.* Canberra: House of Representatives.

Strøm, K. 2003. 'Parliamentary Democracy and Delegation'. In *Delegation and Accountability in Parliamentary Democracies,* eds K. Strøm, W. C. Muller and T. Bergman. Oxford: Oxford University Press.

Uhr, J. 1989. *Public Expenditure and Parliamentary Accountability: The Debatable Role of Senate Estimates Committees.* Papers on Parliament no. 6. Canberra: Department of the Senate.

Weaver, R. K. 1986. 'The Politics of Blame Avoidance'. *Journal of Public Policy* 6(4): 371–98.

Weller, P. 2007. *Cabinet Government in Australia, 1901–2006.* Sydney: UNSW Press.

Wheare, K. C. 1963. *Legislatures.* London: Oxford University Press.

6. The Pattern of Forced Exits from the Ministry

Keith Dowding, Chris Lewis and Adam Packer

Introduction

Ministers leave office for all sorts of reasons. The most dramatic exits are those that are forced. We define a forced exit as one that happens at a time not of the prime minister's choosing. The prime minister might demand a resignation because of some scandal, but she did not want that scandal to emerge and compel her to ask for the minister's resignation. A forced resignation can also occur when a minister resigns because they disagree with government policy, because of a personality clash or simply as part of a strategic ploy to enhance his or her own leadership ambitions. We do not include cases where a minister is asked to leave at a time of the prime minister's choosing—for example, John Howard's penchant for asking ministers to step down during the Christmas break (see below and Chapter 2). Forced exits therefore include cases of what Woodhouse (1994, 33–8) calls 'sacrificial responsibility'—part of individual ministerial responsibility, but also where ministers depart of their own volition because they cannot abide by collective cabinet responsibility.

In this chapter we examine the pattern of individual resignations in the Australian Commonwealth Government since 1949, from the incoming Menzies Government to the end of Kevin Rudd in 2010. We have collected data on all resignations and non-resignations over the period (see below and Appendix 6.1 for details). Our analysis is largely descriptive, to examine the lie of the land, so to speak. But one of our aims is to see whether the pattern of forced exits has changed over time.

Many commentators believe that Australian prime ministers are too reluctant to sacrifice ministers following scandal (Mulgan 2002). John Howard was particularly criticised for his reluctance to dispose of ministers in his later years in office. In a letter to the *Herald-Sun* (12 November 2007), two former prime ministers, Gough Whitlam and Malcolm Fraser, wrote:

> In the last two decades the constitutional principle that ministers should be held accountable for the failings of their policies or administration has been seriously undermined.

> No matter how grave their failings may be, ministers no longer resign.

Academic commentators are more circumspect. Page (1990) and Thompson and Tillotsen (1999) have documented when Australian federal ministers have resigned, but they also note that it has never really been the Australian tradition for ministers to resign for departmental or policy failings (nor indeed has it been in other Westminster systems: see, for example, Dowding and Kang 1998; McLeay 1995, Ch. 5; Woodhouse 1994). Indeed, as Richard Mulgan points out in Chapter 9, the textbook account of ministerial responsibility means that all prime ministers are bound to fail it. Nevertheless, it is worthwhile examining the pattern of forced exit over time to see whether we can discern changes in how prime ministers respond to criticism of their ministers. In order to do that we need to look not only at cases where ministers do resign, but also those where they do not.

Calls to Resign

Sacrificial responsibility is the ultimate public face of ministerial accountability and, as the letter from Whitlam and Fraser suggests, is often thought to be the mark of ministerial responsibility. One way of ensuring that a prime minister's government looks unaccountable is, however, to make lots of calls for resignation. It is clear from our data that many calls are trivial. Rather than use our own subjective judgment about what is trivial and what important, we chose to use our source as a guide. From our original data—which collected all calls for resignation from parliamentarians, elite figures, organisations such as trade unions or from newspaper columnists—we culled those that were not repeated in the media over two or more days. So we only report here cases where the media reported the call and then discussed the issue over several days. We do not claim that all of the cases in the data reported here are 'objectively serious' but we have excluded many cases that are clearly trivial.[1]

Figure 6.1 demonstrates that the number of resignation calls has increased over time (and that increase is even larger if the trivial items are included). Later we will categorise these calls and see where they have been increasing. Figure 6.1 shows a sharp rise in the early 1970s, corresponding with Whitlam's administration, and a further rise under Fraser. We also see large rises under Howard's administration. The figure shows the actual number of calls annually and a smoothed trend line. The trend line is important as it demonstrates how parliamentarians, elites and the media are more likely to call for resignations over time. The trend line falls towards the end but it is too soon to tell if this is a temporary or more permanent phenomenon.

---

1   For example, in the data we report here we have 35 cases of non-resignation distilled from 94 in our full set; we use 12 cases of departmental error of 25 in our full set; 13 financial scandals out of 42, and so on.

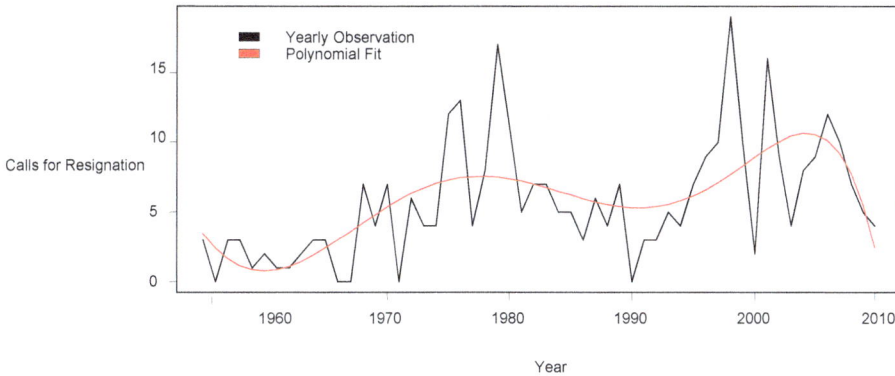

Figure 6.1 Calls for Resignation Over Time

Proximate Causes of Forced Exit

In this chapter we are examining the proximate causes of forced exit—that is, the specific events that led to a minister resigning at the time he did. Proximate causes are contrasted with ultimate causes, which would include factors shown to have been important in ministerial turnover, such as the age of the minister, previous scandals in cabinet, the relative popularity of the government in the polls, and so on (Berlinski et al. 2007, 2010, 2012; Dewan and Dowding 2005). Our aim is to describe the proximate causes of forced exit, examining trends over time, not to explain the ultimate causes and underlying conditions that lead to forced exit.

It would be a mistake to examine only ministerial resignations when attempting to identify the proximate cause of forced exits. Selecting the dependent variable might lead one to conclude that certain proximate factors lead to resignation when in fact a very small percentage of such cases leads to resignation. To overcome that fact we have coded all cases from 1947 to 2010 where there has been a call for a minister to resign. Such 'resignation issues' are composed of resignations and 'non-resignations' where a call has come but the minister has remained in place. The calls have been recorded from those reported in the newspapers (*The Age*, *The Australian* and the *Sydney Morning Herald*), and all cases have been coded according to a set of categories (see Appendix 6.1 for details of the coding methods).

In this chapter we consider a minister to be anyone with ministerial responsibility reporting to either house, thus including people in both inner and outer ministries. The number of ministers has changed over time, with 19 under Menzies' first government, while Howard had 18 in his last cabinet plus 14 in the outer ministry. The number of ministers may vary over any given administration, but not by much.

In what circumstances are ministers forced out? We do not include the 30 departing ministers who have been coded as retirement/outside appointment/ shuffled out. We note here that 10 of these cases occurred under Robert Menzies and eight under Howard; both had long administrations so faced ageing cabinets that needed reinvigorating now and then. One example is Walter Cooper who resigned in December 1960 as Minister for Repatriation; he was then seventy-two (though he remained in Parliament for another eight years). Under Menzies, nine ministers resigned or announced their intention to resign during a government term to take up other positions, including five who left to take up diplomatic posts; most were in their sixties or seventies. Towards the end of his time in office, Howard would take the Christmas break to consider his cabinet and have a reshuffle in late January. No other prime minister moved on ministers in quite such a measured, post-Christmas manner. Note that one reason ministers might be moved on is because they faced earlier resignations calls; nevertheless, they did not go at the time of those calls, but later, at the prime minister's own choosing.[2]

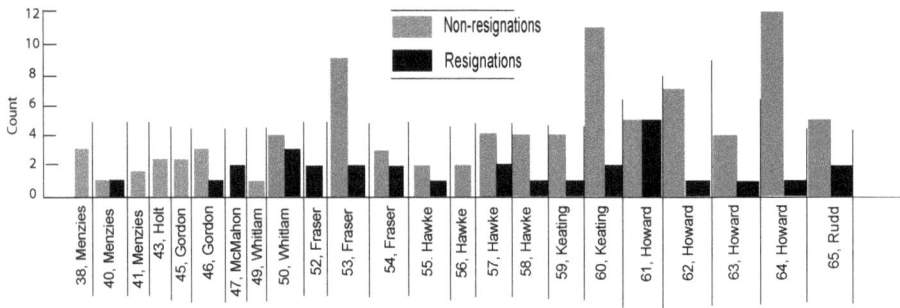

Figure 6.2 Resignations and Non-Resignations by Government, 1949–2010

Figure 6.2 compares the number of resignations with non-resignations by government; we have removed those short-term governments with no resignations or non-resignations. There appears to be no particular pattern to the resignations: some parliaments have few, others 10 or so. But it is clear that the number of non-resignations has increased dramatically over time. There are some peaks in the mid-1970s—notably the fiftieth government (Whitlam's third administration) and the fifty-third (the third Fraser administration)—but the largest rise comes with the sixtieth government (Keating's second administration), with further rises under Howard. This pattern of increasing numbers of calls

---

2 Such earlier non-resignations feature in the ultimate explanation of ministerial turnover, but not in consideration of proximate cause.

for resignations matches trajectories in other countries (Dowding and Dumont 2009a; Dowding and Kang 1998; Fischer et al. 2006) and is certainly due in part to increased media attention to ministerial behaviour—though we note the few calls in Rudd's two and a half years. Of course, as we mentioned in the introduction, Howard was criticised for allowing standards of sacrificial accountability to slip: ministers did not resign following problems within their departments, with decisions they made or general behaviour.

There are many reasons for the increase in calls. There are a greater number of controversial issues as the policy agenda has grown, particularly since the time of Gough Whitlam (Dowding et al. 2010). Issues such as share-ownership and travel expenses have become controversial and worthy of press comment whereas in the past they were ignored (Dowding and Lewis 2012). Many calls in recent years are simply appended to criticisms of ministers' policies. Furthermore, the press and opposition have become more vitriolic in their criticism.

Figure 6.3 breaks the resignations and non-resignations down by prime minister, but since prime ministers serve for different periods we weighed the number of calls for resignation by the number of days in office. Here we see the charge against Howard loses some force. Whitlam had the same number of calls per day (though a slightly higher number of resignations per day in office) with Fraser not so far behind.

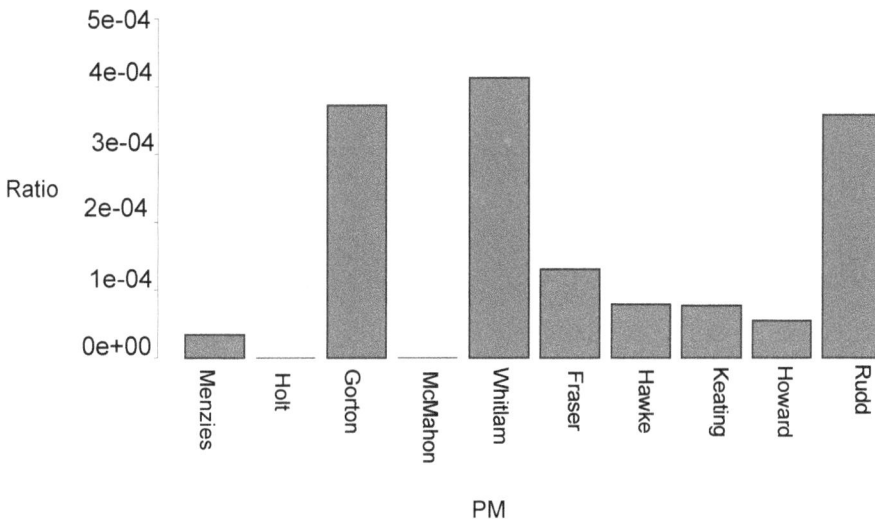

Figure 6.3 Proportion of Resignations to Calls for Resignation by Prime Minister, Weighted by Days in Office, 1949–2010

One way of considering the issue would be to look at the proportion of resignations relative to the number of calls for resignation. This has been called the 'honour ratio' (Dowding and Kang 1998) though the title is perhaps misleading given that even in our restricted set some calls for resignation might be considered mischievous.

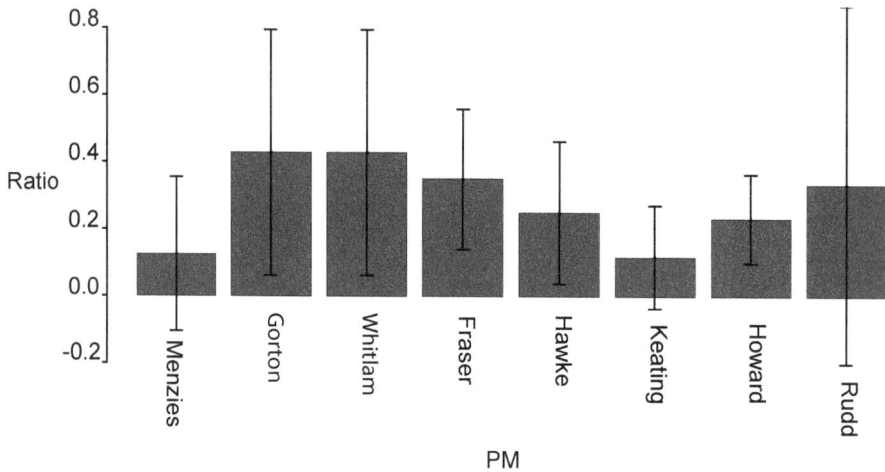

Figure 6.4 Proportion of Resignations to Calls for Resignation by Prime Minister, 1949–2010

Figure 6.4 shows the proportion by prime minister. We see here that in fact Howard has fewer calls per resignation than Keating or Menzies; however, given the small numbers and the increasing calls over time we cannot make much of this. We also put 95 per cent confidence intervals on the figure. The 95 per cent confidence intervals are estimated by the binomial distribution, which approximates a normal distribution for n larger than about 25–30, and so are not very accurate except for the Fraser, Hawke, Keating and Howard entries.[3] This shows that even with the caveats already made, Keating's upper bound is within the proportions for Hawke and Howard, showing a slightly more than 95 per cent probability that Keating's rate of turnover is within the average range for Hawke and Howard. This means we cannot assume from the figure (even ignoring the caveats above) that Keating's ministers were less accountable than Hawke's or Howard's.

---

3   For n trials and p probability of success, the confidence interval is given by $p +- 1.96^*(p^*(1 - p)/n)$.

Reasons for Resigning

What are the proximate reasons that force ministers to exit? We see in Figure 6.5 that by far the greatest number of resignation calls relate to personal error. Personal error includes all decisions made by a minister in his or her capacity as a minister. An example is Gerry Hand's non-resignation over misleading Parliament about funding for the National Aboriginal and Islander Health Organisation. Hand did in fact offer to resign but Hawke supported him and would not accept the resignation. The resignations in this category are: Reg Withers (Administrative Services), August 1978; Mick Young (Special Minister of State), July 1983; John Brown (Arts and Environment), December 1987; Ros Kelly (Environment, Sports and Territories), February 1994; Ian Campbell (Environment), March 2007. The McGregor Royal Commission on electoral redistribution in Queensland found Withers had acted improperly to get the name of an electorate changed, and Fraser dismissed him when he refused to resign. Young was asked to resign by Hawke following the former's admission that he had leaked to a lobbyist that the Government was about to expel a Soviet diplomat. Young was later reinstated after party pressure, despite a report tabled in Parliament that Justice Hope believed that his actions gave rise to a real danger of damaging national security. John Brown resigned in December 1987 for misleading Parliament over the 1988 Expo in Brisbane. Ros Kelly resigned in February 1994 after she admitted that she had approved a sports grant her department considered ineligible. Her problem was not simply the pork barrel, which has long been a practice of Australian politicians, but her failure to keep proper documentation, and her failure to answer questions in Parliament because she was 'rostered off' for that Question Time. Perhaps what eventually led her to resign was the charge that she had misled Parliament and the fact that the affair had rumbled on for most of February, with her resignation coming on the last day of that month. Ian Campbell resigned four days after reports that he had met with the controversial Brian Burke, a former Labor premier of Western Australia and then a lobbyist for WA business interests. With ministers in Western Australia banned from speaking to Burke by the Premier, Geoff Gallop (an edict rescinded by his successor, Alan Carpenter), and the Corruption and Crime Commission investigating Burke's affairs, the Howard Government was attempting at this time to embarrass Labor's new leader Kevin Rudd over his own meeting with Burke. When Treasurer, Peter Costello, asserted that 'anyone who deals with Burke is morally and politically compromised', Campbell resigned quickly to end any Liberal embarrassment.

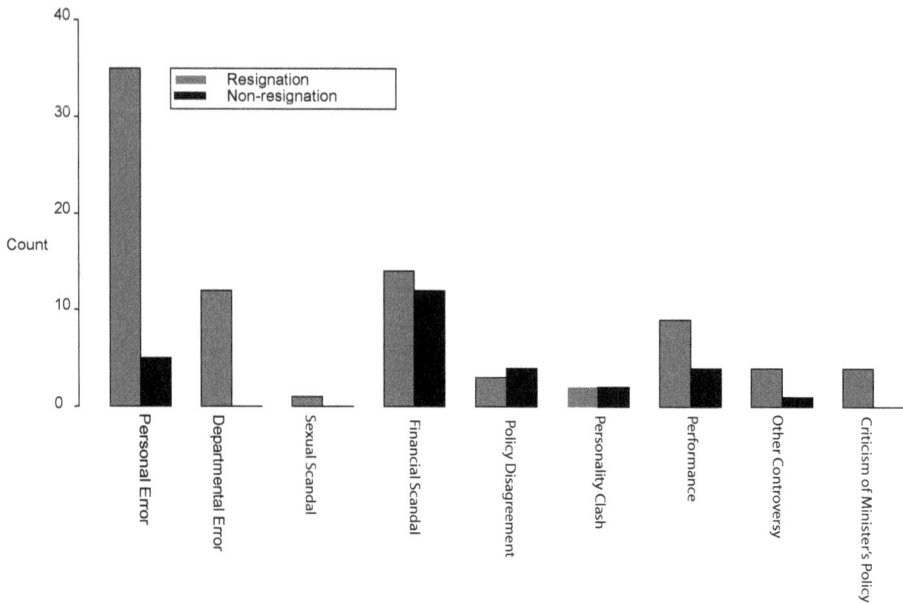

Figure 6.5 Reasons for Call to Resign by Event, 1956–2010

Non-resignations in Howard's government in this category include Alexander Downer (in April 2006)—Rudd suggested Downer had misled either Parliament or the Cole corruption inquiry into the Australian Wheat Board kickbacks scandal (McConnell et al. 2008, 208; Overington 2007; Volcker 2005); De-Anne Kelly in December 2004, despite Howard's admission she had broken the ministerial code of conduct in unlawfully approving grants to electorally sensitive areas unconnected with her portfolio; Robert Hill, who had failed to act on senior Australian military lawyers' reported concerns over the treatment of prisoners in Iraq; Bronwyn Bishop (March 2000), following reports she had misled Parliament the previous year when she had said spot checks on nursing homes would continue when in fact they had not started; there were additionally several calls for Howard to resign following claims he had misled Parliament over the children overboard affair (Keating 2003; Marr and Wilkinson 2003; Weller 2002) and, earlier, over meetings with businessman Dick Honan.

The next largest category of non-resignations is financial scandal though it has the highest number of resignations. This category has the highest proportion of resignations to resignation issues (resignations and non-resignations combined), demonstrating the seriousness with which financial scandals are treated, even when relatively trivial. The earliest resignation over financial matters occurs in July 1975. Whitlam forced Jim Cairns to resign after the minister first denied and then claimed to have no memory of authorising businessman George Harris to investigate the raising of overseas loans. It was part of the loans affair that was instrumental in the fall of Whitlam's government, and the day after Cairns resigned Queensland Premier, Joh Bjelke-Petersen, called on the Coalition to demand Whitlam's resignation. Rex Connor was also caught up in the loans affair, though he was actually dismissed on the basis that he had misled the Prime Minister over continued links with Tirath Khemlani after his authority to seek overseas loans had been withdrawn.

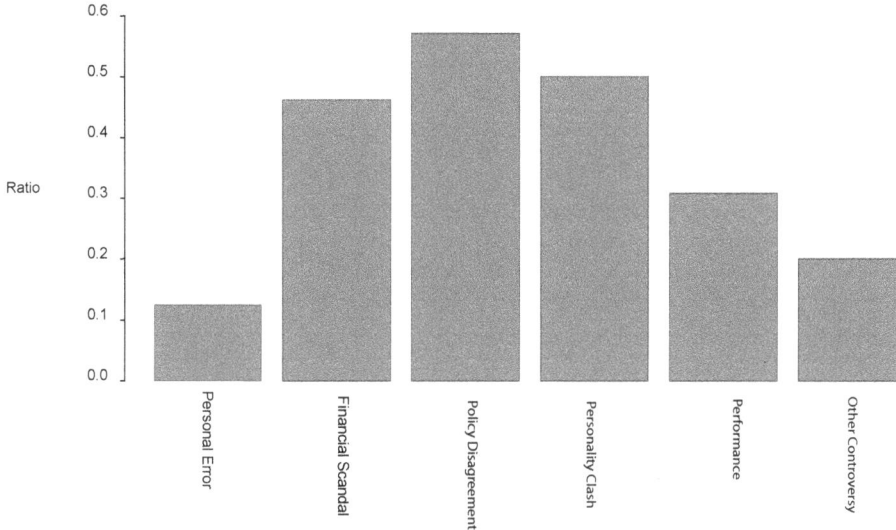

Figure 6.6 Proportion of Resignations to Calls for Resignation by Reason

Victor Garland resigned over the relatively trivial matter of an independent senate candidate giving $500 in expenses at Garland's office. Garland was cleared of any wrongdoing six weeks after resigning. Phillip Lynch resigned, despite having the full confidence of Prime Minister Malcolm Fraser, because of allegations about his family's business interests. He was likewise vindicated, just a month after resigning.

Ian Sinclair finally went in September 1979 after the *Finanne Report* concluded he had not been honest in his business dealings or his explanation of arranging loans from a group of companies of which he was de facto managing director. He had survived three earlier calls to step down (May and October 1978, and June 1979) when his business dealings were under investigation. Michael MacKellar resigned as Health Minister and John Moore as Business and Consumer Affairs Minister responsible for customs in April 1982 after four days of criticisms following MacKellar's admission that six months earlier he had made a false customs declaration to avoid paying duty on an imported television. Fraser demanded both resignations though Moore argued he had done nothing wrong. Mick Young resigned in February 1988 following a police investigation into Labor's failure to disclose a $10 000 election campaign donation. Prime Minister

Hawke accepted the resignation reluctantly, saying that sections of the media had treated Young 'appallingly badly'. Graham Richardson resigned as Minister for Communications over his failure to register his interest that he was a director of a radio station and his failure to quit the directorship immediately he was appointed to the ministry. The issue broke on 30 April though Richardson did not resign until 19 May. A further factor was Richardson's denial (on 29 April) that he had knowledge of his cousin-in-law Greg Symons's business interests,[4] confounded by the revelation on 8 May that he had written a letter of recommendation to the Government of the Marshall Islands to help Symons in his business there. Alan Griffiths resigned in January 1994 following allegations about the possible misuse of funds received for party political purposes to meet the debts of a shop of which he was a part-owner. Joel Fitzgibbon resigned in June 2009, as we shall discuss below.

Eight resignations due to financial scandal came under Howard, the first two (Jim Short and Brian Gibson) snared by Howard's new ministerial code (Howard 1996). Short owned extensive banking shares whilst being responsible for banking matters; Gibson owned bank shares, though he argued he was not responsible for banking policy. (John Moore faced calls for resignation over share-ownership at the same time, but managed to survive.) They began the series of forced exits in Howard's first administration. Santo Santoro went late in Howard's final administration for failing to register shares. Bob Woods resigned over parliamentary expenses; John Sharp and David Jull over false travel allowance claims, followed by Peter McGauran a few days later. Bruce Scott also faced calls for his resignation but weathered the storm. We include Mal Brough, though he was forced to stand down before he was sworn in as minister because of allegations of electoral rorting during a State election in Queensland. Howard relaxed his code following the rush of resignations in his first term, but they almost certainly gave a taste for blood to the Opposition and press.

We will not discuss all the calls for resignation that did not lead to exit, some for relatively trivial issues, but we note that Mick Young faced such a call in July 1984 for making a false customs declaration—a similar, though perhaps not as serious, case as that which led to two ministers resigning under Fraser. John Dawkins and John Button did not resign after claims of conflict of interests. Dawkins was Minister of Trade and admitted knowing his mother owned shares in a company, and Button held shares when Minister of Technology and Commerce. Chris Hurford survived, despite a story that he had promised scoops in return for a regular radio spot on an Adelaide commercial radio station, though there is some doubt about how serious this allegation really was. John Brown did not resign after it emerged that his wife had cashed in a first-class

---

4   As this is a separate issue that went away, but came back and was relevant to his final resignation, we have coded the issue of 29 April as a non-resignation.

ticket issued to her as an MP's wife for economy-class tickets for her and her sons. Bruce Scott (September 1997) faced calls to resign over travel rorts (and was almost certainly not promoted because of the issue); Peter Reith (October 2000) over the use of his telecard by his son; Ian MacFarlane and Peter Costello (August 2003) over a claim that they tried to defraud the Tax Office of GST liabilities for a Liberal Party dinner; Helen Coonan (December 2002) for using ministerial letterheads in personal correspondence with an insurance company; Wilson Tuckey for pressurising South Australia's Police Minister to quash a fine incurred by his son; John Anderson (September 2004) over allegations (that he was cleared of) that he tried to bribe an independent MP to give up his seat, and again (June 2005) over selective handouts to Coalition electorates in his role as Transport and Regional Services Minister. Under Rudd, Joel Fitzgibbon did not resign in March 2009 following details of his association with Chinese businesswoman Helen Liu, though he did go three months later after further revelations about their association and that with Fitzgibbon's brother and the fact defence officials felt they were being pushed to do business with Fitzgibbon's brother. Both Rudd and Wayne Swan are also non-resignations in this category (June 2009) over the OzCar scheme where they were accused of pushing business to specific car dealerships.

We can see with regard to financial scandals that, whilst they are more likely to lead to resignations, in some cases ministers do not go even though these cases seem equally as scandalous as ones in which resignation ensues. Howard introduced his code of conduct following his criticisms of ministers in the previous administration for not declaring interests and holding shares; however, he then faced even greater problems over these issues in his own administration and later felt obliged to relax the guidelines. Sometimes resignations occur over relatively trivial sums of money, largely because ministers have been shown to have given misleading statements, and the issue of honesty rather than the original 'crime' is what leads to resignation. Of course, another issue is how important the minister is to the party and the prime minister. Ministers considered to be good or who are close to the prime minister are less likely to go than those the prime minister might be pleased to see the back of, but we do not consider that aspect of forced exits in this chapter.

The main categories that financial scandals fall into are: first, campaigning irregularities; second, inappropriate use of public money, such as travel rorts; and three, suspicious business activities either personally or in the minister's immediate circle. The first lead to resignations if proven; the second tend to lead to resignations, though are more acceptable if ministers can demonstrate lack of personal knowledge. Whether resignations occur in the third seems to depend upon the seriousness of the claims and whether the minister is shown to have been dishonest in his first response to the allegations. In all three areas the attitude of the prime minister and the political circumstances of the time are key determinants in how the case unfolds.

The line between a policy dispute and 'personality clash' is a fine one. In the main, policy disputes are those where policy disagreement of some sort is aired in public. We have coded some cases as policy dispute where disagreements within cabinet have been made public by the opposition or media, even though sometimes these might be of a relatively trivial nature. The normative constitutional convention is clear enough in this case. Disputes within government, even when becoming public through leaks, should not lead to resignation no matter what hostile oppositions or the media make of them. Publicising them is mischief making by opposition or the media. We have coded as personality clashes those cases where personal ambition has led to resignation. So personality clash also includes power battles between members of the cabinet, notably leadership battles.

In Australia, as in the United Kingdom and other countries, few ministers resign over 'performance' despite many calls for them to do so. Those who call for a resignation based on the poor performance of a minister rarely expect the minister actually to resign; rather the call is simply a means of getting criticism of the government into the news. We will not report the myriad cases of non-resignation, but mention here those exits we have so coded. The first is Frank Crean in November 1974. After the 1974 election, Cairns was elected Deputy Leader of the Labor Party and asserted his right to a bigger role in economic policy, eventually claiming the Treasury after Crean had been virtually sidelined over the 1974 budget. We have also included the dismissal of the Whitlam Government by the Governor-General in November 1975. There has been much debate over this controversial action, but we have simply coded it as one case due to 'performance'. We code as performance John Dawkins' resignation as Treasurer in December 1993, following months of speculation after his budget had been savaged, which he described as the worst month in his political career. Geoff Prosser resigned in July 1997, telling Prime Minister Howard that he had become a liability to the Government. As indicated above, he had survived earlier calls to resign over his business affairs but question marks remained.

Two things are notable about these data for Australia in comparison with the similar data collected for the United Kingdom. The first is the relative lack of sex scandals. We have coded one non-resignation as a sex scandal, though in truth it is a minor affair compared, for example, with the fuss made in the United Kingdom and the United States (Garment 1991; King 1986; Markovits and Silverstein 1988; Tiffen 1999); indeed it was not presented in the newspapers at the time as explicitly about sex. We code it thus more to make the point that sex scandals do not figure much at the federal level.[5] In fact, it was a call in February 1975 by the Country MP Ralph Hunt for Jim Cairns to resign unless there were to be a public inquiry into the appointment of Junie Morosi as Principal Private Secretary to Cairns—a post usually held at that time within the Treasury by a public servant. What is interesting about this 'sex scandal' in comparison with British and US ones is that, whilst the sexual nature of their relationship was guessed by elites in Canberra, it was not aired in the press until almost 30 years later. Australian newspapers do not seem inclined to pursue Commonwealth politicians with the zeal of their US and British counterparts—unless it is that Australian politicians are less inclined to become involved in such tawdry matters.

The second aspect of the Australian data that is particularly noticeable in relation to the United Kingdom is the necessary addition of a new category of resignation issue. In Figure 6.5 there are five entries where there has been a call for a minister to resign over their policy (and another 42 recorded in the full set). None has done so, which is as significant as the coding itself. Ministers in Australia are much more closely aligned with specific policies than in the United Kingdom. Any such calls for resignation in the United Kingdom would be directed more at the Prime Minister for failures in government policy or possibly at the Chancellor of the Exchequer (Treasurer), or directed at more general performance issues. Specific calls for ministers to resign due to their policies—not the failure of those policies as such but their nature—are, however, common in Australia.

Conclusions

This chapter is largely descriptive, presenting some general data on ministerial resignations and non-resignations in Australia over a 60-year period. Like all such descriptive studies using data in this manner there are many judgment calls to be made over how to precisely code the events. Sometimes the point of the coding and discussion is to bring out the nature of the event and how unusual it is, such as the case of Cairns. We note that rarely do ministers resign due to 'performance', though arguably prime ministers can sometimes be thought to do so; however, such cases also involve power struggles.

There are a number of features worth noting in our findings. First, the number of resignation issues has increased dramatically over the period. (There was a falling off during the Rudd years, though it is too early to say if this is a trend.) Whilst there has been a slight increase in the number of ministers over that time,

---

5 They have featured at the State level in the past decade or more.

this increase cannot explain the dramatic rise. There are a number of factors that might. Whilst the standard constitutional issues—calls for resignation over personal and departmental errors, over the general performance of the minister, over policy disagreements—have been around from the start, calls for resignation (in our data set) over financial irregularities started only in the mid-1970s, over personality clashes from the late 1960s (probably due to Menzies being in control for so long) and, whilst we do have one call for a minister to resign over his policies from as far back as 1959, that case is Harold Holt as Treasurer over economic policy. Calls for resignation of ministers due to their policies (we note again this is not policy failure as such, simply criticism of the policy the minister has adopted) started in the late 1960s (with three cases) and then took off dramatically from Whitlam's government in the 1970s. No minister has ever resigned after such a call.

We suggest that the increasing number of resignation issues over time is due to increased media attention, and also to Australian oppositions becoming much more ruthless as they view a potential resignation as a political prize to be pursued. Certainly the call to resign over policy has increased dramatically and is relatively unusual in world terms. With the exception of calls in the United Kingdom for the Chancellor of the Exchequer (the Treasurer, in Australia) to resign during economic crises, such calls are only made on the Prime Minister. Similarly, such calls are rare in Ireland, Germany, Belgium, Canada and other countries for which such dedicated data have been collected (Dowding and Dumont 2009a).

We have discussed the proximate causes of resignation in terms of the reasons for the call for resignation. But we note that the attitude and political judgment of the prime minister are vital. Using Australian data, McAllister (2003) reports that resignations are correlated with falls in government popularity, and, if causal, this ought to make prime ministers reluctant to fire ministers. Dewan and Dowding (2005), however, using British data, argue that it is the resignation issue that is bad for a government's popularity—that resignations in fact provide a corrective effect, increasing government popularity relative to what it would have been. They recognise, however, that prime ministers cannot always sack and the 'political scalp' aspect usually leads prime ministers to defend ministers unless it is clear that the public disapproves. We also note that dishonesty about an issue is often more important than the nature of the issue itself when it comes to whether a minister resigns.

In this chapter we have mapped the outlines of forced exits in the Australian Commonwealth Government in the postwar period. More detailed analysis of our data is required before we can supply a more thorough analysis of the cause of forced exits, but this overview provides a start in examining the changing nature of ministerial resignations and public perceptions about those resignations and thus the true nature of sacrificial ministerial accountability.

Acknowledgements

We thank Anne Gelling, Richard Mulgan, John Nethercote, Rodney Tiffen and John Wanna for their comments. The research reported here was made possible by the Australian Research Council Discovery Grant DP09851986.

Bibliography

Berlinski, S., T. Dewan and K. Dowding. 2007. 'The Length of Ministerial Tenure in the UK, 1945–1997'. *British Journal of Political Science* 37(2): 245–62.

Berlinski, S., T. Dewan and K. Dowding. 2010. 'Performance Evaluation of British Ministers'. *Journal of Politics* 72(1): 1–13.

Berlinski, S., T. Dewan and K. Dowding. 2012. *Accounting for Ministers: Scandal and Survival in British Government 1945–2007*. Cambridge: Cambridge University Press.

Dewan, T. and K. Dowding. 2005. 'The Corrective Effect of Ministerial Resignations on Government Popularity'. *American Journal of Political Science* 49(1): 46–56.

Dewan, T. and D. P. Myatt. 2007. 'Scandal, Protection, and Recovery in Political Cabinets'. *American Political Science Review* 101(1): 63–78.

Dowding, K. 1995. *The Civil Service*. London: Routledge.

Dowding, K. and P. Dumont (eds). 2009a. *The Selection of Ministers in Europe: Hiring and Firing*. London: Routledge.

Dowding, K. and P. Dumont. 2009b. 'Structural and Strategic Factors Affecting the Hiring and Firing of Ministers'. In *The Selection of Ministers in Europe: Hiring and Firing*, eds K. Dowding and P. Dumont. London: Routledge.

Dowding, K. and W.-T. Kang. 1998. 'Ministerial Resignations 1945–97'. *Public Administration* 76(3): 411–29.

Dowding, K. and C. Lewis. 2012. 'Culture, Newspaper Reporting and Changing Perceptions of Ministerial Accountability in Australia'. *Australian Journal of Politics and History* 58: 236–50.

Dowding, K., A. Hindmoor, R. Iles and P. John. 2010. 'Policy Agendas in Australian Politics: The Governor-General's Speeches, 1945–2008'. *Australian Journal of Political Science* 45: 533–57.

Fischer, J., A. Kaiser and I. Rohfling. 2006. 'The Push and Pull of Ministerial Resignations in Germany, 1969–2005'. *West European Politics* 29: 709–35.

Garment, S. 1991. *Scandal: The Culture of Mistrust in American Politics*. New York: Times Books.

Howard, J. 1996. *Guidelines on Ministerial Conduct*. Canberra: Australian Government Publishing Service.

Keating, M. 2003. 'In the Wake of "A Certain Maritime Incident": Ministerial Advisers, Departments and Accountability'. *Australian Journal of Public Administration* 62(3): 92–7.

King, A. 1986. 'Sex, Money and Power'. In *Politics in Britain and the United States*, eds R. Hodder-Williams and J. Ceaser. Durham, NC: Duke University Press.

McAllister, I. 2003. 'Prime Ministers, Opposition Leaders and Government Popularity in Australia'. *Australian Journal of Political Science* 38(2): 259–77.

McConnell, A., A. Gauja and L. Botterill 2008. 'Policy Fiascos, Blame Management and AWB Limited: The Howard Government's Escape from the Iraq Wheat Scandal'. *Australian Journal of Political Science* 43(4): 599–616.

McLeay, E. 1995. *The Cabinet and Political Power in New Zealand*. Auckland: Auckland University Press.

Markovits, A. and M. Silverstein (eds). 1988. *The Politics of Scandal: Power and Process in Liberal Democracies*. New York: Holmes and Meier.

Marr, D. and M. Wilkinson. 2003. *Dark Victory*. Sydney: Allen & Unwin.

Mulgan, R. 2000. 'Accountability: An Ever Expanding Concept'. *Public Administration* 58(3): 555–74.

Mulgan, R. 2002. 'On Ministerial Resignations (and the Lack Thereof)'. *Australian Journal of Public Administration* 61(2): 121–7.

Overington, C. 2007. *Kickback: Inside the Australian Wheat Board Scandal*. Melbourne: Allen & Unwin.

Page, B. 1990. 'Ministerial Resignation and Individual Ministerial Responsibility in Australia 1976–1989'. *Journal of Commonwealth and Comparative Politics* 28(2): 141–61.

Thompson, E. and G. Tillotsen. 1999. 'Caught in the Act: The Smoking Gun View of Ministerial Responsibility'. *Australian Journal of Public Administration* 58(1): 48–57.

Tiffen, R. 1999. *Scandals, Media, Politics, and Corruption in Contemporary Australia*. Sydney: UNSW Press.

Volcker, P. 2005. 'Manipulation of the Oil-for-Food Programme by the Iraqi Regime'. Washington, DC: United Nations. <http://www.iic-offp.org/documents/IIC%20Final%20Report%2027Oct2005.pdf>, viewed August 2010.

Weller, P. 2002. *Don't Tell the Prime Minister*. Melbourne: Scribe.

Woodhouse, D. 1994. *Ministers and Parliament: Accountability in Theory and Practice*. Oxford: Oxford University Press.

Appendix 6.1

All ministers from the beginning of Menzies' fourth ministry (1949) were listed. In this chapter we make no distinction between inner and outer ministries. We then carried out a systematic search for all 'resignation issues' in various newspaper databases. A 'resignation issue' is defined as any issue over which there was a call for a minister to resign by a parliamentarian, a responsible agent such as a professional organisation, lobby group or trade union, or in an editorial or column in one of our newspapers. Cases where ministers resigned prior to any public discussion also constitute resignation issues. The information was downloaded and a short descriptive paragraph of each event written up. From those descriptions all cases were coded into 10 categories: Personal Error; Departmental Error; Sexual Scandal; Financial Scandal; Policy Disagreement; Personality Clash; Performance; Other Controversy; Ill Health; Criticism of Minister's Policy. Whilst some cases had secondary as well as primary causes coded, we utilise only the primary categories in this chapter. These categories were based on those used for a similar study in the United Kingdom (Dowding and Kang 1998) though, as discussed in the text, it was necessary to create additional categories.

In some cases an issue emerges, goes away and then returns. In such cases, if there is a gap of a week or more in reporting, we code it first as a non-resignation and then as a resignation. Similarly, if two issues are bundled together, we code the earlier as a non-resignation and the second that leads to the exit as resignation.

For consistency over the period, we concentrated upon information from the *Sydney Morning Herald* (*SMH*), though for parts of the period further information (not cases) was also taken from other newspapers—notably, *The Age* and *The Australian*. The Factiva database (<Factiva.com>) was utilised to access articles from September 1986 to December 2007. The *SMH* was available from 1 September 1986, *The Age* from 19 January 1991 and *The Australian* with articles available from 8 July 1986. The *SMH* archives site (<http://archives. smh.com.au/>) was utilised for the 1955–95 period. For articles prior to 1955, information was obtained via microfiche files from the National Library of Australia's Canberra facilities. Relevant information in relation to ministerial resignations from Internet databases (1955–2007) was obtained by typing the minister's name in Factiva followed by the word 'resign*' (for example, 'Keating resign*'). Information for the period 1949–54 was acquired though a microfiche search. All entries for individual ministers were noted from the *SMH* index books from the National Library of Australia, and by manually viewing the first three pages of all *SMH* newspapers on microfiche. All material was collected by one researcher who also initially coded the data. The coding was subsequently checked and discussed with another researcher.

Other sources of information used to support data search and check information were: Department of Parliamentary Library, *That's It—I'm Leaving and Other Kirribilli Tales, Ministerial Resignations and Dismissals 1901–1991*, the Parliament of the Commonwealth of Australia (<http://www.aph.gov.au/index.htm>); and Wikipedia and Google searches of different Australian federal governments and ministers. Further background information on cases was also collected from various biographies and secondary sources.

7. Ministers and Scandals

Scott Brenton

Sharp and Jull resigned. Labor led the Coalition two goals to nil.

— *Sydney Morning Herald*, 6 October 1997

Typifying the media commentary surrounding ministerial resignations, politics is often reported like a sporting contest. During Liberal Prime Minister John Howard's first term of office, the use and misuse of politicians' travel entitlements—which the media quickly dubbed 'travel rorts'—became the theme of a series of scandals. Transport Minister, John Sharp, voluntarily amended his travel claims and repaid almost $9000, but did not publicly disclose this information; neither did the Administrative Services Minister, David Jull, who oversaw the amendment and repayment. The Coalition initially closed ranks, emphasising Sharp's 'good bloke factor' and the voluntary nature of the rectifications, as they tried to protect one of the National Party's rising stars. The Government was, however, having 'mid-term blues' and Sharp lost the Prime Minister's support. Both he and Jull were asked to resign, with Howard proclaiming that 'I have acted to uphold not only the reality of standards, but also the perception of standards and that is why what has happened has occurred' (*The Australian*, 25 September 1997). While Howard was not the first prime minister to use such standards to sanction a minister, he became the first to explicitly define the standards and, perhaps inadvertently, enabled opponents to define contraventions of them as scandals with equivalent certainty.

The History of Scandals

While the first written account of a scandal in ancient Greece is almost as old as democracy itself, and scandals have long been a feature of liberal-democratic politics (Clark 2003; Neckel 2005), the involvement of Australian ministers in publicised scandals and the increasing frequency with which they occur are relatively recent phenomena. Both rumours and factual stories about the private lives of former prime ministers have entered political folklore but went unreported at the time: John Curtin was a (recovering) alcoholic and had been imprisoned during World War I; Ben Chifley had an affair with his personal secretary; Robert Menzies had an affair with a prominent newspaper proprietor's wife; Harold Holt had been drinking with a woman who was not his wife before his disappearance in the ocean; John Gorton was also an alcoholic; and Billy

McMahon enjoyed the company of young male sailors. As Dowding, Lewis and Packer chronicle in Chapter 6, in the few decades of the postwar period, Australian politics was characterised by stable conservative government and the more sensational resignations were due to breaches of cabinet solidarity and leadership instability after Prime Minister Robert Menzies retired, rather than the types of indiscretions that now make headlines. The election of a more radical government under Labor Prime Minister Gough Whitlam in 1972 stimulated new political tactics: the targeting of individual ministers in order to challenge the legitimacy and competence of the government, and the fitness of the leader to continue as prime minister.

As the incidence of political scandals has increased, the role of the mass media has changed, while scandalous allegations are being used as offensive political weapons (Williams 1998). In the final year of the Whitlam Government preceding the constitutional crisis, the questionable appointment of Junie Morosi as Deputy Prime Minister and Treasurer Jim Cairns' Principal Private Secretary sparked rumours of a sexual relationship. More significant was Cairns' involvement, along with Minerals and Energy Minister, Rex Connor, in what became known as the 'loans affair'. The scandal centred on attempts to secure loans from Middle Eastern businessman Tirath Khemlani, rather than using the Treasury's normal channels through the Loan Council. For the Opposition and sections of the media, calls for resignation were part of legitimately holding the Government to account. The Governor-General's dismissal of the Whitlam Government confirmed the effectiveness of such offensive political tactics and demonstrated that a government could be brought down by scandal.

Prime Minister Malcolm Fraser's Coalition government was comparatively less scandal-ridden, but increasingly behaviour outside the strict confines of ministers' portfolio responsibilities was being scrutinised. Most notably, Health Minister Michael MacKellar became embroiled in controversy over incorrect customs declaration forms on an imported colour television set, and eventually resigned along with the minister responsible for customs, John Moore.

During Bob Hawke's prime ministership, spanning almost nine years, there were only three resignations due to scandals, and only one during Paul Keating's first two years as prime minister. Strikingly, during the second term of the Keating Labor Government there were five such resignations and many more controversial affairs where ministers resisted calls to resign (termed non-resignations). One of the most notable was that of NSW right factional powerbroker Graham Richardson, who was instrumental in helping Keating depose Hawke. The business dealings of Richardson's cousin by marriage Greg Symons, and Richardson's alleged interventions to assist him, came under scrutiny. Richardson's response was defiant:

Obviously over the years I have hurt them [the Opposition] and they think the Government would be weakened if they got rid of me. They know I am close to Paul Keating and they are trying guilt by association and they will try to extend it further to Paul. (*The Australian*, 6 May 1992)

Howard, at the time a shadow minister, was one of Richardson's chief critics in Parliament, arguing that '[t]here is no more serious parliamentary offence than a minister lying to the Parliament. That is what has happened on this occasion' (*Sydney Morning Herald*, 9 May 1992). During the previous 17 years, four ministers had been accused of 'misleading the Parliament'; all were forced to resign from their ministries. In a speech to Parliament, Howard explicitly linked ministerial conduct to prime ministerial leadership:

Under questioning from the Opposition, and not as an act of ministerial contrition and coming clean, we heard his story. If he had come into the Parliament and said, 'Look, I have really stuffed this one up. I did not give a full account, and here is the full story' perhaps we on this side of Parliament may have a different attitude...

He is a legendary member of the 'mates', and they operate on the basis of never apologising and never resigning. It is not surprising therefore that the Prime Minister should be trying to tough this one out. But, at the end of the day, he has to realise that he stands in a long line of prime ministers, from both sides, who, when the crunch finally comes, have normally done the right thing.

Gough Whitlam, with all his weaknesses, had the guts to sack Rex Connor because he inadvertently misled the Parliament. He had the guts to sack Jim Cairns because he, inadvertently or otherwise, misled the Parliament and his Prime Minister. We want to know whether Paul Keating has the guts to sack Senator Richardson because he misled the Senate...

The supreme test of the courage and probity of the Prime Minister is whether he insists on ministers observing the basic requirements of a minister; that is, that they tell the Parliament the truth. Senator Richardson has failed to do this. (*Sydney Morning Herald*, 9 May 1992)

Howard argued that:

He [Senator Richardson] is too strong to dismiss. The Prime Minister is bound body and soul to his factional mate and can't get rid of him for that reason. It's got nothing to do with the merits of the issue…It's got everything to do with the dominant role that…Richardson played in getting Paul Keating the job. (*The Canberra Times*, 11 May 1992)

These events illustrated the narrative of an ailing government losing its way and a leader losing control over his ministers. Howard effectively appropriated the issue of ministerial propriety as a central campaign theme when he subsequently became Opposition Leader, promising higher standards of ministerial conduct when he won office in 1996. He became the first Australian prime minister to institute a ministerial code of conduct based on a publicly available document, entitled *A Guide on Key Elements of Ministerial Responsibility* (McKeown 2009). It was not just a codification of the public's expectations of ministerial behaviour, but also explicitly detailed what Howard as leader expected. While there were criticisms that the document lacked legal, regulatory or parliamentary authority, and that Howard was the sole authority as author, arbiter and interpreter (Uhr 1998), it concomitantly meant that Howard's authority was also called into question when ministers breached the code. Furthermore, as a Liberal prime minister with the power to choose his own ministers, Howard's judgment in selecting appropriate ministers could also be scrutinised.

What Is a Political Scandal?

One of the most common definitions in the field of 'scandology'—as the study of scandals has become known—is that political scandals involve 'the gross violation of cultural and [or] legal norms that limit the use of positions of public trust for private purposes' (Logue 1988, 257). Political scandals can occur only in liberal democracies, as freedom of speech, an open and aggressive media and strong political competition are necessary conditions enabling scandals to flourish. Moreover, scandals occur at the intersection of power with the processes and procedures that are so fundamental in liberal democracies (Markovits and Silverstein 1988). The defining characteristic of a political scandal is not the degree of personal gain, but the violation of process and procedure in the quest for greater political power. Simply using public office for individual gain is not scandalous, as most politicians are rational, materially self-interested individuals attracted to the benefits of power; *noblesse oblige* motivates few (Logue 1988). Rather it is the extent to which rules and regulations attached to public office are violated.

Processes and procedures are also fundamental components of accountability, and therefore scandalous transgressions are often erroneously, or at least simplistically, linked to questions of accountability. Scandals are not, however, *really* about ministerial accountability; rather they are tests of prime ministerial leadership. Being called to account in response to a scandal is often reduced to a simplistic question of should the minister resign/be sacked. Yet sanctions are only part of accountability. Sanctions are about punishment and, as in the earlier case of 'travel rorts', about political point-scoring. Accountability involves not simply questioning the transgressor and the transgression and debating the consequences, but a deeper questioning of the processes and procedures and how these can be abused through the exercise of power. This did not occur, and rarely does. The system of travel and other entitlements remained open to abuse and the political saga continued unabated. Only days after the resignations of Sharp and Jull, the Opposition refocused its attention on the travel claims of Veterans' Affairs Minister, Bruce Scott, but could not gain traction in the media; however, another Nationals minister was already in their sights. Labor shadow minister Simon Crean interrogated Science and Technology Minister, Peter McGauran, in Question Time over his travel claims, and warned that the Opposition would keep scrutinising his claims until he resigned (*The Australian*, 24 September 1997).

Game on: Winning ministerial 'scalps' and claiming momentum

Oppositions are not interested in explanations or justifications or any other form of accounting for one's actions, and will generally always call for the minister to resign or be sacked. McGauran's responses, like those of Sharp and Jull before him, were secondary: the real focus was on what the leaders knew, should have known or did not know and how they handled the situation. At first, Howard and the National Party leader, Tim Fischer, defended McGauran. Howard, however, later requested a full audit of McGauran's travel claims and charter allowances. Fischer conceded that the minister's actions were 'prima facie…unacceptable' (*The Australian*, 24 September 1997), and that McGauran initially misled Parliament. After the audit Howard told Parliament that his office was informed a few months previously about incorrect travel claims by two ministers, but, he claimed, 'I personally knew nothing of the matters until the past few days' (*The Australian*, 24 September 1997). Howard's senior members of staff Graham Morris and Fiona McKenna were sacked and McGauran finally tendered his resignation to the Prime Minister. This was a decisive leadership action, with an element of personal sacrifice in dismissing trusted senior advisers.

The Government had already been tarnished by the 'shares affair' in the preceding year. Assistant Treasurer, Jim Short, resigned from the ministry in 1996 after granting a banking licence to a subsidiary of a bank in which he held shares. Parliamentary Secretary to the Treasurer, Senator Brian Gibson, also resigned in 1996 after granting futures market access to a company in which he held shares. In 1997, Small Business Minister, Geoff Prosser, resigned over perceived conflicts of interest due to his continued private business dealings. Resources Minister, Senator Warwick Parer, also became embroiled in a similar scandal and eventually ceded control of mining shares and other investments. With 'travel rorts', Labor was beginning to master a damaging political strategy, with a complicit media also fanning populist anti-politician sentiment, which was particularly strong when it came to taxpayer-funded entitlements and resources. While often dismissed as trivial distractions from 'serious' political issues, the focus of political competition has shifted to trivial issues in general (Apostolidis and Williams 2004). Williams argues that many consumers of the mass media find policy details and differences complex and boring, whereas scandalous allegations are simpler to report and are generally regarded as being more interesting (Williams 1998). Political scandals do not require detailed political knowledge and can enliven discussions in forums like talkback radio, in contrast with the arid, abstract policy discussions that can create a barrier to popular involvement (Clark 2003).

Each scandal also has its own momentum, which is crucial in determining its longevity and the potential damage, and is also dependent on the discovery of new pieces of information. Innuendo and suggestion are habitually used to develop momentum until new information is discovered, particularly when the initial facts seem mundane; scandal momentum is often related to sheer sensationalism (Garment 1991). Momentum is closely related to the news cycle and what other issues are on the media agenda at the time. The life of scandals is not determined by the nature of the offence, but by the interaction of political strategies and media practices, which each function according to their own logics and sets of interests (Tiffen 1999). Often rumours have been circulating behind the scenes for some time and the instigator chooses a specific moment to publicise the gossip, with the timing planned to divert attention from other issues or to link the scandal to particular political agendas (Clark 2003). Rumours and gossip can also be suppressed until the politician is perceived to be a real threat to opponents, such as when they are promoted to a leadership or ministerial position.

While the momentum of a single scandal can be broken by a resignation or the diversion of media attention to other issues, there is a cumulative effect and the next scandal can be even more damaging. The opposition will continue to fossick for damaging information on other ministers under the guise of raising standards of accountability, in order to whittle away the prime minister's moral authority and keep party leaders on the defensive. It is not in the raw political interests of the opposition for processes and procedures to be fundamentally reformed to prevent future abuses; rather it is in their interests for abuses to occur and be exposed—unless their own members are involved, enabling the government side to raise the spectre of mutually assured destruction. In this case, not only can the overall political momentum be broken, the scandalous issue can be taken off the agenda. The Government 'successfully' turned defence into offence by questioning the travel claims of Labor shadow minister Senator Nick Sherry. Sherry attempted suicide, which became the circuit-breaker for an uneasy truce. The Opposition relented as they realised that the most effective political prosecutor is the media.

'It's Not a Hanging Offence'

In 2000, *The Canberra Times* journalist Emma Macdonald broke the story that in late 1993 Peter Reith (by this stage the Minister for Employment, Workplace Relations and Small Business) gave his parliamentary telecard code number to his son, Paul, to contact him in an emergency while in Western Australia on holiday. His son used it for four years, making $950 worth of calls; however, 11 000 phone calls from 900 locations around the world, costing nearly $50 000, were made on the telecard over six years from 1994 to 1999. Reith told the Prime Minister, who referred the matter to the Australian Federal Police, while a whistleblower informed Labor Senators John Faulkner and Robert Ray at about the same time as Howard was initially told (*The Australian*, 12 October 2000). The behind-the-scenes actions led to criticisms that there was a lack of public accountability during the 14-month secret investigation.

The Director of Public Prosecutions did not find sufficient evidence to lay any charges. The Commonwealth Director of Public Prosecutions found that Reith's son was not criminally liable, and the Australian Federal Police and the Commonwealth Director of Public Prosecutions cleared Reith of criminal liability. The Commonwealth Solicitor-General, David Bennett, also cleared Reith and his son of liability for most of the debt (except the $950) after finding that a court would most likely prefer Paul Reith's version of events; however, before the final report was released, Reith paid the entire debt by taking out a loan, without claiming a work-related tax deduction (after earlier refusing to rule out that possibility). Reith said that '[t]he responsibility I'm accepting is a political one, not a moral one, whilst acknowledging my first mistake, a mistake anybody else could reasonably have made' (*Sydney Morning Herald*, 16 October 2000).

Reith appeared to breach a number of clauses in the Prime Minister's code of conduct, particularly that '[m]inisters should ensure that their actions are calculated to give the public value for money and never abuse the privileges, which, undoubtedly, are attached to ministerial office' (*The Australian*, 14

October 2000). Yet Reith said he had not considered resigning. Howard would not sack Reith because it was not a 'hanging offence' although he said Reith had been foolish (*Sydney Morning Herald*, 27 October 2000). Some Coalition Members of Parliament were unhappy with Reith's handling of the incident, calling for Howard to sack him from the ministry to limit damage to the Prime Minister's credibility (*The Australian*, 20 October 2000; *Daily Telegraph*, 23 October 2000).

An unnamed Labor source claimed the party wanted to vigorously pursue Reith and Howard, but not to the point where their own practices would be scrutinised (*Sunday Telegraph*, 15 October 2000). Notably, Labor did not pursue the issue when their senators were first informed, as their strategy appeared to be to encourage the media to take the lead, giving the public the sense that it was a non-partisan exercise. *The Canberra Times* (20 October 2000) editorialised that:

> The media was crucial, eventually, in Reith's decision to pay back the $50,000...Everyone was waiting to see what the media, through editorials, talkback radio and public-opinion polls, had to say about the matter. Talkback radio concluded that Reith should pay up...The overall impression is that ministers and their leaders wait to see what they can get away with rather than take a principled decision.

In Howard's first two years as prime minister there were seven resignations in response to scandals, while there was none in the next four years and only three during the remainder of Howard's prime ministership. This was despite frequent scandals and calls for resignation. One such scandal centred on the Minister for Revenue and Assistant Treasurer, Senator Helen Coonan, and her spouse's property investments and principal residences. Coonan claimed her incorrect pecuniary interest declaration was due to a typographical error, but admitted that she mistakenly declared her principal place of residence as an investment property. The Opposition then alleged a conflict of interest between Coonan's ministerial duties and her directorship of a mediation company. Coonan claimed that she resigned as a director when she became a minister, although her spouse, the company's secretary, did not so advise the Australian Securities and Investments Commission until 11 months later. It also emerged that Coonan used her ministerial letterhead for personal purposes. She used it to pursue a personal insurance claim, to complain to the local council and to a builder, and to (successfully) request that the council waive a supplementary development application fee. Howard conceded that the use of ministerial letterhead for personal affairs was 'not normal practice' and 'I encourage ministers not to do it', but argued that it was not a 'hanging offence' (*Sydney Morning Herald*, 14 December 2002). He said that Coonan was not in breach of his ministerial code of conduct.

Another non-resignation involved the Minister for Regional Services, Territories and Local Government, Wilson Tuckey. Tuckey used his ministerial letterhead to assert to the SA Police Minister that 'his constituent'—Tuckey's son—should have been given a warning rather than a fine for failing to carry a logbook for his truck (*The Canberra Times*, 23 August 2003). Tuckey initially told Parliament that: 'I wrote to the minister saying that I thought a warning should be appropriate…I did not press the matter any further', triggering accusations that he was misleading Parliament, as a Labor backbencher revealed a series of letters (*Sydney Morning Herald*, 20 August 2003; *The Canberra Times*, 23 August 2003).

This time Labor was more active in pursuing the issue, particularly after the last non-resignation. Labor accused Tuckey of breaching Howard's code of conduct, which stated that ministers should 'avoid giving any appearance of using public office for private purposes', and that '[m]inisters should not exercise the influence obtained from their public office, or use official information, to gain improper benefit for themselves or another' (*The Canberra Times*, 23 August 2003). Howard's ministerial code of conduct was also subjected to media scrutiny, with criticisms that it had become meaningless (*Daily Telegraph*, 21 August 2003). Howard's response was 'I thought the minister was quite foolish and wrong, he was very foolish indeed to have written this on his ministerial letterhead', but it was not 'a hanging offence' (*The Canberra Times*, 23 August 2003).

Resignations or sackings are viewed as a win for the opposition or a 'scalp', and important in gaining 'momentum'. Thus, ministers and prime ministers initially adopt a defensive strategy—a position, once adopted, that becomes hard to shift from. The choice for the government is based on whether a prolonged distraction is giving the opposition more momentum than a resignation would. The extent of the distraction is not necessarily related to the actual transgression or degree of culpability, but rather what other issues the scandal is competing with for political and media attention at the time. If a scandal ends in resignation (which is uncommon), the government frames it as a noble gesture on the part of the minister to end the distraction to the government and its policy focus. The other common outcome is a cabinet reshuffle, which is again framed in positive terms, like refreshing the government. Tuckey was eventually demoted from the ministry in a reshuffle only a month after the scandal.

Howard's responses to scandals later in his prime ministership often followed the same theme. He repeatedly defended ministers—Reith, Coonan and Tuckey—on the grounds that the behaviour in question was not a 'hanging offence'. His reluctance to demote ministers can be viewed in purely political terms, as evidence of his determination not to give the Opposition a 'scalp'. Presumably government strategists decided that it was less damaging to defend ministers than to force resignations and allow the Opposition to claim small victories and gain momentum. Scandals do eventually run out of steam as new political issues take prominence, so determined ministers can avoid resignation.

Keating, too, was very reluctant to dismiss his scandal-ridden minister Graham Richardson, until the issue became too distracting for the Government. Keating displayed a similar attitude towards Sports Minister, Ros Kelly, in what became known as the 'sports rorts affair', after accusations that she bypassed process in approving sports grants for marginal Labor electorates and then misled Parliament in response to questions. At the time even Kim Beazley, later to become Labor leader, conceded that misleading Parliament is a 'hanging offence'.

Limiting the Damage

Scandals create opportunities for considerable political damage by distracting the politician, their party, the media and the public from other political issues of the day. The political damage is in proportion to the extent of the distraction. Timing is therefore a significant factor. When a scandal breaks, the gravity of the transgression and the standing of the politician will be compared with the importance of other issues currently on the political agenda to determine whether the scandal is given the opportunity to develop momentum and become a distraction. These comparisons will be made both strategically and more passively by various groups, principally political opponents, the media and the public. Often those groups will differ in their interpretations, which may mitigate the severity of the damage.

The magnitude of the scandal does not necessarily dictate the extent of the distraction, as there are other more important factors at play. It is when that distraction interrupts the politician's ability to effectively continue in their position that it becomes career threatening or career destroying. That decision is not made by the media or even the public (except at election time), but by the politician and more importantly the politician's party and leader. The other aspect of this issue is that a scandal can be damaging even if there is no tangible evidence of harm done to the politician's prospects. It is the *perception* that it could potentially be a problem that is damaging. Scandals can dominate the limited and precious media time given to federal politics each day, and deprive party leaders of opportunities to discuss other issues. Political discourse, at least in the electronic media, is often reduced to 10-second sound bites and in this environment a political scandal is an unnecessary distraction.

Most ministers actually survive scandals, so it is perhaps more instructive to examine why the politicians whose political careers ended as a result of scandals sustained such significant damage. The overall impact of scandals has generally not been felt at the ballot box, but rather has been mitigated or intensified during the normal course of politics as parties seek to attack and counterattack their rivals (with the media ever present). While public support is ultimately necessary for political survival, it is the support that the politician's party provides (or does not) that is most crucial. Scandals alone do not cause the political distraction; rather the overall handling of the scandal beyond just the verbal response is what determines the level of damage. Resignations can be the most damaging outcome for a government, creating the impression that ministers are incompetent, whereas by weathering the controversy ministers and prime ministers can suggest that scandals are part of the 'rough and tumble' of politics and that they are tough enough to handle this. Howard's repeated defence of his ministers, perhaps counter-intuitively, did not lose its effectiveness over time: those familiar words did not appear to remind voters of previous ministerial indiscretions during his prime ministership or indicate a lack of discipline.

A scandal does not necessarily end a minister's career, and long-term damage can be limited. There are many political factors beyond the immediate control of the politician that can mitigate the damage. First, the support of the party is crucial, as the politician's chance of winning a seat as an independent is minimal. Furthermore, strong and publicly expressed support from the party is required, as its absence is noticeable. This can send a message to the public that there is something seriously wrong with the behaviour of the politician, if even his or her party is unforgiving. Second, the timing will determine the amount of potential media attention, and this is beyond the control of the politician and their party. Third, major-party senators (in the States) enjoy the advantage of six-year terms and generally safer seats, which makes it more likely they will have their party's support to weather any storms. Fourth, complicated scandals where simple narratives cannot be applied, as in the case of Coonan, are unlikely to excite public interest. Fifth, the public cares less than might be expected. Politicians are already held in low regard, so scandals are not shocking in that sense. Furthermore, during election campaigns other issues assume more public importance. Finally, a politician may be able to survive a scandal by providing a sense of closure. Resigning from a ministerial or leadership position is one way; he or she might also repay money or in some other way move to repair the damage. Such acts can also provide a socially acceptable ending to the story. Significantly, most scandals do not have long-term political impacts.

Ministers are held to a higher standard of personal and professional behaviour than other parliamentarians. Ministers are called to resign from the ministry, but rarely from parliament altogether. Similarly, there is no 'punishment' for backbenchers who may commit the same offence as a minister, such as incorrectly claiming an entitlement. Public expectations are heightened to some degree by frequent opposition promises of improved ministerial codes of conduct. As Thompson (2005, 47) observes, 'the occurrence of scandal tends to have a cumulative effect: scandal breeds scandal, precisely because each scandal further sharpens the focus on the credibility and trustworthiness of political leaders'. This focus becomes incorporated into the political cycle as political parties and their leaders pledge to improve standards of conduct after their opponents fail the credibility test.

Just as one of Howard's major campaign themes before winning government in 1996 was around this issue, Labor leader Kevin Rudd campaigned on increasing accountability and released his own version of the ministerial code of conduct after winning government in 2007. Both Howard and Rudd criticised previous governments for condoning lower standards of ministerial behaviour and promised reforms once in government. First-term governments are particularly vulnerable as they provide test cases for the effectiveness of the new reforms, compounded by ministerial inexperience; however, after a few 'scalps', prime ministers lower the standards themselves. After Howard lost a few ministers in his first term, he changed tactics. While inexperienced Labor ministers did not succumb to the same fate in their first term as their Coalition predecessors, Rudd did lose his Defence Minister, Joel Fitzgibbon, after the Defence Department conducted unauthorised covert investigations into his friendship with a businesswoman. While this was not deemed sufficient to warrant resignation, it invited increased media scrutiny and it emerged that his brother, who headed a health fund, had met department officials to pursue business opportunities. Fitzgibbon resigned to 'protect the integrity of the government' (*The Australian*, 4 June 2009). Months later, Environment Minister, Peter Garrett, was criticised for his department's administration of the Home Insulation Program, which resulted in several deaths and house fires; in an election year, Garrett was demoted, remaining in the ministry but with his portfolio downgraded.

Backbenchers are better placed than ministers to successfully emerge from scandals because they do not have to front the media in the execution of their normal duties. Furthermore, public discussion is also limited: unknown backbenchers are less interesting unless the transgression is particularly unusual. The media is generally very aggressive with ministers, but quickly loses interest in backbenchers, and is less likely to pursue leads involving them in the first place. In most cases it is not the transgression or its magnitude that causes the scandal, but the standing of the politician that attracts media attention.

The Role of the Media

There is a tendency to simplistically view the media as one homogenous entity, particularly in Australia where media ownership is so concentrated, and even more so in relation to politics, which is principally covered by a relatively small Canberra Press Gallery. Scandals, however, consist of multiple narratives and, for public discussion to be genuinely fostered, there need to be contested interpretations. As Lull and Hinerman (1997) observe, scandals are *polysemic*—that is, they are never uniformly interpreted. While there may be a diverse range of opinions expressed in editorials, political columns, letters to the editor and panel discussions on radio and television programs *after the facts have emerged*, in the actual reporting of the incident in the initial stages of the scandal a 'pack mentality' can easily develop. Once the scandal breaks, the media's objectivity can become compromised in the sense that their interest is in finding new information to provide more evidence of guilt rather than objectively considering the possibility of innocence (Garment 1991). It is the nature of contemporary media competition, with each media organisation worried about being 'scooped' by rivals. As Tiffen (1999) observes, unlike in a court of law, in the media, evidence presented is not subject to clear rules, and thus the timing is only dependent on availability, opportunity and an erratic sense of newsworthiness. Tiffen also notes another important difference between media coverage and judicial due process: media coverage shifts focus as issues develop and can lose clarity about what the alleged offence actually is.

There has also been a 'tabloidisation' of existing media, as broadsheet newspapers have gone downmarket in an attempt to arrest declining revenues (with a particular interest in sex scandals), which has contributed to increasing personalisation of politics (Dobel 1998; Tumber 2004; Tumber and Waisbord 2004a, 2004b). Tumber and Waisbord describe 'tabloidisation' as the focus on titillation, drama, rumour and sensationalism, at the expense of substance and the higher journalistic standards of rigour and veracity. Media advisors to politicians are complicit in this process, with press releases and rehearsed 'sound bites' conforming to, and thus perpetuating, tabloid standards. Gamson (2004) argues that market forces have pressured mainstream news organisations to adopt tabloid-style topics and presentation strategies. Tabloidisation is not exclusive to the newspaper industry, with television news programs also following similar trends, aided by spin doctors and shrinking audience attention spans. Increased competition from cable news channels that have successfully embraced tabloid-style presentation techniques has persuaded higher-quality news programs to do the same. As Williams (1998) observes, unlike complex policies, personal wrongdoing can be simply reported and is more likely to generate interest.

Unlike the traditional inverted-pyramid style of news reporting—that is, where articles are structured from the beginning with the most important point, continuing to the least important—scandals are narrated like a story (Bird 1997). The media imposes narrative frames providing characters, structure and longevity (Lull and Hinerman 1997). As Tomlinson (1997) notes, journalists use human-interest angles to appeal to the widest possible audience. Scandals are stories that can often overshadow the facts in attempting to arouse the curiosity of the widest possible audience, who then seek more information from the media (Lull and Hinerman 1997). In this way, narrativisation encourages speculation, as the emphasis shifts from reporting what actually happened to debating what will happen next. Thus, the initial transgression can become less and less important as the scandal ensues, to the point where it is (almost) forgotten.

The plot and character developments resemble familiar storylines and structures to facilitate greater identification from the audience, while the storylines themselves are quite simple albeit sensationalised. Kenski (2003) observes that scandals focus on the dramatic and are framed in terms of winning and losing, where the politician's status or reputation is at stake; however, as briefly mentioned in the previous section, there is never only one storyline (in major scandals at least). Williams (1998) argues that major political scandals do not take the form of a single, unbroken narrative, as there is competition between the various players—such as the initiator, the transgressor, the media and political opponents—for ownership and control of the scandal. Williams (1998, 128) contends that scandals consist of 'disconnected, fragmented, overlapping, multiple narratives'. The audience or, more precisely, audiences are also disconnected, fragmented and overlapping.

One notable trend is for journalists to use scandals to psychoanalyse leaders and to raise questions of judgment that have only tenuous connections with ministerial accountability. The prime minister's political judgment in selecting and retaining the minister is then called into question. If anything, the administrative errors or issues more directly related to the minister's portfolio or performance are easier to get away with, as there are more people to blame and chains of events are often complicated. It is more difficult for the largely politically uninterested public to follow these than, for example, the more salacious sex scandals. Journalists sometimes also assume the role of amateur psychologist. Former leader of the Australian Democrats turned Labor frontbencher Cheryl Kernot (2002, 150), herself subject to many scandals, is unsurprisingly critical: 'The editor of the *Canberra Times*, Jack Waterford, voices concerns about a different trend: that of psychological speculation in political reporting, where journalists, as amateur psychologists, theorise at length on the motives for politicians' actions and decisions; this is often as a substitute for factual reporting.'

In most cases, it was not the opposing party that publicly initiated and aggressively pursued the issue. The media has often uncovered and publicised the information, as in the cases of Helen Coonan (the *Sydney Morning Herald*'s Mark Riley); John Sharp (the Nine Network's Laurie Oakes); Chris Ellison (the *Sunday Telegraph*'s Peter Rees, with investigative committee work by Labor Senator Robert Ray); and Peter Reith (*The Canberra Times*'s Emma MacDonald).

Most of these scandals involved the misuse of taxpayer-funded entitlements, which supports the argument that the opposition has been reluctant to become too overtly involved, lest their own practices be made public. While a scandal might be damaging for its subject, it can also harm the initiator, as the targeted politician has someone (the initiator) to identify and blame. That does not mean, however, that the media might not receive tips or leaks from the opposing party.

While the emergence of new and alternative media has been cited as a factor in the proliferation of political scandals in contemporary politics, its role in Australian politics has been limited. It is generally the 'old' media that breaks scandals and is instrumental to their continued momentum; however, the 'old' media may still have been responding to competitive pressures caused by the changed media landscape. Even so, many politically focused blogs continue to publish rumours and innuendo that have not been repeated in the mainstream media. There are other important differences between the Australian media culture and the American media culture, upon which much of the scandological theory is based. Australia does not have a prevalence of locally based talk shows or topical comedy programs, and has only a couple of 24-hour news channels (and even those include many overseas news programs and stories). Local and talkback radio are prominent, but do not operate on a 24-hour news cycle in the same way. Furthermore, as previously mentioned, media ownership is more concentrated in Australia and competition is thereby reduced. In these respects, Australian politicians enjoy more protection than their American and British counterparts.

Conclusion

Scandals are never exactly the same partly because the seriousness of the offence is not always the best predictor of the outcome, and actions can produce differential consequences depending on the context (Tiffen 1999). As Tiffen (1999) observes, in the 'court of public opinion' penalties vary and there is inconsistency between the punishments, which are often disproportionate to the severity of the offences and related more to political expediency or accidents of circumstance. Public opinion itself is inconsistent and there are varying points of view amongst the public. Furthermore, it depends when this court of public opinion is *in session*—that is, the timing of the offence. It also depends on whether the court is distracted by other issues, which is again related to the timing of the event. Thus, luck can be a factor. The outcome will depend on the status of the politician involved and how distracting the incident is to the party's polling performance more broadly. Again, internal party dynamics appear to be an important factor, specifically the authority that a politician wields within the party and how powerful his or her factional allies and opponents are. While it is difficult to definitively ascertain, it appears that many scandals emanate from within the politician's own party. With limited ministerial positions for ambitious backbenchers, the goal is often to damage the standing of the politician within the party rather than in the electorate.

Ministers can and do come back and scandals need not be politically damaging in the first instance; however, there is a cumulative effect, and multiple scandals can be politically fatal, as politicians become more susceptible and also more open to scrutiny. Kernot is a classic example of how frequent scandals raise questions about a politician's competence, as the 'benefit of the doubt' is gradually exhausted. Ultimately, the scandals discussed here were viewed through the prism of leadership—that is, while the minister's response was important to some degree, in each case the reactions of the leader deeply affected the political dynamics. Most ministers initially resist calls for resignation, opting for some form of explanation, and the focus shifts to the prime minister and how he or she handles the situation. This becomes the primary focus of the scandal, with the accountability of the minister of secondary concern.

References

Apostolidis, P. and J. A. Williams (eds). 2004. *Public Affairs: Politics in the Age of Sex Scandals*. Durham, NC: Duke University Press.

Bird, S. E. 1997. 'What a Story! Understanding the Audience for Scandal'. In *Media Scandals: Morality and Desire in the Popular Culture Marketplace*, eds J. Lull and S. Hinerman. Cambridge: Polity Press.

Clark, A. 2003. *Scandal: The Sexual Politics of the British Constitution*. Princeton, NJ: Princeton University Press.

Dobel, J. P. 1998. 'Judging the Private Lives of Public Officials'. *Administration and Society* 30(2): 115–42.

Gamson, J. 2004. 'Normal Sins: Sex Scandal Narratives as Institutional Morality Tales'. In *Public Affairs: Politics in the Age of Sex Scandals*, eds P. Apostolidis and J. A. Williams, pp. 39–68. Durham, NC: Duke University Press.

Garment, S. 1991. *Scandal: The Culture of Mistrust in American Politics*. New York: Times Books.

Kenski, K. M. 2003. 'The Framing of Network News Coverage during the First Three Months of the Clinton–Lewinsky Scandal'. In *Images, Scandal, and Communication Strategies of the Clinton Presidency*, eds R. E. Denton jr and R. L. Holloway. Westport, Conn.: Praeger.

Kernot, C. 2002. *Speaking for Myself Again: Four Years with Labor and Beyond*. Sydney: HarperCollins.

Logue, J. 1988. 'Appreciating Scandal as a Political Art Form, or, Making an Intellectual Virtue of a Political Vice'. In *The Politics of Scandal: Power and Process in Liberal Democracies*, eds A. S. Markovits and M. Silverstein. New York: Holmes & Meier.

Lull, J. and S. Hinerman. 1997. 'The Search for Scandal'. In *Media Scandals: Morality and Desire in the Popular Culture Marketplace*, eds J. Lull and S. Hinerman. Cambridge: Polity Press.

McKeown, D. 2009. *A Survey of Codes of Conduct in Australian and Selected Overseas Parliaments*. Canberra: Department of Parliamentary Services.

Markovits, A. S. and M. Silverstein (eds). 1988. *The Politics of Scandal: Power and Process in Liberal Democracies*. New York: Holmes & Meier.

Neckel, S. 2005. 'Political Scandals: An Analytical Framework'. *Comparative Sociology* 4(1–2): 101–14.

Thompson, J. B. 2005. 'The New Visibility'. *Theory, Culture and Society* 22(6): 31–51.

Tiffen, R. 1999. *Scandals: Media, Politics and Corruption in Contemporary Australia*. Sydney: UNSW Press.

Tomlinson, J. 1997. '"And Besides, the Wench Is Dead": Media Scandals and the Globalization of Communication'. In *Media Scandals: Morality and Desire in the Popular Culture Marketplace*, eds J. Lull and S. Hinerman. Cambridge: Polity Press.

Tumber, H. 2004. 'Scandal and Media in the United Kingdom'. *American Behavioral Scientist* 47(8): 1122–37.

Tumber, H. and S. R. Waisbord. 2004a. 'Political Scandals and Media across Democracies, Volume I'. *American Behavioral Scientist* 47(8): 1031–9.

Tumber, H. and S. R. Waisbord. 2004b. 'Political Scandals and Media across Democracies, Volume II'. *American Behavioral Scientist* 47(9): 1143–52.

Uhr, J. 1998. 'Howard's Ministerial Code'. *Res Publica* 7(1): 1–11.

Williams, R. 1998. *Political Scandals in the USA*. Edinburgh: Keele University Press.

8. A Recent Scandal: The Home Insulation Program

Chris Lewis

Introduction

The policy debacle that was the Rudd Labor Government's Home Insulation Program (HIP) cannot be disputed.[1] First, four young Australians died installing insulation in homes before the program was cancelled on 22 April 2010. Further, about $1 billion (approximately 40 per cent) of the $2.45 billion cancelled scheme was, in the end, used to cover its costs, including safety and quality inspections for about 200 000 homes fitted with ceiling batts or foil (Berkovic 2010f). As of 10 December 2010, the number of fire incidents attributed to the HIP since May 2009 had reached 202, including 165 attended by fire authorities, with another 37 confirmed through roof inspections, although 87 per cent of incidents (176 households) resulted in no structural damage (DCCEE 2010).

The HIP came under fire from many quarters. In July 2010 a senate committee called for a royal commission in order 'to unravel the gross and systematic failures in the development and implementation of the Program' (Environment, Communications and the Arts References Committee 2010, ix). Julia Gillard, who replaced Rudd as Prime Minister on 24 June 2010, stated during the election campaign that 'the insulation scheme was an absolute mess' (Karvelas and Franklin 2010). And the Auditor-General, while acknowledging its role as part of the Government's response to the global financial crisis (GFC) in terms of generating economic stimulus and employment (and possible energy efficiency gains), concluded that 'stimulus objective overrode risk management practices that should have been expected given the inherent program risks'. The Auditor-General stated that the HIP 'has been a costly program for the outcomes achieved', that there 'still remains a range of safety concerns' with 'serious inconvenience to many householders', that reputational damage had been caused to the insulation industry, and events had 'harmed the reputation of the Australian Public Service for effective service delivery' (Auditor-General 2010, 26–7).

---

1   This chapter refers to the Home Insulation Program (HIP) throughout; the scheme was known as the Home Owner Insulation Program until September 2009.

In analysing the HIP as a case study, focusing on the Rudd Government's determination to implement a program speedily without adequate consultation and planning, this chapter argues that the HIP did not give sufficient attention to key measures advocated by widely used texts on Australian public policy, even allowing for differences between them. For instance, the *Australian Policy Handbook* (Althaus et al. 2007) (hereinafter *APH*) provides a normative/ guidelines approach to public policy by illuminating various stages of policy planning and implementation, while Hal Colebatch (2006, 1), in *Beyond the Policy Cycle: The Policy Process in Australia*, cautions that 'the world of policy is populated by a range of players with distinct concerns, and that policy-making is the intersection of these diverse agendas, not a collective attempt to accomplish some known goal'.

Both these texts advocate policy recommendations that would have improved the operation of the HIP if implemented. Instead, as this article will highlight, the HIP proved a debacle on three counts. First, in terms of leadership, the Rudd Government's determination to implement a policy speedily undermined any chance of formulating a more balanced and effective policy approach while also placing immense pressure on the Commonwealth Department of Environment, Water, Heritage and the Arts (DEWHA) and State/Territory governments. Second, the Government downplayed the importance of the consultation—a crucial dimension to the HIP given that various safety and training concerns were expressed by a number of industry players. Third, there is the art of judgment: the Government displayed a lack of commonsense in failing to anticipate the possibility of substantial fraud and rorts.

The Role of Government Leadership

With any public program, the quality of ministerial leadership is crucial to success. In this regard, the *APH* and Colebatch approaches are similar: they both acknowledge the influence of powerful ministers and departments. As Scott Prasser observes, 'the public bureaucracy is now expected to be more responsive to the demands of elected governments and their policy agendas' (2006, 268–9). The *APH* also states that 'the policy domain speaks through the heads of central agencies such as [the Department of the] Prime Minister & Cabinet (PMC), the Department of Finance and Administration (Finance) and Treasury, though policy itself is typically developed within the relevant policy department. The central agencies also speak for the final domain, administration' (Althaus et al. 2007, 26).

For the Rudd Government, the major goal was speedy implementation rather than a policy that was supported by all involved players. It has been documented that DEWHA had earlier favoured a five-year roll-out of the HIP given its nature and size, yet the Government wanted a two-and-a-half-year roll-out (Auditor-General 2010, 69). The Government's decision—approving the HIP as part of the $42 billion Nation Building and Jobs Plan (Rudd 2009a, 2009b)—followed Treasury's advice that the GFC provided an unprecedented external negative shock that needed a stimulus package to counter its likely impact in 2010–11 given that gross domestic product (GDP) would fall and unemployment would increase (SERC 2009, E3–E4).

The Government promoted large-scale participation as quickly as possible. The HIP included a rebate of $1600 for householders (intended to run until 31 December 2011); Medicare was responsible for online registration and payment to installers where approved by DEWHA (Auditor-General 2010, 49). According to DEWHA, the $1600 rebate was designed 'to achieve maximum impact in line with the economic stimulus and employment objectives of the program' (DEWHA 2009b, 14). The Insulation Council of Australia and New Zealand (ICANZ), in 2007, estimated that it would cost $1200–1500 to have ceiling insulation professionally installed in an average home, and that a $500 rebate would achieve only a 28 per cent uptake over three years (D'Arcy 2010, 72; Deloitte Insight Economics 2007, 6; ICANZ 2010a, 11).

To manage risk, DEWHA did follow part of the policy framework suggested by the *APH* by commissioning (in March 2009) Minter Ellison to undertake a *Risk Register and Management Plan*. Completed in April 2009, and publicly released in February 2010, the *Risk Register* listed 19 individual risks. These included an extremely limited time frame for moving from a system where householders paid the installer and then claimed $1600 reimbursement to a full rebate system with no upfront payment (by 1 July 2009); inadequate regulation to prevent fraudulent or inappropriate behaviours; inadequate training; and quality issues (Minter Ellison 2009, 1).

Although Minter Ellison urged that the start of the rebate scheme be delayed three months to 30 September 2009 given the above concerns (Minter Ellison 2009, 1), DEWHA decided not to do so on the basis it had addressed the risks identified. From 1 July 2009, if the contracted price was less than the $1600 rebate limit, householders paid nothing for insulation. Installers were paid directly through Medicare's claim-processing system (Environment, Communications and the Arts References Committee 2010, 10). Further, under the *Risk Register and Management Plan*, fraud risk was transferred from the Commonwealth to providers where possible; installers were required to be insured properly and indemnify the Commonwealth against claims/loss arising from installers' actions (Minter Ellison 2009, 1).

The above measures demonstrate the Government's determination to implement the HIP with minimal delay. As one document reveals, the Nation Building and Jobs Plan was overseen by the Commonwealth Coordinator-General (then within the Department of the Prime Minister and Cabinet, PM&C), whose purpose was to 'break red tape and get work happening on the ground as quickly as possible' (Australian Government 2009, 12). Michael Mrdak, former Coordinator-General, has stated that

> the Government had clearly set out a very ambitious program for the rollout of a number of these infrastructure initiatives…The time frames were set out in the National Partnership Agreement, which was agreed by COAG [the Council of Australian Governments]. There certainly was a strong view by government and by senior officials that we should continue to press on to meet the time frames that had been set out by the government. (Mrdak 2010, 10)

On 18 February 2009, a representative of the Office of the Coordinator-General informed an industry consultation that '$2.7 billion worth of funding is in part structured around the Government going into deficit for a short period of time. Clear statements from [the] Treasurer and the Prime Minister state that funding is required to be spent within 2.5 years with a cap of $1600 per household' (ICANZ 2010b).

The Government's determination to implement the HIP speedily defied the significant apprehensions of various State governments, who were simply expected to fall in line. South Australia's Coordinator-General, Rod Hook, told his Commonwealth counterpart, Michael Mrdak, then a deputy secretary in PM&C, that he had concerns about the program 'from day one in February 2009'. Hook told the ABC of concerns about safety and how the Commonwealth 'was going to audit the program to ensure it was getting value for money and proper installation' (Berkovic 2010c). According to Western Australia's Treasurer, Troy Buswell, DEWHA officials told officers of State consumer agencies via a phone hook-up in April 2009 that a 10 per cent failure rate was to be expected (up to 100 000 homes) (Tillett et al. 2010). The ABC (and other sources) revealed that DEWHA officials, during April 2009, told State and Territory officials that the extensive roll-out of insulation posed a risk to lives and property, and that the program would effectively be unregulated (Berkovic with O'Brien 2010; Hudson 2010a; *The Canberra Times* 2010c).

State officials were concerned that the Commonwealth had not mandated qualifications for insulation installers, had no criteria for companies being listed on a federal register of installers, and that being on the register would be seen by consumers as government endorsement. They were also not impressed with the prospect of responsibility for any accident, death or blaze caused by the program (Probyn and Tillett 2010). The NSW Government was so alarmed by the HIP that just a month after it started it urged the Commonwealth to pay to have 10 per cent of work inspected. This was revealed by previously confidential documents (obtained under freedom of information) sent to Peter Garrett, the Commonwealth minister responsible for the program, in September 2009 because of concern about 'a spike in the number of house fires' linked to the HIP (Farr 2010).

The Rudd Government's approach to the HIP was very much top down: DEWHA and other levels of government were expected to fall in line. As revealed by an anonymous insider from DEWHA on ABC TV's *Four Corners* (in April 2010), 'we were told many times by senior management that the technical and safety issues were of less importance than getting this programme up and running and creating jobs' (Carlisle 2010).

Consultation

The Rudd Government's determination to implement the HIP speedily raises the question of how adequate was consultation with various key industry players.

Both the *APH* and Colebatch approaches emphasise the importance of consultation; significantly, the *APH* notes the problem 'of how to weight differing voices' (Althaus et al. 2007, 98). The *APH* makes a number of points. First, consultation provides 'an opportunity for policy makers to invite and obtain stakeholder input into the calculation of whether any particular policy is feasible' (Althaus et al. 2007, 98). Second, consultation serves 'to improve the quality of policy decisions through access to relevant information and perspectives, including exchange of problem and solution definitions, alternatives and criteria' (Althaus et al. 2007, 119). Third, consultation promotes 'understanding, acceptance and legitimacy of proposed policies' and 'promotes consensus about policy choices...by providing transparency, accountability and opportunities for participation' (Althaus et al. 2007, 119–20). Fourth, consultation boosts a policy's feasibility by improving 'the confidence of decision makers that a policy is not going to be riddled with embarrassing problems even before it commences the implementation phase' (Althaus et al. 2007, 98). Similarly, Prasser notes that

> every policy issue has its own particular group of interests, so one of the tests of good politics and good policy is that there is overall support for any new proposal from these groups. The range of interest groups will vary from issue to issue, and across different policy areas. The task is to

recognise what groups are important and to gauge their influence and power. This will partly depend on the party in power. (Prasser 2006, 273–4)

The reality is that the HIP applied to an industry where the need for extensive consultation was essential if only for the major safety risks. While it has been noted that the home insulation industry previously had few special regulations, besides being 'subject to normal work and safety provisions and employers' duty of care', with insulation 'frequently installed by householders themselves' (Tiffen 2010), greater attention to consultation should have been a given because the insulation of Australian homes was moving from the previous historical rate of about 65 000–70 000 per year to 2.7 million homes in 2.5 years (Combet 2010a, 2149–51; ICANZ 2010a, 6). Further, any malpractice within the insulation industry was likely to multiply owing to the likelihood that the number of installer companies would increase substantially from an estimated 200 established businesses installing insulation prior to the HIP (Auditor-General 2010, 65–6).

It defies belief that the DEWHA did not listen more to members of the electrical industry during the design stage of the HIP, even allowing for the restricted time frame for implementation. The Auditor-General (2010, 67) noted that 'consultation would most likely have enhanced the department's awareness of safety issues indicated'.

The safeguards that were introduced proved inadequate, as was predicted by many industry groups (see below). From 1 July 2009, installer businesses were required to be registered with DEWHA, to have occupational health and safety (OH&S) training, and to comply with relevant Australian Standards for insulation materials and installation (Installer Advice nos 9, 12). There was mandatory minimum occupational health and safety training for all personnel involved in installation; installers had to comply with State/Territory workplace and occupational health and safety laws; and installation practices were governed by relevant Australian Standards and State/Territory regulations for laying thermal insulation and working around electrical wiring (DEWHA 2009b, 5, 26). The Construction and Property Services Industry Skills Council also produced a range of training resources for registered training providers, including a 'pocket book' for installers available from 1 August 2009, which contained information about common installation hazards including electrical hazards (CPSISC 2009, 2).

While the Auditor-General has suggested that 'strong and divergent views among stakeholders made it difficult for DEWHA to make a judgement on how stringent to make the terms and conditions' (Auditor-General 2010, 77), there is considerable evidence that important concerns from a variety of industry players were virtually ignored.

There had been—with substantial justification—extensive concern about electrical safety prior to the HIP's implementation, even though the ICANZ argued that it did not support compulsory electrical inspections on the basis that 'experienced insulation installers know what to do and have managed this safely over the years' (ICANZ 2010a, 17). The Master Electricians Australia (MEA) expressed concern about inadequate training given the various electrical risks. These included pre-existing faults in wiring in the roof space and faulty installation of aluminium foil (a conductor of electricity) (Garrett 2010a; MEA 2009, 3).

On 18 May 2009, the MEA warned about 'a very serious fire risk' being caused by the incorrect installation of woollen batts, 'especially in older homes' (MEA 2009, 3). The National Electrical and Communications Association (NECA), having stated in February 2009 that 'there is a significant risk of electrical equipment overheating especially in the event of downlights in ceilings being covered if insulation is installed inappropriately', recommended that a licensed electrician check wiring before installation (Bostrom 2010, 53–4; NECA 2009). The NECA's Chief Executive, James Tinslay, wrote to Peter Garrett (on 9 March) about the 'inherent dangers' of installing insulation near electrical cables in regard to fires, and the need to train installers (Berkovic with O'Brien 2010; Hudson 2010a; NECA 2009), while also stressing that there were 'inherent dangers' with foil insulation (Balogh et al. 2010). The National Secretary of the Electrical Trades Union, Peter Tighe, reported that his union raised concerns about poor electrical safety aspects early in 2009 during discussions with a departmental advisory group reporting to Garrett; 'they ignored our advice and gave the impression they thought our concerns were excessive' (*The Canberra Times* 2010b).

The Government also ignored knowledge that plastic staples had been recommended in New Zealand since 2007 (NZMED 2007). Moreover, ICANZ noted on 18 February 2009 that a similar program in New Zealand 'had to be suspended because three people electrocuted themselves' (ICANZ 2010b).

Expressing concerning about training standards given the risks of insulation installation, Dave Noonan, National Secretary of the Construction Forestry Mining and Energy Union (CFMEU), reported:

> We made it very clear that people working in this program would need to be trained to identify potential electrical risks and they'd need to be aware of the risks involved in working at heights and in confined

spaces…We also made it clear this program would attract young, vulnerable workers with no experience in the construction industry. We said they'd also need proper training regarding unsafe work practices and their right to refuse to work in an unsafe environment. (Beeby 2010a)

The CFMEU was so concerned about inadequate funding for training installers under the program that, with the exception of New South Wales, its registered training organisations throughout Australia refused to participate in the program. Assistant National Secretary, Lindsay Fraser, a member of the technical working group appointed in 2009 to advise the Government on job opportunities and training, stated that 'they were not prepared to fund the training to the level we argued was necessary' (Beeby 2010c).

With the deaths of installers—the first on 19 October 2009—the Rudd Government adopted tougher requirements. From 2 November 2009, metal fasteners were banned; plastic staples were made compulsory. It also became mandatory for covers to be placed over downlights and other ceiling appliances, and an electrical safety inspection program was announced for foil installations in Queensland (Garrett 2009a). After the fourth insulation-related death, the Government suspended the use of foil insulation from the HIP (9 February 2010) (*The Canberra Times* 2010a). The HIP closed on 19 February 2010 for safety and compliance reasons (Garrett 2010b), and was ultimately axed on 22 April 2010 after the Government received a report by Dr Allan Hawke (2010) that expressed 'grave concerns about the wisdom of proceeding' and 'safety and quality risks' that 'cannot be fully abated' (Combet 2010b).

It was only on 17 December 2009, following the third insulation-related death, that the Government announced that training requirements now applied beyond supervisors to all employees involved in installation, although this was not to take effect until 12 February 2010 (Garrett 2009b, 2009c). Any company unable to provide proof of training in one of the three competency criteria by their workers would be suspended (Auditor-General 2010, 108; Rehn 2010). As of February 2010, only 2738 (37 per cent) of registered installers could provide evidence of minimum competency requirements; the Auditor-General has suggested that this low figure may be explained by higher costs of compliance with the new requirements (Auditor-General 2010, 108).

As for potential industry benefits, Brian Tikey, representing the Aluminium Foil Insulation Association (AFIA), wrote to Prime Minister Rudd in February 2009 about the rebate. Tikey argued that the subsidy would open the door to a flood of cheap fibreglass imports and do little to benefit Australian manufacturers. Neither Rudd nor Garrett replied; there was also no departmental acknowledgment that the letter had been received or considered (Beeby 2010b). Although ICANZ predicted that any reliance on imports would be minimal (ICANZ 2010b), AFIA also warned the Government (in February 2009) that 'cheap imports' would not meet Australian Standards or be 'compliant to the Building Code of Australia' (AFIA 2009, 2).

In time, the Polyester Insulation Manufacturers Association of Australia (PIMAA), although focusing not only on imports, claimed that 30–40 per cent of homes used non-compliant products (Zuzul 2010, 10)—a claim that ICANZ strongly disputed (Thompson 2010, 58). Although ICANZ estimated that only about 8 per cent of HIP materials were Chinese, about 40 per cent of the Chinese materials (about 3 per cent of the HIP total) failed thermal claims (ICANZ 2010b; Thompson 2010, 58). PIMAA also felt compelled to warn Garrett about excessive levels in imports of formaldehyde—a substance (although not specifically banned) that has been linked to respiratory problems and cancer (Hudson 2010b). At the senate inquiry, DEWHA noted that any complaint by householders about non-compliant materials was a matter for State/Territory fair trading authorities (DEWHA 2009b, 30).

The Art of Judgment

The Rudd Government's determination to implement the HIP speedily, and downplay many warnings from those involved during the consultation stage, also raises the question about its capacity for sound judgment.

The need for careful judgment is recognised by both the *APH* and Colebatch. The *APH* notes that 'it is difficult to test behavioural assumptions before a policy is implemented' (Althaus et al. 2007, 7). It states the need for careful judgment given that 'policies must make assumptions about behaviour', with 'incentives that encourage one behaviour over another, or disincentives to encourage particular actions', and 'must incorporate guesses about take-up and commitment, and mechanisms to deal with shirking and encourage compliance' (Althaus et al. 2007, 7). Colebatch observes that 'policy does not exist in a vacuum, but in relation to some identified field of practice, and this implies knowledge, both of the problem area and of the things that might be done about it' (Colebatch 2002, 10).

To some degree, the Auditor-General mitigates DEWHA's culpability by suggesting that the HIP proved 'more complex than anticipated', with risk-treatment options proving inadequate over time 'to manage the emerging risks' (Auditor-General 2010, 76). The report suggests that

> there may have been a perception by householders that installers who were listed on the register had gone through a more stringent registration

process than agreeing to the terms of conditions of registration and an Australian Business Number validation check, which was all that was required until 1 September 2009 [a period that involved 70 per cent of registrations].

It was only from 1 September 2009 that all new installers were required 'to provide copies of OH&S certificates for all installers associated with their business, verification of public liability and property damage insurance, verification of workers' compensation insurance (where applicable) and evidence of competency for those installers in a supervisory role' (Auditor-General 2010, 105).

The HIP debacle reinforces a reality that should always be present in policy making. This is the need to take account of human nature, to understand that all action occurs in an imperfect world. This is not a new insight. The *Federalist Papers*, for example, warn that 'if men were angels, no government would be necessary'. And, further, 'if angels were to govern men, neither external controls or government would be necessary' (Madison et al. 1987, 319–20).

Realistic appraisal of the HIP based on what could go wrong would have told ministers and administrators that the program would be open to abuse. The scale of the funding warranted an active obligation to minimise risk; it should certainly not have been assumed that all installer companies would do the right thing.

The Government's haste to implement the HIP (and promote extensive take-up) overrode other sensible approaches that placed a greater burden on the purchaser and helped to minimise rorting. Until 30 June 2009, two independent quotes along with a site inspection (with exemptions for remote areas) were required. It was naive to remove this requirement on 1 July 'to allow the market and householders to interact without the involvement of the department' (DEWHA 2009b, 8, 15; HIP 2009, 5). Nor was it sensible to place the burden on the consumer to choose a suitable installer and insulation type, enter into a contract with the installer and express satisfaction with the work by signing a work order form to enable the installer to be paid through the online payment system (Environment, Communications and the Arts References Committee 2010, 10).

The likelihood that the HIP would be rorted should have been evident from the start, long before the Hawke report (in April 2010) recognised that 'the lack of an upfront payment and no requirement for quotes (between June and November 2009) meant there was little incentive for householders to take the normal level of responsibility for the quality and performance of the installers' (Hawke 2010, 29). As two submissions to the senate committee noted, paying the first 25 per cent of the cost of insulation would have encouraged rational decision-making behaviour by consumers and some 'buy-in' from them in the outcome (Autex 2010, 6; PIMAA 2009, 6). One Sydney builder, who had been fitting home insulation for five years before the scheme began, commented that, once the Government announced the money, the insulation market was like a spaghetti western movie:

> [T]here were so many cowboys out there. People who had no experience were being hired to do the work and everybody was billing for the total amount of the grant rather than what the job actually cost. It was a giant rort and nobody in authority seemed to care. (Reilly 2010)

Similarly, John Muldoon, owner of The Solar Guys in Brisbane, who has been working in the solar power industry for more than a quarter of a century, said such rebate schemes attracted 'shoddy operators and shoddy work' because 'whenever you give a significant rebate you attract the wrong people into the industry', whether it be 'rainwater tanks, insulation, solar…there is a common theme, people come into the industry because they think there is a quick buck to be made' (Chalmers and Elsworth 2010).

While the Government may have underestimated the possible increase in insulation installer companies (from about 200 companies to 6313 by 6 December 2009: DEWHA 2009b, 21–3), it should have done much more to minimise the likelihood of dodgy businesses being established to take advantage of the program. After all, the Government's requirements for installers to be registered with DEWHA from July 2009 allowed qualification by three options: 1) demonstrating minimum trade-related competencies including being a licensed builder, electrician, carpenter, bricklayer, plasterer, painter or plumber, or equivalent where no licensing requirements exist; 2) demonstrating insulation-specific competency by either a statement of attainment from a registered training organisation or a training package relating to insulation installation; or 3) two years of work experience installing insulation (Installer Advice no. 9). It was only mandatory for the supervisor to have insulation-specific competencies (Auditor-General 2010, 107; DEWHA 2009a).

One company, Sky green, noted that a supervisor could have a large crew of untrained people performing the installations and simply arrive at each installation to sign off on the form (Sky green 2009, 10). Not only did new installation businesses emerge from businesses such as pest controllers, gyprockers and pool and spa companies (Berkovic 2009), even convicted criminals were able to benefit from the HIP because of minimal checks on those receiving public money. Paul Raymond Stanshall (of Stanshall and Sons Proprietary Limited) accessed taxpayer funds for 10 months despite previously serving seven years in prison from 2000 for eight violent crimes, including conspiracy to murder and false imprisonment (Berkovic 2010b). An arsonist convicted in 2002 who had previously torched a kebab shop for insurance money was director of a company that installed government-subsidised roof insulation until being deregistered in February 2010 after causing a house fire through insulation placed over the downlights in a roof (Wilson 2010).

With few checks on the rebate scheme, and the rebate only reduced from $1600 to $1200 from 2 November 2009 (Garrett 2009a),[2] the number of HIP installations exploded after July 2009 once costs for consumers were basically eliminated with no upfront payment, particularly in months when the rebate amount was reduced or the program suspended (November 2009 and February 2010). The HIP installation figures for 2009 were: March, 3321; April, 7917; May, 18 175; June, 23 642; July, 78 375; August, 108 169; September, 136 838; October, 165 104; November, 209 267; and December, 136 402. For 2010: January, 139 850; and February, 186 095 (Environment, Communications and the Arts References Committee 2010, 19).

Despite the *APH*'s recommendations, the Government implemented few measures to encourage consumers to adopt their own checks to enhance quality and value for money by paying some of the fee, fostering a climate significantly amenable to fraud and/or poor quality, along with much waste of the public purse. While DEWHA noted that only 0.65 per cent of participants complained about their experience (Thompson 2010, 24), the Australia Institute found that, among householders approached by insulation businesses in the previous 12 months, 16 per cent were told that insulation needed to be replaced regularly (misinformation that suggests attempts to defraud the Commonwealth) (Australia Institute 2010, 2–3).

It took months of negative media publicity before the Government acted, notwithstanding compelling evidence about the abuse of the HIP. During March 2009, Justin Beck, manager of installation company Patnicar, reported that new insulation companies were cutting corners, quoting for jobs using Google Earth and not specifying materials (Berkovic 2009). In June 2009, the Australian Competition and Consumer Commission (ACCC) announced that it was already investigating reports that the necessary second quote could be obtained by telephone or from a subcontractor, without a home visit, and that one insulation company had 'partnered' another company to provide the necessary quotes (Maley 2009).

---

2   Installers could, however, continue to claim up to $1600 until 30 November 2009 if four criteria were met: the quote for installation had been accepted by the householder prior to 2 November 2009; installation was completed between 2 November and 16 November 2009; the online component of the claim was lodged by the installer prior to the manual component; and online and manual components of the claim were lodged prior to 30 November 2009 (Auditor-General 2010, 121–2).

Yet, it was only from December 2009 that new mandatory risk assessment was required for each job before work started, which included filling in a form to prompt the installer to look for the listed hazards, and giving advice about how to respond to them (Garrett 2009c). New guidelines also required two independent quotes and a site inspection (with exemptions for remote areas) (DEWHA 2009b, 8, 15), while installers attempting to access grant/s were now subject to 'stringent' Australian Business Number and background checks (Vasek 2009).

Commonsense should have also prevailed regarding the possibility that new installer businesses, without adequate safety training, would provide a much greater risk to the public and help undermine long-established successful businesses. The Auditor-General acknowledged that 'learning on the job and allowing qualified and experienced individuals to supervise the work of inexperienced trainees is an acceptable practice within the general construction industry', but pointed out that 'installing insulation, which requires working in a roof space (particularly near electrical wiring), is hazardous and presented a high level of risk for inexperienced and untrained workers' (Auditor-General 2010, 107).

As the MEA noted in its submission to the senate committee, its more than 70 years' experience representing the electrical contracting industry showed clearly that unskilled labour combined with electrical cabling was a recipe for tragedy (MEA 2009, 3). Several organisations noted that foil had been used safely for 50 years, and that recent fatalities were caused by the influx of inexperienced workers (AMI 2010, 2; Renouf 2010, 78). Silverline Insulation founder Peter Venn, who employs 25 people in Queensland and had been installing foil insulation for 23 years without accident, noted that the Government had 'rushed ahead and allowed every unqualified person to come into the industry, that's what happens' (Berkovic 2010a). AFIA's Vice-President, Michel Bostrom, also argued that 'in 54 years since the first roll of foil was sold in Australia…there has not been, to my knowledge, a single case of electrocution installing foil until now' (Maiden 2010). With foil better suited to Queensland's climate than fibreglass, some 100 000 Queensland homes had been fitted with foil during the past 30 years without any electrical safety issues (Berkovic 2010d).

Others noted how installers in the past had always relied on staff learning how to work safely on the job (AMI 2010, 2); that most in the insulation industry would not have allowed installers to go out after only a two-day course (Arblaster 2010, 21); that brief formal training (six hours to two days) could not adequately replace supervised experience or surpass a stipulation that at least one person in a roof should be either a tradesperson or someone with at least six months' experience in the industry (Bostrom 2010); that training up to October 2009 was scant to non-existent for most installers, with many new entrants having little experience (MEA 2009, 3); and that exemptions from competency requirements defied logic on the basis that a 'free pass' was presented to a number of trades given their limited direct dealings with insulation (AFIA 2009, 6).

Evaluation and Lessons Learned

Following the *APH*, there is a need to evaluate a policy or program to draw lessons. While it was hoped that the HIP would insulate a further 2.7 million homes (Auditor-General 2010, 65), just 1.1 million roofs were insulated (at a cost of $1.45 billion) before the HIP was axed (Auditor-General 2010, 26). It has already been noted that about $1 billion—approximately 40 per cent of the $2.45 billion cancelled scheme—will be needed to cover the costs of the HIP (although any surplus amount will be returned to the budget), including safety and quality inspections of about 200 000 homes fitted with ceiling batts or foil. This included $424 million for the Foil Insulation Safety Program and Home Insulation Safety Program, and $56 million for various industry assistance packages (Auditor-General 2010, 26).

Substantial rectification of completed work was needed. As of March 2010, of 13 808 roof inspections conducted, about 29 per cent had identified installations 'with some level of deficiency, ranging from minor quality issues to serious safety concerns' (Auditor-General 2010, 26). By 25 July 2010, 489 homes had foil insulation removed (Auditor-General 2010, 99).

There were a significant number of complaints. While total complaints (11 874) represented less than 1 per cent of total installations, there were 2883 instances of no insulation being installed, 1348 concerns about fire or safety risks and 193 complaints of work order forms being signed but no installation done. There were also 1051 complaints about incomplete work, 1317 about questionable installer practices, 375 about property damage, 222 about overcharging, 292 about installing without consent and 150 about using non-compliant material (Auditor-General 2010, 90–1).

There was some benefit in terms of employment, although the actual number of jobs created from the HIP was 'not monitored or reported against in any disciplined way' (Auditor-General 2010, 37). While DEWHA estimates that an additional 6000–10 000 new jobs were created by the end of 2009 (Auditor-General 2010, 37), Fletcher, which produces about 40 per cent of Australia's insulation, estimated during July 2010 that 8000 jobs will be lost from the industry (Rolfe 2010). It is highly probable that a more gradual expansion of the HIP could have sustained a steady increase of employment over a longer time frame, albeit initial job creation would have been lower.

More gradual take-up of the HIP would also have helped domestic insulation batts production keep up with demand, resulting in less dependence upon imports. While it is difficult to know precisely how much material was imported as statistics do not separate glass-wool batts from total fibreglass products (DEWHA 2009b, 21), ICANZ estimated that about 40 per cent of HIP installations used products imported from China, the United States, the United Kingdom, Malaysia and Thailand (ICANZ 2010b).

The HIP disaster also led to costly business decisions. One company, projecting increased demand for fire-retardant downlight barriers, increased production from 500 units a day to 5000 a day, taking on more staff and installing more equipment. When the HIP was axed, the owner was left with $65 000 worth of unsold stock and forced to lay off staff (Lower 2010).

It is difficult to calculate energy efficiency and greenhouse benefits obtained by the HIP. It had been estimated 'that, on average, for each home that received new ceiling insulation, 1.65 tonnes of carbon dioxide equivalent (CO_2-e) will be saved each year', equating to an estimated 1.9 million tonnes of CO_2-e per annum nationally based on 1.16 million installations (0.4 per cent of Australia's annual national greenhouse gas emissions in 2007) (Auditor-General 2010, 37, 100). According to the Auditor-General, this assumption cannot be determined with any accuracy given 'problems with installation quality, the removal of insulation where safety risks were a problem, and potentially fraudulently claimed installations (Auditor-General 2010, 37, 100).

The jury is still out on the final extent of suffering and waste. Of fires, the senate committee's final report concluded that 'it is impossible to say whether the rate of defective-installation-causing-fire is higher or lower in HIP jobs than in earlier jobs' (Environment, Communications and the Arts References Committee 2010, 56). The committee cited other information that suggested it would require knowledge of the average 'incubation period' of an insulation-related fire (Combet 2010a, 2151; Environment, Communications and the Arts References Committee 2010, 56; ICANZ 2010a, 6). One source, comparing Australian Bureau of Statistics (ABS) data for 2008 with fires under the HIP to February 2010, noted that there had been 80–85 fires per year before the HIP in regard to an average 67 500 installations per year, compared with 93 fires under the HIP by February 2010 from about 1.1 million installations (Possum Comitatus 2010). Other data are less supportive. By 17 March 2010, the eighteenth insulation-related fire of that year in the Melbourne metropolitan area had occurred. There had been seven such fires from January to June 2009 and 31 from July to December 2009 (Webb 2010).

In terms of deaths, more adequate training may have prevented the four deaths (although the construction industry had an average of 35 fatalities a year in

Australia despite high OH&S standards and severe penalties for non-compliance) (CPSISC 2009, 2). When more adequate training was made compulsory for all installers from 12 February 2010, with 7300 insulation firms having to re-register under new rules (Bita 2010), little more than one-third of businesses met the training standards (Berkovic 2010e).

The four deaths resulting from the HIP have led to legal action. One Queensland company, Arrow Property Maintenance Proprietary Limited, pleaded guilty to safety breaches following the electrocution of Reuben Barnes, sixteen years old, while installing fibreglass insulation in central Queensland, on 18 November 2009. Though the Rockhampton Industrial Magistrate's Court heard that there were no 'specific or documented procedures in place for installation of insulation', the company had allowed work to proceed without the house's electricity being turned off, had not provided workers with first-aid training in the event of electric shock and had not offered proper induction training (AAP 2010).

There was also abuse of workers in regard to wages. While the Auditor-General noted just 13 complaints from staff about not being paid (Auditor-General 2010, 91), an audit by the Fair Work Ombudsman of more than 200 companies (mostly in Queensland), following complaints from unions and workers since April 2010, found that 58 businesses had underpaid their workers. Hence, 79 workers were repaid nearly $50 000 (Barry 2010).

In terms of fraud, by April 2010 there were 961 cases where more than one insulator had submitted a claim for payment for insulating the same premises, all of which were referred for further investigation (Medicare Australia 2010).

So what can be learned from the HIP experience? Certainly the Rudd Government should have taken advice from DEWHA officials who urged a much slower roll-out of the HIP over five years or more, in line with industry warnings (Auditor-General 2010, 69; Berkovic 2010d). The Government should have learned more from the Victorian Government Insulation Rebate program (13 August 2007 to 31 March 2009), which budgeted $1.2 million for 3000 rebates, provided a rebate of 30 per cent (up to $300) for non–concession card-holders and 50 per cent (up to $500 for concession card-holders). Further, in contrast with the HIP, in Victoria, all installers were required to sign a contract specifying their obligations and complete a six-hour training session conducted by a technical college; participating companies had prior experience in insulation installation; and 5–10 per cent of each installer's work was audited for safety and quality by an experienced building inspection company (Auditor-General 2010, 53).

Both the Warm Front (United Kingdom) and Warm Up (New Zealand) schemes, started in 2000 and 2009 respectively, also had extensive checks on installers prior to registration, including safety practices, reliability, quality of work, experience, price, service and financial position; outsourced delivery models that used companies with experience in the insulation or energy efficiency industries; five to 10 per cent of insulation installations audited for quality; and longer delivery timeframes and were of a smaller scale. (Auditor-General 2010, 53)

The Auditor-General's report contains a number of recommendations. First, DEWHA, supported by Medicare, could have collected information from installers as part of a better process for claims, compliance and audit to develop risk profiles of installers to 'better detect and address instances of serious non-compliance and potential fraud' (Auditor-General 2010, 35). Second—and although just 0.7 per cent of deregistrations were due to installer non-compliance with program terms and conditions (Auditor-General 2010, 35), and while any deregistration process should incorporate 'principles of natural justice'—the deregistration process was far too long (Auditor-General 2010, 132). With the first payment withheld in late August 2009 and the first installer deregistered for non-compliance on 6 October 2009, such penalties did not occur until months after the HIP began (Auditor-General 2010, 135). One installer, referred to the compliance committee on 7 October 2009, was not deregistered until 21 December 2009; another, first discussed by the compliance committee in regard to fraud on 12 November 2009, was not deregistered until 15 January 2010. Six installers were discovered to have duplicate registrations, enabling them to operate after being deregistered for non-compliance (Auditor-General 2010, 148).

Other recommendations urged a more appropriate time frame in terms of diminishing risk and ensuring best outcomes; quicker advice and options given to ministers about possible policy constraints during implementation; responsible departments having 'in-depth knowledge of the industry or business environment'; more thorough consultation with key players about relevant issues; a greater understanding of what effect a policy will have on the behaviour of industry and consumers; measures to encourage 'the right incentive structures for participants' (such as withholding a proportion of payments or requiring co-payment from those benefiting); governance arrangements that clearly define roles and responsibilities to encourage 'appropriate mobilisation of resources and addressing emerging problems in a timely and effective manner'; and appropriate levels of skilled staff and resources to support policy implementation (Auditor-General 2010, 173–6).

Conclusion

The HIP is a significant case study demonstrating what can happen when best-practice public policy recommendations are given scant attention. Had more attention been paid to known standards of public policy, the Rudd Government's HIP would have benefited. As it was, the HIP confirms the worst fears held by both the *APH* and Colebatch. The Government did not give adequate attention to serious safety and quality concerns. The *APH*, in this respect, warns that 'consulting may just be cherry-picking acceptable responses' (Althaus et al. 2007, 105), and Colebatch observes that the consultation stage is often swamped by the reality that participation can remain 'a powerful rhetorical theme in policy practice' (Colebatch 2006, 5–6). The *APH* notes the need for 'creative thinking and high level skills are needed to resolve the tensions in practice' (Althaus et al. 2007, 105); this expectation was misplaced where the HIP was concerned.

In the end, while the Rudd Government implemented the HIP in order to offset predicted lower private-sector economic activity caused by the GFC, the failure of the program was derived from its determination to implement the HIP speedily; the lack of consultation with industry players over safety, quality and rorts; and poor judgment about likely industry and consumer behaviour.

Acknowledgement

This is a revised version of 'The Home Insulation Policy Debacle: Haste Makes Waste' (*Public Policy* 6[2]: 83–100). I thank John Nethercote for his encouragement, advice and reading of numerous drafts in regard to this chapter.

Bibliography

Aluminium Foil Insulation Association (AFIA). 2009. Submission 23, Attachment, Letter to Prime Minister, 9 February 2009. Canberra: Parliament of Australia. <http://www.aph.gov.au/Senate/committee/eca_ctte/eehp/submissions.htm>

Amalgamated Metal Industries (AMI). 2010. Submission 25, 19 January 2010. Canberra: Parliament of Australia. <http://www.aph.gov.au/Senate/committee/eca_ctte/eehp/submissions.htm>

Althaus, C., P. Bridgman and G. Davis. 2007. *The Australian Policy Handbook*. Sydney: Allen & Unwin.

Arblaster, A. 2010. Australian Cellulose Insulation Manufacturers Association. Committee Hansard, 17 February 2010. Canberra: Parliament of Australia.

Australia Institute. 2010. Submission 46. Canberra: Parliament of Australia. <http://www.aph.gov.au/Senate/committee/eca_ctte/eehp/submissions. htm>

Auditor-General. 2010. *Home Insulation Program*. Audit Report no. 12 2010–11. Canberra: Australian National Audit Office.

Australian Associated Press (AAP). 2010. 'Insulation Company Pleads Guilty'. *Brisbane Times*, 14 September, <http://news.brisbanetimes.com.au/ breaking-news-national/insulation-company-pleads-guilty-20100914-159uh.html>

Australian Government. 2009. *Nation Building Economic Stimulus Plan*. Commonwealth Coordinator-General's Progress Report, 3 February 2009 – 30 June 2009. Canberra: Australian Government.

Autex. 2010. Submission 10. Canberra: Parliament of Australia. <http://www. aph.gov.au/Senate/committee/eca_ctte/eehp/submissions.htm>

Balogh, S., J. Pierce and P. Hintz. 2010. 'Double the Homes Endangered by Foil: Government Will Pay to Check Every Installation'. *The Courier-Mail*, 11 February, p. 10.

Barry, S. 2010. 'Insulation Companies Underpaid Workers'. *ABC*, 27 November, <http://au.news.yahoo.com/local/qld/a/-/local/8400947/insulation-companies-underpaid-workers/>

Beeby, R. 2010a. 'On the Fast Track to Tragedy'. *The Canberra Times*, 13 February, p. 6.

Beeby, R. 2010b. 'Garrett Insulates Himself with Personnel Amid Calls to End Scheme'. *The Canberra Times*, 18 February, p. 1.

Beeby, R. 2010c. 'Union Warned Govt on Inadequate Safety Plan'. *The Canberra Times*, 27 February, p. 6.

Berkovic, N. 2009. 'Warning on Rip-Offs by Dodgy Pink Batt Installers'. *The Australian*, 16 March, p. 2.

Berkovic, N. 2010a. 'Garrett Removes Foil from Roof Scheme'. *The Australian*, 10 February, p. 4.

Berkovic, N. 2010b. 'Criminal Escaped Rebate Radar'. *The Australian*, 18 February, p. 1.

Berkovic, N. 2010c. 'Rudd Insulated from Warnings'. *The Australian*, 19 February, p. 1.

Berkovic, N. 2010d. 'ALP Urged to Strip Foil Insulation from Homes'. *The Australian*, 3 March, p. 4.

Berkovic, N. 2010e. '7000 Batts Firms Not Checked'. *The Australian*, 13 March, p. 4.

Berkovic, N. 2010f. 'Full Cost of the Bungles Revealed'. *The Australian*, 12 May, p. 4.

Berkovic, N. with A. O'Brien. 2010. 'Garrett Admits to Insulation Warnings'. *The Australian*, 12 February, p. 1.

Bita, N. 2010. 'Lives Lost in Haste to be Seen as Green'. *The Australian*, 20 February, p. 4.

Bostrom, M. 2010. Amalgamated Metal Industries, Committee Hansard, 17 February 2010. Canberra: Parliament of Australia.

Carlisle, W. 2010. 'A Lethal Miscalculation'. *Four Corners*, ABC TV, 26 April, <http://www.abc.net.au/4corners/content/2010/s2882985.htm>

Chalmers, E. and S. Elsworth. 2010. 'Garrett Feels the Heat—Industry Insider Says Rebates Attract Dodgy Tradies'. *The Courier-Mail*, 19 February, p. 10.

Colebatch, H. K. 2002. *Policy*. Second edition. Maidenhead, UK: Open University Press.

Colebatch, H. K. 2006. 'Mapping the Work of Policy'. In *Beyond the Policy Cycle: The Policy Process in Australia*, ed. H. K. Colebatch, pp. 1–19. Sydney: Allen & Unwin.

Combet, G. 2010a. House of Representatives Hansard, 10 March 2010. Canberra: Parliament of Australia.

Combet, G. 2010b. Insulation Component of the Renewable Energy Bonus Scheme Will Not Proceed. Media release, 22 April 2010, Parliament House, Canberra.

Construction and Property Services Industry Skills Council (CPSISC). 2009. *Submission 5, Construction Industry Pocket Book—Resource for Installers of Ceiling Insulation*, 10 December 2009.

D'Arcy, D. 2010. Committee Hansard, 17 February 2010. Canberra: Parliament of Australia.

Deloitte Insight Economics. 2007. *An Economic Assessment of the Benefits of Retrofitting Some of the Remaining Stock of Uninsulated Homes in Australia, Summary of ICANZ's $500 Subsidy Proposal*, June 2007. Australia: Deloitte Insight Economics.

Department of Climate Change and Energy Efficiency (DCCEE). 2009a. *Installer Advice no. 9*, 29 September 2009. Canberra: Australian Government. <http://www.climatechange.gov.au/en/government/programs-and-rebates/hisp/installer-advice/previous-installer-advice.aspx>

Department of Climate Change and Energy Efficiency (DCCEE). 2009b. *Installer Advice no. 12*, 26 October 2009. Canberra: Australian Government. <http://www.climatechange.gov.au/en/government/programs-and-rebates/hisp/installer-advice/previous-installer-advice.aspx>

Department of Climate Change and Energy Efficiency (DCCEE). 2010. Fire Incidents Linked to the Home Insulation Program. Media release, Parliament House, Canberra. <http://www.climatechange.gov.au/en/government/programs-and-rebates/hisp/fraud-and-compliance/incidents.aspx>

Department of Environment, Water, Heritage and the Arts (DEWHA). 2009a. *Energy Efficient Homes Package—Competency Requirements for Registration on the Installer Provider Register*. September 2009. Canberra: Commonwealth of Australia.

Department of Environment, Water, Heritage and the Arts (DEWHA). 2009b. Submission 19, 23 December 2009. Canberra: Parliament of Australia. <http://www.aph.gov.au/Senate/committee/eca_ctte/eehp/submissions.htm>

Environment, Communications and the Arts References Committee. 2010. *Energy Efficient Homes Package (Ceiling Insulation) Report*, July. Environment, Communications and the Arts References Committee. Canberra: Parliament of Australia.

Farr, M. 2010. 'Garrett Didn't Act on Warning'. *Daily Telegraph*, 30 April, p. 26.

Garrett, P. 2009a. Insulation Changes: Safety, Consumer Protections and Value for Money. Media release, 1 November 2009, Parliament House, Canberra.

Garrett, P. 2009b. Insulation Safety Standards to Get a Further Boost. Media release, 30 November 2009, Parliament House, Canberra.

Garrett, P. 2009c. Update on Insulation Training Requirements. Media release, 17 December 2009, Parliament House, Canberra.

Garrett, P. 2010a. Foil Insulation Suspended from Home Insulation Program. Media release, 9 February 2010, Parliament House, Canberra.

Garrett, P. 2010b. Significant Changes to Commonwealth Environmental Programs. Media release, 19 February 2010, Parliament House, Canberra.

Hawke, A. 2010. Review of the Administration of the Home Insulation Program, 6 April 2010. Canberra: Department of the Prime Minister and Cabinet.

Home Insulation Program (HIP). 2009. *HIP Program Guidelines. Version 5*, 1 December 2009. Canberra: Australian Government.

Hudson, P. 2010a. 'Deadly Alarm Raised Often'. *Herald-Sun*, 12 February, p. 6.

Hudson, P. 2010b. 'New Garrett Shame: Insulation Boss Reveals: I Told Minister of Poison Batts Threat'. *Herald-Sun*, 13 February, p. 3.

Insulation Council of Australia and New Zealand (ICANZ). 2010a. Submission 18. Canberra: Parliament of Australia. <http://www.aph.gov.au/Senate/committee/eca_ctte/eehp/submissions.htm>

Insulation Council of Australia and New Zealand (ICANZ). 2010b. Answers to Questions On Notice no. 8 from Senate Hearing 17 February 2010 (received 16 March 2010): Minutes of an Industry Consultation Meeting, 18 February 2009. Canberra: Parliament of Australia. <http://www.aph.gov.au/senate/committee/eca_ctte/eehp/submissions.htm>

Karvelas, P. and M. Franklin. 2010. 'Gillard, Abbott Face Brisbane Grilling'. The Australian, 18 August, <http://www.theaustralian.com.au/national-affairs/gillard-abbott-face-brisbane-grilling/story-fn59niix-1225907009879>

Lower, G. 2010. 'Insulation Confusion a Barrier to Safety'. *The Australian*, 13 July, p. 4.

Madison, J., A. Hamilton and J. Jay. 1987 [1788]. *The Federalist Papers*. Isaac Kramnick (ed.). Harmondsworth, UK: Penguin.

Maiden, S. 2010. 'Garrett Misses Roof Meeting to go Bush'. *The Australian*, 15 February, p. 1.

Maley, P. 2009. 'Insulation Subsidy Scheme Rorted'. *The Australian*, 20 June, p. 6.

Master Electricians Australia (MEA). 2009. Submission 20, Attachment, Media release, 18 May 2009. Canberra: Parliament of Australia. <http://www.aph.gov.au/Senate/committee/eca_ctte/eehp/submissions.htm>

Medicare Australia. 2010. Answer to Question 9 On Notice from Hearing 26 February 2010, Received 9 April 2010. Canberra: Parliament of Australia. <http://www.aph.gov.au/Senate/committee/eca_ctte/eehp/submissions. htm>

Minter Ellison. 2009. *Risk Register and Management Plan*, 9 April 2009. Australia: Minter Ellison.

Mrdak, M. 2010. Committee Hansard, 26 February 2010. Canberra: Parliament of Australia.

National Electrical and Communications Association (NECA). 2009. Submission 39. Canberra: Parliament of Australia. <http://www.aph.gov.au/Senate/ committee/eca_ctte/eehp/submissions.htm>

New Zealand Ministry of Economic Development (NZMED). 2007. *Installing Under Floor Thermal Insulation—Electric Shock Hazard*, 21 June 2007. Wellington: Ministry of Economic Development.

Polyester Insulation Manufacturers Association of Australia (PIMAA). 2009. Submission 11, 18 December 2009. Canberra: Parliament of Australia. <http:// www.aph.gov.au/Senate/committee/eca_ctte/eehp/submissions.htm>

Possum Comitatus. 2010. 'Did the Insulation Program Actually Reduce Fire Risk?'. *Crikey*, 24 February, <http://blogs.crikey.com.au/pollytics/2010/02/24/did-the-insulation-program-actually-reduce-fire-risk/comment-page-1/>

Prasser, S. 2006. 'Aligning Good Policy with Good Politics'. In *Beyond the Policy Cycle: The Policy Process in Australia*, ed. H. K. Colebatch, pp. 266–92. Sydney: Allen & Unwin.

Probyn, A. and A. Tillett. 2010. 'Garrett Got Insulation Warning'. *West Australian*, 11 February, p. 5.

Rehn, A. 2010. 'Batt Man Returns but Only to His Cave'. *Daily Telegraph*, 17 February, p. 4.

Reilly, T. 2010. 'Roof Inspections Just the Latest Delay in Green Home Program'. *Sydney Morning Herald*, 12 February, p. 10.

Renouf, T. 2010. Committee Hansard, 17 February 2010. Canberra: Parliament of Australia.

Rolfe, J. 2010. 'One Big Broke Batt Mountain of Tears'. *Daily Telegraph*, 20 July, p. 9.

Rudd, K. 2009a. Prime Minister: Energy Efficient Homes—Ceiling Insulation in 2.7 Million Homes. Media release, 3 February 2009, Parliament House, Canberra.

Rudd, K. 2009b. $42 Billion Nation Building and Jobs Plan. Media release, 3 February 2009, Parliament House, Canberra.

Senate Economics References Committee (SERC). 2009. *Government's Economic Stimulus Initiatives*, 9 October 2009. Canberra: Commonwealth of Australia.

Sky green. 2009. Submission 12. Canberra: Parliament of Australia. <http://www.aph.gov.au/Senate/committee/eca_ctte/eehp/submissions.htm>

The Canberra Times. 2010a. 'Repair Job: $50m Heat on Garrett'. [Editorial], 11 February, p. 5.

The Canberra Times. 2010b. 'Inquiry into House Fires after Insulation Doubts'. [Editorial], 12 February, p. 4.

The Canberra Times. 2010c. 'Battflip: Pressure Builds but Garrett Stands Firm amid Opposition Calls to Stand Down'. [Editorial], 20 February, p. 10.

Thompson, M. 2010. Committee Hansard, 22 February 2010. Canberra: Parliament of Australia.

Tiffen, R. 2010. 'A Mess? A Shambles? A Disaster?'. *Inside Story*, 26 March, <http://inside.org.au/a-mess-a-shambles-a-disaster/>

Tillett, A., A. Probyn and R. Taylor. 2010. 'Besieged Garrett Deflects Blame'. *West Australian*, 12 February.

Vasek, L. 2009. 'Deregistered Insulation Firms to Escape Scrutiny on Name-and-Shame List'. *The Australian*, 1 December, p. 4.

Webb, C. 2010. 'Time Bomb Warning Over Botched Insulation'. *The Age*, 17 March, p. 3.

Wilson, L. 2010. 'Arsonist Worked Despite Fire'. *The Australian*, 20 February, p. 4.

Zuzul, T. 2010. Committee Hansard, 17 February 2010.Canberra: Parliament of Australia.

9. Assessing Ministerial Responsibility in Australia

Richard Mulgan

I

Ministerial responsibility remains a key constitutional convention in Australia, as in all Westminster-derived systems. But its role continues to be contentious and disputed. Is it effective as an instrument of public accountability? Is it an outmoded principle that promises accountability but, in practice, allows both ministers and their officials to evade public scrutiny? Answers to these questions are elusive, in part because the actual requirements of the conventions of ministerial responsibility are a matter of dispute. Without agreement on what ministerial responsibility requires of ministers, one cannot expect to reach any straightforward conclusions about whether ministerial responsibility is doing its job. Moreover, ministerial responsibility is only one element in a complex system of government accountability and needs to be assessed within this larger context. Other accountability mechanisms have been subject to considerable evolution over the past 50 years, affecting the role played by ministerial responsibility. Concepts of 'traditional' ministerial responsibility drawn from an earlier era may no longer be applicable and may lead to distorted judgments about its present-day performance.

This chapter therefore begins by discussing the main issues surrounding the definition of ministerial responsibility, including a number of well-entrenched misunderstandings of the concept—for example, the supposed dependence on a distinction between 'policy' and 'administration' and its supposed requirement that ministers resign for mistakes made solely by their departmental officials. I then illustrate the effectiveness of present-day ministerial responsibility through analysis of a recent major public policy, the ill-fated Home Insulation Program (HIP) discussed by Chris Lewis in the previous chapter. Conventions of ministerial responsibility will be seen to have played a major role in securing public accountability of this program—though in the process they have distorted some of the attributions of personal responsibility and blame.

II

According to standard constitutional doctrine, as represented in textbooks of constitutional law and political science (for example, Ratnapala 2007, 40; Summers 2006, 76–7), ministerial responsibility is a defining element in the conventions of responsible government. It includes collective ministerial responsibility, which obliges ministers to give public support to cabinet colleagues, especially the prime minister. It also covers individual ministerial responsibility, the subject of this chapter, which requires ministers to take responsibility for their portfolios, answering to parliament for the conduct of their departments and resigning in the case of failure or impropriety. In practice, this means that ministers are obliged to inform parliament and the public about any action taken by themselves or their officials and to impose remedies when failures have come to light. Resignation becomes an issue when the minister can be said to be personally responsible, particularly for matters of individual impropriety, illegality, negligence or incompetence. Whether ministers do resign depends on a range of factors, including the seriousness of the alleged failure, the extent of the minister's personal responsibility and a political calculation (ultimately by the prime minister) about the consequences for the government's standing of either accepting or rejecting the resignation (Mulgan 2002; Page 1990; Thompson and Tillotsen 1999; Weller 1999).

Both elements of this account—answering for departments and resignation in the case of failure—have been the subject of debate and criticism. Ministers' obligation to be responsible or accountable for the actions of their departments was traditionally taken to imply that public servants should remain anonymous, leaving the minister to be the sole public spokesperson for the department. The result was to shield public servants from direct scrutiny of their actions and prevent them from giving information about the inner workings of government departments. While ministers might be the right people to articulate and defend the general directions of departmental policy, public servants were often directly responsible for giving policy advice to ministers and for making routine administrative decisions for which they could not be held publicly accountable. Criticism of the monopolistic nature of ministerial responsibility as a mechanism of executive accountability led to the introduction of a number of supplementary mechanisms, including the ombudsman, freedom-of-information legislation, an expanded scrutinising role for parliamentary committees, the extension of government audit from financial compliance to the efficient and effective performance of government agencies, and increased judicial review of administrative actions. All such mechanisms had the effect of making public servants more directly accountable to the public.

These accountability innovations were adopted throughout the 'Westminster' world, though the United Kingdom was a slower and more reluctant reformer because of more deeply entrenched commitment to traditional notions of ministerial responsibility and more pervasive fears that the rights of ministers might be diminished (Woodhouse 1994). Such objections, however, were overstated. The new mechanisms sought to preserve the sole responsibility of ministers for government 'policy' and to confine their own scope to matters of 'administration' where ministers and government policy were not directly involved. The distinction between 'policy' and 'administration' was never clear-cut and has always been interpreted according to the political dynamics of the particular context. But it has proved useful in discouraging the new accountability mechanisms from venturing too far into politically controversial areas.

The distinction between policy and administration, it should be noted, was not essential to the traditional conventions of ministerial responsibility. An influential recent analysis (Hughes 2003, 32–3, 244–6) implausibly links the Westminster model and ministerial responsibility to a model of traditional bureaucracy grounded in Weberian theories of bureaucracy and Woodrow Wilson's distinction between the realms of politics and administration. On this view, the Westminster model supposedly made ministers responsible for policy and bureaucrats responsible for administration—an unworkably rigid separation of functions that is then claimed to invalidate the conventions of ministerial responsibility because they rest on a fallacious assumption.

No such sharp division of roles, however, is required under traditional Westminster concepts where ministers were publicly accountable for all aspects of their departments, both general policy directions and more routine matters of administration. The distinction has only come to the fore with the new, supplementary accountability mechanisms, which seek to expose departmental officials to direct scrutiny while still protecting ministers' rights to control their departments. Officials are exempted from commenting on 'policy' and required to answer questions on 'administration' only. The distinction is often contested, particularly in parliamentary committees. Opposition politicians, anxious to embarrass the government politically, seek to extract damaging information about ministers from their officials. Public servants, on the other hand, being professionally loyal to the government of the day, use the concept of 'policy' as an excuse not to comment on politically contentious issues.

Even now, however, while public servants are excused from commenting on 'policy', the right of ministers to answer questions on matters of 'administration' remains intact. The new mechanisms supplement, rather than necessarily restrict, the accountability of ministers. Admittedly, under certain managerial practices associated with the new public management, such as the use of executive agencies and outsourcing, the responsibility and accountability of ministers have sometimes been restricted to setting policy, leaving the implementation (administration) to other, separately accountable officials or organisations. But the imposition of such a sharp differentiation of roles has been a deliberate attempt to *restrict* the traditional scope of ministerial responsibility (Mulgan 2003, Ch. 5). Indeed, public expectations of ministerial responsibility—that ministers should answer for all actions of their departments and not pass the buck to subordinates—have regularly undermined the managerialists' aim to keep politicians out of policy implementation (Polidano 1999; Woodhouse 1994, Ch. 12).

Any current assessment of ministerial responsibility therefore needs to recognise that it retains the ministers' right to answer for departments but no longer offers public servants the levels of anonymity and protection from scrutiny that it did in the past. It does not purport to be the sole channel of executive accountability and should not be criticised on these grounds. Instead, it needs to be seen simply as one element within an extensive range of accountability mechanisms to which executive government is now subject. Its effectiveness is therefore to be judged within this wider context in terms of its contribution to a general structure of accountability.

Controversy also attaches to the requirement that ministers should accept responsibility and resign in the case of failure. Individual ministerial responsibility has often been interpreted as if ministers are expected to exercise a form of 'vicarious' responsibility for their departments in the sense that they supposedly take on personal responsibility for all the actions of their departmental officials as if they were their own. On this view ministers must not only inform the public and see that administrative errors are rectified (*informatory*, *explanatory* and *amendatory* responsibility in Woodhouse's [1994] useful terminology) but they must also take the blame for and resign over all major failures committed by their officials (*sacrificial* responsibility). The notion that ministers should resign over the failures of their subordinates is widely held among members of the public and the commentariat, and provides ready ammunition for a claim that ministerial responsibility is ineffective. Because ministers never (or no longer) resign when they are not personally at fault, ministerial responsibility is said to be dead.

Vicarious responsibility, however, is a red herring, involving a misinterpretation of some key UK precedents (Dowding and Kang 1998; Marshall 1989; Woodhouse 1994, Ch. 2). All cases where ministers have been called on to resign over departmental failure involve a claim that the ministers in question personally share at least some of the responsibility for the failure, whether through their own negligence or incompetence or through their responsibility for the general policy and budgetary settings within which the failure occurred. Resignation without any personal blame at all is not, and never has been, a binding obligation on ministers. Repeated complaints that ministers 'no longer' exercise ministerial responsibility because they do not resign for faults wholly committed by their subordinates are ill informed.

Leaving vicarious responsibility to one side, ministers still frequently face calls for resignation for departmental failure when they can be said to share at least some of the blame. Actual resignation on these grounds is rare (Woodhouse 1994, 33–9). Indeed, in the Australian Commonwealth, no clear cases have occurred (Dowding, Lewis and Packer this volume; Page 1990; Thompson and Tillotsen 1999). Thus claims, such as those made by former prime ministers Gough Whitlam and Malcolm Fraser (quoted in Chapter 6 of this volume) that 'ministers *no longer* resign' for 'the failings of their policies or administration' (emphasis added), are without foundation. Ministers in Australia have never resigned for such failings.

The complete lack of observance of this principle, however, does not necessarily invalidate it: ministers *ought* to resign for presiding over departmental failure to which they have contributed personally. If the principle were invalid, ministers themselves, when called on to resign for such reasons, would surely argue that they had no such obligation and that their opponents were relying on an outmoded myth. In fact, they do not. Instead, they tend to resort to the red herring of vicarious responsibility and claim that ministers are not required to resign over matters that are entirely the fault of public servants. Thus, John Howard, as Prime Minister, facing a large number of calls for his ministers to resign (see Chapter 6), stated that 'it's never been the ministerial principle that you resign if something goes wrong in your department' (*The Australian*, 14 February 2001, quoted Mulgan 2002). But his wording was typically canny and designed to mislead, implying situations where ministers are not personally involved ('something goes wrong in your department').

As already noted, resignation never arises in such contexts. But this does not mean it could not do so if something went wrong in the department *to which the minister had contributed in some way*. In such cases, ministers do not deny the principle. Instead, they attempt to exonerate themselves by justifying their actions and rebutting charges of failure, toughing it out rather than accepting fault. Thus all sides appear to accept that ministers can be blamed for their part in departmental failures and would be obliged to resign if the failures were sufficiently serious and their role in them incontrovertible.

The responsibility of ministers for their departments is essentially similar to the corporate responsibility of chief executives in other sectors—for instance, heads of commercial companies, school principals, bishops or chairmen of cricket associations. All such people are expected to exercise general oversight of all aspects of their organisations, to answer to the public for their organisation's performance and to accept personal responsibility for matters directly within their control. When their organisations fail, they can expect to face calls for their resignation. As with ministers, however, such calls are seldom accepted. Most chief executives either seek to rebut the charges of failure or, while accepting that their organisation may have performed badly, argue that they should remain in office to repair the damage. Because responsibility for most collective failures lies with various individual members as well as with corporate culture and processes, pinning blame on a single person is notoriously difficult (the problem of 'many hands': Bovens 1998). Corporate leaders, though personally tarnished by failure, can usually escape any obligation to shoulder sole or major blame (Mulgan 2002).

That ministers similarly do not respond positively to calls for their resignation in cases of collective failure is therefore hardly surprising. More anomalous, perhaps, is that the obligation to resign figures so prominently in standard definitions of ministerial responsibility. In the case of a company executive or a bishop, we do not usually say that their role is twofold: first, to manage their company or diocese well and, second, to resign in the case of personal fault or collective failure. An obligation to resign may be implicit in a general obligation to manage competently and honestly, but it is not singled out for special mention in the job description.

Indeed, the obligations of ministers can be similarly stated without explicitly mentioning resignation, as in the Government's own statement of *Standards of Ministerial Ethics* (Department of the Prime Minister and Cabinet 2010), which summarises the responsibility and accountability of ministers without reference to any obligation to resign. Nonetheless, the emphasis on resignation, including resignation for departmental failure, in standard accounts of ministerial responsibility, while arguably anomalous, cannot be ignored. It continues to be kept alive in public discourse and political culture, not only by opportunistic opposition politicians but also by members of the general public. It must therefore be considered a central element in the conventions, even if it is never acted on.

III

The Home Insulation Program (originally the Home*owner* Insulation Program; HIP) was announced in February 2009 as part of the Federal Government's package of economic measures designed to counter the effects of the global financial crisis of 2008 (for a detailed account of the program, see Auditor-General 2010). Like other policies in the package, the HIP was intended to generate short-term employment and stimulate consumption while leaving behind a long-term benefit—in this case, improved insulation and energy efficiency in domestic housing. The program provided financial incentives for the installation of home insulation, through payments of up to $1600 for homeowners or $1000 for landlords or tenants.

The initial phase of the program ran from February to June 2009 and required homeowners to seek reimbursement for work completed (more than 73 000 rebates were paid out in the five-month period—an average of about 15 000 per month). During the second phase, beginning on 1 July 2009, payment procedures were streamlined, allowing installers to claim directly through the Medicare network. In the nine months till the program was suspended at the end of March 2010, a further 1.16 million payments were made (an average of nearly 180 000 per month, or about 12 times the rate of payments in the first phase). During the same period the number of insulation installation businesses increased from about 200 before the program to more than 10 800 at its peak (Auditor-General 2010, 99, note 106).

Primary responsibility for administering the program lay with the Department of the Environment, Water, Heritage and the Arts (DEWHA), under its minister, Peter Garrett. To manage the program, the department established a Project Control Group, including representatives from other departments, such as Medicare, which handled the registration of installers and payment of rebates. It also called on a range of consultants, including Minter Ellison for risk assessment, KPMG for the business model design, Protiviti and PriceWaterhouseCoopers for compliance and audit, and Ernst and Young for a fraud control plan. The Project Control Group reported to the Office of the Coordinator-General, in the Department of the Prime Minister and Cabinet, which oversaw all the stimulus initiatives, with a particular view to making sure that spending targets were being met. While State governments were not directly involved in the administration of the program, State fair trading organisations and consumer affairs departments were relied on for dealing with individual complaints from the public.

Initial complaints about the program came from relevant stakeholders, including established members of the insulation trade and electrical contractors concerned about the threats to standards and safety raised by an influx of inexperienced installers. During the second phase, from mid-2009, problems also arose over shortages of ceiling batts; certain major suppliers were accused of monopolising stock and crowding out smaller competitors. Unscrupulous operators were reported to be claiming for work that was inadequately carried out. In mid-October 2009, the death of an installer, followed by two more deaths in November, raised major safety concerns. In response, the department introduced a number changes to the scheme, including targeted safety inspections of foil installations in Queensland, the mandatory use of downlight covers and the banning of metal staples. In December, further training materials from installers were released and installers were required to provide evidence of minimum training (Auditor-General 2010, Appendix 2).

In early February 2010, a fourth fatality followed by increasingly strident public criticism of the scheme prompted further changes, including the suspension of foil insulation (on 9 February) and electrical inspections of all installed foil insulations (on 10 February). Finally, on 19 February the entire program was scrapped. Shortly thereafter, responsibility for winding up the program and dealing with the outstanding issues of inspection and compensation was transferred to another department, the Department of Climate Change and Energy Efficiency (DCCEE), under the direction of the Minister for Climate Change, Greg Combet.

Public accountability for the program developed through a number of processes. To begin with, most discussion took place through the normal channels of consultations with stakeholders. Departmental officials held regular meetings with relevant industry representatives and received feedback from interested parties and disgruntled consumers; however, after the reporting of deaths associated with the program in October and November 2009, the program began to attract public criticism in Parliament. In mid-November, a number of backbench Opposition MPs used their allotted time in adjournment debates to raise issues from their constituencies about the faulty implementation of the scheme—for instance, rorting and intimidation by installers and stockpiling of batts by major suppliers (Coulton 2009; Marino 2009; Schultz 2009).

The first major parliamentary attack on the program came the week after the third death on 25 November (*House of Representatives* Hansard 12873). Greg Hunt, the shadow minister for climate change, environment and water, raised the Government's whole environmental and water programs as 'a matter of public importance' (*House of Representatives* Hansard 12873), devoting most of his speech to the insulation program. He criticised the minister, Garrett, for being responsible for a flawed program that was open to fraud and substandard work as well as to major safety risks. Hunt relied heavily on information from the electrical contractors' professional association, the National Electrical and Communications Association (NECA), which said that it had written to the minister as early as March 2009, pointing out the dangers of fire and electrocution from careless installation of insulation. Hunt also called for an immediate inquiry by the Auditor-General.

In response (*House of Representatives* Hansard 12877), the minister pointed to the overall success of the program, in terms of houses insulated and people employed, and to the constant adjustments being made to reduce opportunities for fraud and to increase safety. He expressed regret over the deaths and other instances of failure but asserted that the Government had given priority to safety concerns, pointing out that safety inspection was a matter for State authorities. There was no need for an immediate audit report, the Auditor-General having agreed to audit the program later 'in the ordinary course of business'.

The tempo of criticism quickened when Parliament resumed after the Christmas break. The Leader of the Opposition, Malcolm Turnbull, who was reported to have been in favour of such a scheme when Minister for the Environment in the previous Howard Government, had been replaced with the more aggressive Tony Abbott. Moreover, a fourth program-related fatality, in early February, reignited safety concerns and deepened the impression of a minister and government with blood on their hands. The Opposition went after Garrett, with all available parliamentary weapons. In Question Time in the House of Representatives, for three consecutive sitting days (February 11, 22 and 23), every Opposition question concerned the minister's conduct of the insulation program. Most were directed to the minister himself; a few were aimed at the Prime Minister, querying his continued support for Garrett.

On the next two days (24 and 25 February), when the Prime Minister had begun to take charge of the issue and Garrett was being sidelined, the focus of questioning moved more to the Prime Minister and away from the minister. But the insulation program itself remained the subject of all Opposition questioning. The Opposition also pursued its attack through motions of censure (11, 22 and 24 February). Media interest was intense, as journalists reflected public anger at the program's failings, especially the four fatalities, and as the press gallery, in particular, scented the possibility that a minister might be fatally damaged. By the time Parliament met again on 9 March, Garrett no longer had any formal responsibility for the program, which had been moved to a different department under another minister. The Opposition's focus at Question Time then moved on to other topics.

While the House of Representatives, which included the minister, the Prime Minister and the Leader of the Opposition, was naturally the key forum of Opposition attack, questions were also raised in the Senate, directed particularly at Senator Mark Arbib. Arbib was not only Senate spokesman for the Environment Minister but was also indirectly involved in the insulation program as minister in charge of the Office of Coordinator-General in the Department of the Prime Minister and Cabinet, which was overseeing progress of all the various programs making up the economic stimulus package. The Opposition was also able to use the Senate Committee on Environment, Communications and the Arts to question senior department officials, particularly about the minister's personal role in overseeing the program.

In their questioning of the minister, the Opposition concentrated on issues where his own personal fault and responsibility might be more readily established. For instance, they quizzed him repeatedly on warnings about safety he had received from NECA and others, and on why he had apparently taken so long to act on them. They also hammered the question of when he had first received a risk assessment prepared for the department by the consulting firm Minter Ellison. They evidently hoped to catch him in a contradiction that would constitute the offence of misleading Parliament. To all such questions the minister replied that the Government had always given priority to safety issues, that his department had regularly and conscientiously reacted to a variety of warnings and risk assessments, and that he himself had acted responsibly on the advice of his department.

The Leader of the Opposition also explicitly referred to familiar debating points about Westminster conventions of ministerial responsibility. Ministers were responsible for the administration of their departments and should not hide behind their officials (for example, 11 February 2010, *House of Representatives* Hansard 1211; 22 February 2010, *House of Representatives* Hansard 1324). The minister's claim to have responsibly followed advice was inadequate, especially when he had been repeatedly warned about safety issues. In addition, obfuscation over the Minter Ellison report amounted to misleading Parliament. Either he should resign or the Prime Minister should sack him.

Senior government ministers came to Garrett's defence by arguing that he could not be responsible for all the details of the program's implementation. According to Julia Gillard, the Deputy Prime Minister, Garrett could not be expected to be up in every roof inspecting each installation (quoted in *The Australian*, 18 February 2010). Lindsay Tanner, the Minister of Finance, was reported to have said that government could not be expected 'to dot the i's or cross the t's' (11 February 2010, *House of Representatives* Hansard 1207). For debating purposes, they thus introduced the red herring of vicarious responsibility, inferring that Garrett was supposedly being held responsible for all actions of officials even when he could have had no personal responsibility for them. Such a charge could then be dismissed as unreasonable.

The Opposition's argument, however, did not rely on questionable notions of vicarious responsibility. They argued on the much stronger ground that the minister was personally negligent and blameworthy for not doing more to ensure tighter safety standards after he had personally received a series of warnings about safety issues. As the extent and seriousness of the program's failures gradually emerged in the media blitz generated by the Opposition's attack, the minister's defence—that he had done all that could be reasonably expected of a responsible minister—rang increasingly hollow. No evidence was found of his actually having misled Parliament over the receipt of documents, but his apparently passive reliance on official advice suggested a lack of responsible leadership. The Prime Minister refused to countenance the minister's formal resignation, presumably because it would have handed an obvious victory to the Opposition. But he was forced to accept the substance of the Opposition's case as a means of defusing the continuing negative publicity. Not only was the program suspended, but also the minister was stripped of formal responsibility for clearing up the mess over which he had presided. He remained in cabinet but with his political reputation seriously, perhaps permanently, damaged.

In the case of the ill-fated HIP, the conventions of ministerial responsibility clearly proved a powerful instrument of public accountability. They channelled the Opposition's desire to damage the Government into a concerted, sharply focused attack on a weak minister defending a badly botched program. The repeated calls for the minister's resignation, sanctioned by well-entrenched Westminster conventions, forced the minister into a desperate and ultimately unconvincing justification of his own personal role. The minister may not have formally resigned but the argument that he *ought* to resign carried great public resonance, particularly in the light of the fatalities. The gripping political drama played out daily in Question Time generated widespread public interest and helped to publicise the program's many problems. In a matter of weeks, the program was seriously curtailed then scrapped altogether, with the Government committed to generous recompense for those who had lost financially or whose homes were at risk of fire or causing electrocution.

Ministerial responsibility provided the spearhead of public accountability of the Home Insulation Program. But the political pressure that it built up also set in train other accountability mechanisms that were able to move at a more deliberate pace. The Senate Standing Committee on Environment, Communications and the Arts had already, in late 2009, begun an inquiry into the Energy Efficient Homes Package. The inquiry received added impetus after the political crisis in February 2010. The committee held a number of public meetings in February and March and eventually reported in July 2010; however, reflecting the partisan passions aroused by the program, the committee divided along party lines, with the Opposition Coalition senators returning a majority report, government senators submitting a minority report and the Greens entering dissenting comments.

In addition, the Department of the Prime Minister and Cabinet commissioned a review of administrative aspects of the program from Dr Allan Hawke, an experienced former secretary of a number of Commonwealth departments. Dr Hawke reported in April (Hawke 2010). While not seeking to exonerate the departmental officials running the program, he did point to a number of extenuating factors beyond their control. He also sought to estimate the benefits, as well as the costs, of the program.

Finally, one of the first actions of the new minister, Greg Combet, was to request the Auditor-General to conduct an audit of the program (a request already made several times by the Opposition spokesman, Greg Hunt). The Auditor reported in October (Auditor-General 2010), providing a comprehensive and balanced assessment of the program, particularly the part played by Commonwealth public servants. Further accountability measures, through State judicial systems, were also undertaken in relation to individual installers.

Later reports naturally added a wealth of further information, additional to the relatively few facts available at the time the minister was being questioned in Parliament. For instance, it is now clear that the documents from the NECA and Minter Ellison, of which the Opposition made great play, were only a fraction of the relevant advice and feedback received and processed by members of the department as they administered the program and reported regularly to the minister.

The most telling general conclusion to emerge from the later reviews is that the prime cause of the program's failure was the urgency imposed on the department (DEWHA) by the need to roll out the program as quickly as possible. Moreover, this imperative was imposed from the outside, through the Department of the Prime Minister and Cabinet (PM&C) in its pursuit of the Government's overall strategy of economic stimulus spending. DEWHA, which lacked experience in direct program delivery, was not given the resources, staff or time to implement the program effectively. Within the Commonwealth Public Service, therefore, administrative responsibility for the failure lies more with PM&C, which helped drive the spending agenda and whose secretary, as head of the Public Service, was known to be very critical of bureaucratic caution and risk aversion in line departments. Political responsibility, in turn, rests with the Prime Minister and his economic ministers, rather than with the Minister for the Environment whose concerns were overruled by senior colleagues.

That excessive speed was a major driver of failure was clear to the Opposition and occasionally mentioned by them in their attacks on the minister. But so long as their focus was firmly fixed on claiming the minister's scalp, the speed factor could not become part of the central thrust of their campaign because it was not something for which the minister could be held personally responsible. Indeed, the more that is revealed about the inner political and bureaucratic dynamics surrounding the program, the less blameworthy Garrett appears. Not only was he doing the bidding of the Prime Minister and his cabinet colleagues in pressing on without delay, but he was also not very well served by his departmental officials who, in the view of the Auditor-General, could have done more to keep him fully informed about the problems facing the program (Auditor-General 2010, 34–5). Garrett could perhaps be accused of excessive loyalty to his party or of moral timidity in not speaking out more forcefully about the program's obvious faults once they emerged. But he was hardly the leading instigator or primary cause of these faults as depicted by the Opposition in their desire to force his resignation.

It was only after responsibility for the program was removed from Garrett that the Opposition began to turn their attention to the Prime Minister himself, who carried primary responsibility for the overall stimulus spending and for the overriding economic imperative to spend funds quickly. By drawing the full initial force of the Opposition's broadside and not passing the buck, Garrett had helped to protect his leader and senior colleagues from their due share of blame for the program while the media frenzy was at its height. Indeed, according to journalist Barrie Cassidy, there were some members of the government caucus who felt that the Prime Minister had unfairly let Garrett take responsibility for the program's failure (ABC 2010). Party gratitude was presumably one factor in Rudd's willingness to keep Garrett in cabinet even though his responsibilities were significantly reduced.

Concentration on the directly accountable minister not only helped to shield other ministers who carried more of the personal responsibility, but it also deflected immediate attention from other organisations and individuals who shared some of the blame—for instance, the departmental officials directly responsible for the day-to-day administration of the program. Even when Opposition MPs had access to senior members of DEWHA in the senate committee, their focus remained fixed on the role of the minister and his office and on trying to find evidence of their negligence. It was only the subsequent Hawke and Auditor-General's reports that clearly documented the department's actions and pointed to serious deficiencies that were the responsibility of the secretary and senior officials rather than the minister. Ministerial responsibility on its own would have left such matters unexamined.

Beyond the Commonwealth Public Service, other contributors escaped even belated scrutiny. For example, the bevy of consulting firms used by DEWHA (including the infamous Minter Ellison) was beyond the terms of reference of both Hawke and the Auditor-General. So too were the relevant State government agencies responsible for occupational health and safety. The ripples of accountability prompted by the Opposition's attack on the minister petered out before a complete account could be made of all the contributing factors.

IV

What general conclusions about the effectiveness of ministerial responsibility as an accountability mechanism can be drawn from this case? To begin with, the exceptional nature of the Garrett affair must be conceded. It involved an unusual intensity of hostile questioning and adverse publicity clearly derived from the scandalous failures of the program, particularly the four fatalities, for which the minister and the Government could be blamed. Nonetheless, it illustrates continuing aspects of ministerial responsibility that may be dormant for much of the time but the prospect of which animates much government and opposition behaviour.

First, oppositions rely heavily on the conventions of ministerial responsibility as a key set of weapons in trying to hold the government accountable and thus improve their own electoral prospects. In this they are followed by the press gallery and the national media, which concentrate on Question Time in their reporting of politics and which find displays of weakness or incompetence by individual ministers particularly newsworthy. The accountability effects of this parliamentary contest are profound. Ministers must answer not only in parliament but also directly to the media. Though they can and do frequently prevaricate and try to avoid answering the questions asked, they must face the public consequences of such evasion.

Second, the thrust of opposition questioning, determined by the electoral incentive of embarrassing their political opponents, is towards the personal responsibility of individual ministers. Questions may seek information about the performance of government departments but typically as a means of securing evidence to undermine the credibility of ministers. Third, the principle that ministers *ought* to resign (or be dismissed) for incompetence in running their departments is widely acknowledged and provides an underlying assumption for opposition attacks on vulnerable ministers (and for ministerial defences of their actions). Though ministers may not actually resign on these grounds, their failure to do so on matters of serious policy failure tarnishes their reputation and inflicts political damage not only on themselves but also on their government as a whole.

At the same time, the concentrated focus on individual ministers can weaken public accountability if it shifts the spotlight of public attention too far away from others who share responsibility for a particular policy or program. By leaving the individual portfolio minister to bear the brunt of public attack, other ministers—especially the prime minister, who carries ultimate responsibility for the government as a whole and therefore for all major policies—can escape immediate scrutiny. Ultimately, no doubt, the voters have the chance to hold the prime minister and the government to account through the ballot box, but such an assessment lacks the sharp focus of direct parliamentary questioning.

In addition, the role of public servants who play a major part in developing and implementing policy tends to be overlooked in the opposition's (and the media's) preoccupation with the fate and reputation of ministers. Such political considerations heavily influence the agenda not only of parliamentary questions but also of parliamentary committees. These committees, in theory, are intended to provide opportunities for directly examining the conduct of public servants and their administration of government agencies. In practice, politically partisan factors predominate (Mulgan 2008). It is for this reason that less politicised accountability agencies, such as the audit office and the ombudsman, are so important. Their avoidance of controversial matters of 'policy' allows them to focus their attention primarily on the actions of public officials.

As is now generally recognised, ministerial responsibility, on its own, cannot provide comprehensive accountability of all the activities of government. Other, supplementary, accountability institutions are also vital. But ministerial responsibility, properly understood in context, is still a very powerful and effective accountability mechanism. From the point of view of the general public and the media, ministers are the most obvious point of contact over matters of community concern. Within the government apparatus, too, the relevant minister remains the natural spokesperson for each agency and loyal support for the minister in this public role is a key value for professional public servants.

These expectations reinforce the centrality of ministerial responsibility in our system of government. Indeed, some commentators complain that ministers and their immediate circle of advisers are too powerful in Westminster-style systems such as Australia's (Hughes 2003). On this view, hierarchical accountability through the minister fosters excessive, top-down bureaucratic control and stifles the development of flexible, bottom-up, citizen-centric government that is possible in more devolved political systems, such as those of the United States or some European countries. But whatever the merits of ministerial responsibility as a principle in institutional design, its continuing impact is undeniable.

References

Auditor-General. 2010. *Home Insulation Program*. Audit Report no. 12 2010–11. Canberra: Australian National Audit Office. <http://www.anao.gov.au>

Australian Broadcasting Corporation (ABC). 2010. *The Drum*, 18 October, <http://www.abc.net.au/thedrum>

Bovens, M. 1998. *The Quest for Responsibility—Accountability and Citizenship in Complex Organisations*. Cambridge: Cambridge University Press.

Coulton, M. M. 2009. *House of Representatives* Hansard 12222, 19 November. Canberra: Parliament of Australia.

Department of the Prime Minister and Cabinet. 2010. *Standards of Ministerial Ethics*. Canberra: Department of the Prime Minister and Cabinet. <http://www.dpmc.gov.au/guidelines/index.cfm>

Dowding, K. and W.-T. Kang. 1998. 'Ministerial Resignations 1945–97'. *Public Administration* 76(3): 411–29.

Hawke, A. 2010. *Review of the Administration of the Home Insulation Program*. Canberra: Department of the Prime Minister and Cabinet.

Hughes, O. 2003. *Public Management and Administration*. Third edition. Basingstoke, UK: Palgrave.

Marino, N. B. 2009. *House of Representatives* Hansard 12234, 19 November. Canberra: Parliament of Australia.

Marshall, G. 1989. 'Individual Responsibility: Some Post-War Cases'. In *Ministerial Responsibility*, ed. G. Marshall, pp. 127–33. Oxford: Oxford University Press.

Mulgan, R. 2002. 'On Ministerial Resignations (and the Lack Thereof)'. *Australian Journal of Public Administration* 61(2): 121–7.

Mulgan, R. 2003. *Holding Power to Account*. Basingstoke, UK: Palgrave Macmillan.

Mulgan, R. 2008. 'The Accountability Priorities of Australian Parliamentarians'. *Australian Journal of Public Administration* 67(4): 457–69.

Page, B. 1990. 'Ministerial Resignation and Individual Ministerial Responsibility in Australia, 1976–89'. *Journal of Commonwealth and Comparative Politics* 28: 141–61.

Polidano, C. 1999. 'The Bureaucrat Who Fell Under a Bus'. *Governance* 12: 201–29.

Ratnapala, S. 2007. *Australian Constitutional Law: Foundations and Theory*. Melbourne: Oxford University Press.

Schultz, A. J. 2009. *House of Representatives* Hansard 11776, 16 November. Canberra: Parliament of Australia.

Summers, J. 2006. 'Parliament and Responsible Government'. In *Government, Politics, Power and Policy in Australia*, eds A. Parkin, J. Summers and D. Woodward, pp. 68–92. Sydney: Pearson Education.

Thompson, E. and G. Tillotsen. 1999. 'Caught in the Act: The Smoking Gun View of Ministerial Responsibility'. *Australian Journal of Public Administration* 58(1): 48–57.

Weller, P. 1999. 'Disentangling Concepts of Ministerial Responsibility'. *Australian Journal of Public Administration* 58(1): 62–4.

Woodhouse, D. 1994. *Ministers and Parliament: Accountability in Theory and Practice*. Oxford: Clarendon Press.

www.ingramcontent.com/pod-product-compliance
Lightning Source LLC
Chambersburg PA
CBHW061245270326

41928CB00041B/3432